Organisational Change and Retail Finance

Financial organisations, like many others, have recently undergone radical transformation, affecting both their organisational processes and the technology that supports such processes. As a result, banks are now at the forefront of new employment practices and in many ways can be viewed as postmodern organisations.

This volume provides a detailed examination of the recent changes in retail finance from sociological, anthropological, management science and technology and organisation perspectives. It reports on the use of sociological ethnography to guide these changes, both in terms of helping to better understand and redraw work processes and through providing a more accurate and flexible understanding of the role played by technology. The authors place the reported research in context by contrasting it with those approaches more commonly associated with change, including business process engineering, participative design and soft system methodologies. The book explains the benefits of ethnography, as well as the potential it has in helping achieve more desirable change in all organisations, financial services included.

Organisational Change and Retail Finance will be of interest to all international researchers concerned with organisational and technological change, as well as managers of organisational development. It will also interest advanced students in sociology, anthropology, management science and organisational studies.

Richard Harper is Director of the Digital World Research Centre, University of Surrey. **Dave Randall** is Senior Lecturer at the Department of Sociology, Manchester Metropolitan University. **Mark Rouncefield** is Research Fellow at the Computing Department, Lancaster University. The authors have published widely in the various disciplines associated with organisational life and technology design, and have built a considerable reputation for bringing new sociological insights into the organisational-change literature.

Routledge International Studies in Money and Banking

1 Private Banking in Europe
Lyn Bicker

2 Bank Deregulation and Monetary Order
George Selgin

3 Money in Islam
A study in Islamic political economy
Masudul Alam Choudhury

4 The Future of European Financial Centres
Kirsten Bindemann

5 Payment Systems in Global Perspective
Maxwell J. Fry, Isaak Kilato, Sandra Roger, Krzysztof Senderowicz, David Sheppard, Francisco Solis and John Trundle

6 What is Money?
John Smithin

7 Finance
A Characteristics Approach
Edited by David Blake

8 Organisational Change and Retail Finance
An Ethnographic Perspective
Richard Harper, Dave Randall and Mark Rouncefield

9 The History of the Bundesbank
Lessons for the European Central Bank
Jakob de Haan

10 The Euro
A Challenge and Opportunity for Financial Markets
Published on behalf of *Société Universitaire Européenne de Recherches Financières (SUERF)*
Edited by Michael Artis, Axel Weber and Elizabeth Hennessy

Organisational Change and Retail Finance

An Ethnographic Perspective

Richard Harper, Dave Randall
and Mark Rouncefield

London and New York

First published 2000
by Routledge
11 New Fetter Lane, London EC4P 4EE

Simultaneously published in the USA and Canada
by Routledge
29 West 35th Street, New York, NY 10001

Routledge is an imprint of the Taylor & Francis Group

© 2000 Richard Harper, Dave Randall and Mark Rouncefield

Typeset in Sabon by Steven Gardiner Ltd
Printed and bound in Great Britain by
T J International Ltd., Padstow, Cornwall

All rights reserved. No part of this book may be reprinted or
reproduced or utilised in any form or by any electronic,
mechanical, or other means, now known or hereafter
invented, including photocopying and recording, or in any
information storage or retrieval system, without permission in
writing from the publishers.

British Library Cataloguing in Publication Data
A catalogue record for this book is available
from the British Library

Library of Congress Cataloging-in-Publication Data
Harper, Richard.
  Organisational change and retail finance : an ethnographic
perspective / Richard Harper, Dave Randall, and Mark Rouncefield.
    p. cm.
  Includes bibliographical references and index.
  ISBN 0-415-20264-7
  1. Bank management. 2. Bank management—Great Britain.
I. Randall, Dave. II. Rouncefield, Mark. III. Title.
HG1615.H356 1999
332.1'068—dc21   99–37474
                                                              CIP

ISBN 0 415 20264 7

For John Hughes

Contents

Preface   xi
Acknowledgements   xiii

1 Introduction   1

Preamble 1
Overview of the book 3
The view from sociology 6
   Financial services and more engaged sociology: CSCW 13
Conclusion 16

PART I

2 Organisational studies and empirical description   21

Introduction 21
Organisational studies 23
   Functionalism and the creation of typologies 25
   Other forms of functionalism 28
   Functionalism, psychology and organisational behaviour 31
   A sociological response 33
Revisiting the auspices of organisational studies 35
   Sense-making in organisations 37
Conclusion 40

3 Approaches to the management of change   42

Introduction 42
Approaches to change 44
   Business Process Re-engineering 44
   Participative Design 49
   Soft Systems Methodology 52

Conclusion: The productivity paradox 54
  Assessing management of change and technology-design perspectives 56

4 **Ethnography and change** 62

  Introduction 62
  What is ethnography? 63
    What is involved in 'doing' ethnography 65
    Ethnomethodologically informed ethnography 67
    Relative merits of the approach 69
  Conclusion 71
    Some problems of ethnography 76

PART II

5 **Taking customers seriously** 81

  Introduction 81
  'Telling' and 'selling' – customer confidence and demeanour-work 82
    The confident customer 84
    Knowledge in action 88
    Visible competence 90
    The satisfied customer and everyday tasks 91
    Breaking the rules 93
  Making sense of the customer: Interviews and local knowledge 94
    Visible competence and interviewing 98
    Back office work 102
  Conclusion 104

6 **The virtual customer** 107

  Introduction 107
  Cooperating with the customer 108
    Local knowledge and the 'customer in the machine' 110
    Demeanour-work and the 'customer in the machine' 113
    Identifying 'difficult customers' in the machine 114
  More than a number: Relationship management and the customer in the machine 115
    Managing change 117
    Reconfiguring the borrower 119
  Conclusion 123

7 **Taking technology seriously**   126

Introduction 126
Technology inside banks 128
  Accounts in trouble 129
  Decision-making applications and 'accounts in trouble' 132
  Advanced technologies and practical actions 134
  Management Information Systems 142
Banking on the old technology: 'Legacy' systems in use 145
  Old systems and ordinary work 146
Conclusion 148

8 **Conclusion**   150

Introduction 150
  A post-disciplinary approach to empirical research 151
  *Placing a post-disciplinary approach to ethnography within a
    spectrum of techniques 158*
Conclusion 158
  The analytic foci of a post-disciplinary approach 159

References   165
Index   179

Preface

Like many books this one is the product of circumstance and happy accident. As successive research assistants to Professor John Hughes, and being fortuitously involved in research in similar fields, we met at conferences, workshops and bars to discuss our work and express our general disappointment, verging on boredom, with the standard sociological accounts of the area – summarised in that well-worn phrase from *Star Trek*, 'it's life, Jim, but not as we know it'. Those like ourselves who took the ethnomethodological 'turn' at some point in their intellectual careers are accustomed to some dissatisfaction with our parent discipline, sociology. As, for historical reasons, each of us began to research organisational life, and in particular the role of technology and its uses in the organisation our 'troubled thoughts' about sociology, organisational theory and concomitant disciplines seemed to multiply. Fashionable views concerning the proper subject matter of the social sciences and the desire to theorise above all were, it seemed to us, accompanied by a somewhat cavalier treatment of 'data' and, in more recent versions, a legitimate concern for the problematisation of 'facticity' has, on occasion, seemed to render data collection irrelevant. The subjection, not to say subversion, of facticity to theoretical purpose in the social sciences through radical constructionist and postmodern approaches has been in our view largely spurious, ignoring as it does the massive reality of the world for those who inhabit it. In turn, ethnomethodology's standpoint has been widely misunderstood, arguably because many writers cannot conceive of an approach which really means what it says when it argues that the 'lived reality' of work, or work as an 'interactional achievement', requires no commitment to any philosophical or sociological theorising.

At much the same time, and with some irony, quite different traditions in organisational study have proliferated. In these traditions, and we include here change-management approaches such as Business Process Re-engineering and 'principled' alternatives such as Socio-technical Systems work and Participatory Design, practical design agendas have predominated to such an extent that theory has hardly been an issue at all. The irony lies in the fact that one might naively imagine that these largely atheoretical stances might be accompanied by the very concern for description that we advocate. We were, to put it mildly, disappointed in that they are not in fact, for the most part, engaged in any serious reflection on appropriate methodologies for description. Their desire to prescribe organisational change seems not to encourage but to discourage methodological rigour.

The field in which we largely work, that of Computer Supported Co-operative Work (CSCW), has been concerned precisely with the role of description in practical, design-oriented studies of organisations. Nevertheless, CSCW itself has manifested a variety of the tensions one might expect where an uneasy set of relations between computer scientists, psychologists, sociologists and ethnomethodologists exists, and its emphasis on technology has been such that 'organisation' sometimes disappears entirely from view. At root, these tensions reflect different views on what the proper subject of interdisciplinary work might be, arguments concerning the role of empirical work in this area and about the nature of empirical study itself.

These various omissions have led us to think about how one might adequately characterise the working life of bank and building society employees with an eye to understanding issues of work, technology and organisation without rushing to judgement. Our interest in the very ordinariness of organisational life – in the practical and mundane character of human activity in organisational contexts – provides, we hope, a corrective to the revelatory character of much social science and gives a picture of 'what it is like' to be a member of an organisation, or to do a job that is otherwise so often missing.

The modest purposes of this book, then, are first to provide the kinds of description we are advocating in an organisational context, that of retail financial services, and to say something about what these descriptions might be for; second, to examine the issues of prescription and description as they pertain to this domain; and last, to allow readers in some small way to feel that they understand, from the point of view of people working in retail financial services, what it is like to do this kind of work. In so doing, we are conscious that there are many aspects of the retail financial-service sector we have said little or nothing about. Its history; the role of legislation; the importance of new regulatory frameworks and the way they pan out into issues of compliance; and analysis of the work of senior management are all missing here. Broadly, this is because many of these issues are dealt with more than adequately by other writers, and because space precludes the treatment of these themes.

Acknowledgements

The authors would like to express their thanks and appreciation to John Hughes, to whom this book is dedicated, for his friendship and support over many years. He has been a mentor to all of us and must take much credit for whatever may be seen as good, interesting or useful in this book. The blame for anything bad, boring or useless resides, as usual, with us, and we will readily attribute it to each other.

The research for much of this book was drawn from a variety of funded research projects including: the COMIC Esprit BRA in CSCW; the DTI-EPSRC funded initiative in CSCW; the EPSRC SEBPC program; and the ESRC 'Virtual Society?' program. We are grateful for the financial support received. We would also like to record our thanks to the staff at the various field sites for their good humour and tolerance of the 'professional strangers' amongst them. We particularly thank Steve Blythin and Roger Scowcroft for arranging and facilitating fieldwork access.

Richard Harper would like to say thanks to Ron Watford, Wally Howe and Peter McCafferty; to Iris Littleboy, and to other colleagues and friends who have put up with us during the research and the writing both at Xerox Research Centre and the University of Surrey.

Dave Randall would like to thank his colleagues and friends Ted Cuff, Dave Francis, Liz Marr, Pete Martin and Wes Sharrock for their powerful argumentation, intellectual stimulation and continued presence in the Grafton. He would also like to thank Ann Burns and Christine Rourke, two ex-colleagues and still valued friends, for providing him with considerable support in trying times and for the necessary 'push'. Above all he wishes to thank Elisabeth, for everything.

Mark Rouncefield offers particular, heartfelt, thanks to Jon O'Brien, Tom Rodden and Peter Tolmie for their constant friendship, patience and unfailing generosity with their time, fieldwork notes and the theft and mangling of their ideas. He would also like to thank the members of 'TeamEthno' at Lancaster University for their support and encouragement to 'tell it like it is' and for their strange and continued tolerance of an 'observational scientist' whose powers of perception regularly and unaccountably disappear. Finally, and most importantly, he would like to thank Caroline Warbrick to whom he owes a debt of gratitude he lacks the ability to calculate or the wit to describe.

1 Introduction

PREAMBLE

We are all familiar with organisational change. Whether such changes are driven by external factors or by new philosophies and management approaches within our organisations, they effect us all. Moreover, response to change feeds more change; the cycle is never ending. The pace of change is variable, of course, with some organisations undergoing more radical transformations than others. In the past decade or so, regulatory, technological and marketplace pressures have resulted in retail financial services organisations, as a case in point, radically altering their internal structures as well as their points of contact with the outside world. We are nearly all users of the services such organisations provide and so are all familiar with many of these changes – though it is very unlikely that many of us have been able to influence them greatly. For those within such organisations (banks for short), planning, implementing and evaluating change has doubtless been a source of headaches and exhaustion, broken or made careers, as well as pleasant surprises and unexpected benefits. To guide these individuals in their 'change management', as it is called, they are likely to have had the help of a wide range of experts: technology vendors claiming to offer solutions to the perennial problem of reducing the cost of customer channels; psychologists offering guidance on how to maintain organisational morale through change; and highly paid business process experts offering techniques to identify and abolish inefficiency and waste.

Sociologists have not been party to these offerings. This is not because banks are uninteresting to sociologists – far from it – nor because sociologists think they have nothing to say to banks. It is rather that most sociological work is distant from the concerns and interests of those who actually work within and are responsible for change in banks. This is not a contrast between academic research on the one hand and practical action on the other; it has to do with how the bulk of sociology is focused on theoretical and analytical concerns internal to sociology itself. In essence, sociology is an inward looking discipline – as has been said by numerous commentators over the years from C.Wright Mills onward. Of course, many

2   Introduction

sociologists would hotly dispute this, and when asked will cite endlessly their political and moral credentials as underscoring both the veracity of their research and its practical contribution to a better society. But in saying this they miss the point. What concerns them and what concerns those who have to make changes in organisations is not the same: for sociologists, or at least the majority of them, what is of concern are grand ideas – how diverse social processes can be seen to fit into a whole, across contexts and situations. For those in banks, and indeed all organisations going through change, what is of concern is what happens in this situation, with this technology, in this context. The simple truth is that the sociological literature on banking has lacked substantive empirical descriptions of what has come to be called 'situated work practice'. Apart from one or two notable exceptions, there is very little ethnographic description, for instance, of contemporary banking organisations. Nor is there any substantive literature on the methodological problems of undertaking field observation in organisations that are subject to chronic, continuous and often radical change.

Such an absence is all the more striking given the fact that research in a variety of other technologically rich domains has begun to demonstrate that sociological techniques for observation and analysis are able to confront these sorts of methodological problems. This research is also showing how a sociological approach can specify organisational action in such a way as to enable better management of change. This research emanates mainly from the domains known as Human Computer Interaction (HCI and in North America CHI) and, to a larger extent, from Computer Supported Cooperative Work (CSCW). This research is showing its utility not by bringing to bear the fruits of over a century's sociological theorising from Marx to Weber to Giddens, or for that matter through providing descriptions of the post-modern condition. It is doing so through providing empirical insights into how people organise themselves to produce the processes we are all familiar with in banks and elsewhere – the rule governed behaviour, the technologically mediated action, the documentary systems that embed our individual identities in bureaucratic form. The kind of sociology that does this is one that views such things as the protocols of technology use, the following of organisational rules and the implementation of change programmes, as 'encountered phenomena'. By this is meant that these phenomena are ones that members of organisations have to identify, work through, and instantiate for themselves.

The sociological reader will doubtless be immediately alerted to various methodological assumptions underscoring this approach; for non-sociologists the assumptions will be of less interest than the output of such research. Besides, the important point is that the increasing success of this research over the past decade or so is indicating that the historical conception of the role of sociology and its relationship to technological design and the management of organisational change needs to be revised. Whereas hitherto, these matters have been the subject of sociological inquiry, a new post-disciplinary approach is emerging where sociology is contributing to and helping guide such changes. Moreover, it is doing so not only through making sociology a more action-oriented discipline. It is also offering correctives to those disciplines more traditionally associated with organisational change and technological design – management science, organisational studies and such approaches as offered by Business Process Engineering (or BPR as it is more familiar to the public at large). The latter, for example, oversimplifies organisational processes and, though it enables senior managers to get a top-down view of the overall structure of their organisation, it does not generate the kind of detail required to understand the role of technology or the arrays of skills deployed at any workplace. This is not to say BPR has no advantages or does not go a long way in terms of offering those concerned with organisational change a way of seeing what choices they might make; it is only to say that such an approach – like many others currently offered – does not do it all. This is something that members of organisations are all too aware of, and thus is one reason why BPR initiatives are invariably allied with a host of other processes and inquiries.

In this regard both what one might call orthodox approaches in sociology and much of what is offered from management science, organisational studies and business consulting share a common fault – insufficiently grounded information about organisational action, technology and work process. In the case of sociologists, this has resulted in them being largely ignored by those undertaking change; as regards the management scientists and such like, it has meant that no particular approach is viewed as complete or comprehensive and is bolstered by various *ad hoc* ways of complementing and testing techniques for change.

In this book we want to explain how the absence of sociology in change programmes, as well as some of the problems within the currently popular approaches to the management of organisational change, can be corrected and changed. We will argue that a particular approach to empirical investigation taken from sociology can be developed and refined in such a fashion as to generate detailed and rich materials about the nature of behaviour in organisations and, related to that, the role of technology. Such an approach can help deepen understanding of what current work involves, whether it be face-to-face interaction at point of sale, or behaviour mediated by technology. It can help in tracking the fate or impact of change programmes, especially when they involve large scale changes in organisational structures and processes. Above all, it can help in providing much more comprehensive understanding of the place of technology in situated, work practices.

OVERVIEW OF THE BOOK

Although we will illustrate our arguments with reference to our own research into retail financial services – high street banks in common parlance – our argument will be that the approach we outline is applicable to any and all organisations wanting to undertake change. To achieve this we will structure our arguments in the following way. Having concluded our overview of the book, we shall give some time in this chapter to overviewing some of the sociologically informed research into banking. As remarked, this is at once extensive and curiously lacking in rich empirical detail. At this point, though, our main interest will be to set out some of the various arguments – driven by theoretical concerns as we say – to highlight both why it is that such research is largely irrelevant to those within banks, and to note at the same time what the main themes in this research are. Our concern will not be to imply that this research is uninteresting; only to point towards why its practical role is limited. Amongst the themes we will sketch are the new aesthetics embodied in the emergence of 'knowledge-based' products in financial services, as well as transformations brought about in conceptions of identity and self in the 'consumer society'. We remark also on some of the research into the role of technology in banks. This will lead us onto our conclusion, in which we report some of the sociologically informed research which does try and focus on technology in such a way as to help inform its design: we refer here to research in the research domain known as CSCW.

In Chapter 2, we elaborate on some of the organisational studies in the literature with a view to placing our own approach in broader context. We will not endeavour to offer a full-blown review of research into organisations but will want to summarise what we feel are its salient features and come to the pessimistic conclusion that much of it is divorced from any practical implications. This is not to say that the research lacks merit but, like sociology generally, it is fixated on theoretical and exclusively academic arguments. In particular, we will sketch some of the early functional approaches to organisations mainly motivated by a desire to create typologies. We will note what implications this approach has for understanding technology and how one paradox is that it tends to make human action seem very mechanical, almost like a technology itself. We will then review the slightly different programme of functionalism which focuses on action in organisation, rather than organisational structure. Here the concern is with psychology, and its relationship with the achievement of organisational goals, suitable levels of motivation, and so forth. This will lead us on to debates about structure and agency, which are more or less central to all current discussions of organisation. As with the functional approaches, the literature on structure and agency is striking for its lack of concern with empirical measures. We will ask whether the research justifies itself in terms of empirical description and whether the same (i.e., those descriptions) could be used to support more pragmatic and practical contributions to organisational life (e.g., through change management).

If our discussions will have been focused largely on the sociology of organisations and related disciplines in Chapter 2, in the next we consider approaches that are expressly concerned with having practical implications on organisations. Its particular concern will be Business Process Re-engineering, Participative Design and Soft Systems Methodology. We will discuss the role of technology and 'process' in these approaches, and argue that all three have certain problems relating to assumptions about the information resources used to understand settings, the relationship between action and process as accomplishment, and also related to the provision of evidence and description of work more generally. We will suggest that they oversimplify the processes and activities involved when technology is actually used 'in anger', and outline alternative viewpoints, the most relevant of which is organisational ethnography.

This will be the topic of Chapter 4. Here we will draw a contrast between describing and explaining and discuss how most approaches to organisational action suffer from what may be described as the 'missing what' of technology use. This relates to the lack of concern with empirical measures and description that we will have highlighted in the previous chapter. We will outline an approach – ethnomethodologically informed ethnography – that emphasises analysis of the 'situated' properties of organisational and technologically mediated action. The chapter will argue for an understanding of organisational action and process that is grounded in observable phenomena. Such an approach can provide numerous benefits to change management programmes, in offering better understanding of work practice, in allowing access to situated skills and the way change processes are folded into work patterns and technology use. We will remark on some of the ways our own research has been part of larger change management programmes.

Chapter 5 will introduce the first empirical materials focusing on the skills and practices that comprise customer-facing work. We will be particularly concerned with how bank staff have to manage on a day-to-day and moment-by-moment basis the unpredictable though nonetheless routine concerns of customers, and how at the same time this is achieved in part through displays of competence. Such competence has to do with how bank staff convey to the customer through their interaction that they know what the customer wants or needs, are familiar with the 'ins and outs' of bank procedures, and are able to deal with almost any request however so presented. We will suggest that these abilities may be thought of as local rationalities, a concern for which we will have outlined in Chapter 4.

In Chapter 6 we will develop some of these themes further, but focus on how such interactions are being replaced by procedures that have much more technological mediation. Here we will talk about the 'virtual customer'; that is, how bank staff have to deal with a person who is understood

6   *Introduction*

through (in large part) the technology that provides information and 'expert advice' about that person. A particular concern will also be to emphasise the 'everyday world' of banking, whether it involves dealing with the virtual or the truly embodied customer. It is in this chapter too, that we will present some examples of lending, the *sine qua non* of banking work and emphasise how lending turns around the use of local rationalities and resources provided by technology.

This will lead us on to a focused examination of technology within banks in Chapter 7. Here, we will show how rather than technology being an unproblematic contributor to, let us say, deskilling, it must be examined as being 'made to work' in the process of use. We will instantiate this idea through descriptions of work with decision-support systems and use of databases offering customer 'notes', as well as further elaborate some of the lending processes described in the previous chapter. A particular theme will be to say that to understand technology use means recognising that computer-mediated action is itself always part of a larger context of artifacts and technologies, including paper. Given the apparent move toward 'paperless banking', this chapter will conclude with some discussion of what may be called the affordances of paper, and how those affordances are likely to render the existence of such an environment unlikely, at least for the immediate future.

Chapter 8 will conclude the book. Here, we will review what we will call the post-disciplinary auspices of the ethnographic approach we will have outlined. We will recapitulate the analytic stances used in Chapters 5, 6 and 7, and will emphasise the sanity, or 'reality' testing aspects of this work. It will reiterate how the importance of organisational knowledge, interdependency in the workplace, the flow of work, and orientation to procedures, all discussed in various ways in the empirical chapters are useful ways of directing analytic focus. We will argue at a more general level, that studies of the social organisation of banking activities can ground a host of concerns including the management and control of organisational change, as well as the design of new technology. The notion of technology use, underscored in the empirical chapters, will be remarked on further, and we will argue that such a concern incorporates a new view of the organisation based on an understanding of practice. In this respect, it will underscore the insights of Suchman (1987) in deconstructing 'plans' and 'situated actions'. We will suggest ways in which the various concerns highlighted in the empirical chapters can be woven together to provide a more coherent understanding of the role of technology organisations, and not just banks.

THE VIEW FROM SOCIOLOGY

Although commonly viewed as purely economic (and occasionally political) institutions, financial services and banks in particular have been the focus of increasing and considerable sociological investigation. In part this is because, in the face of massive economic, social and cultural change, banks have been seen to be undergoing changes that are far more radical than those occurring in other sectors (Llewelynn 1996). In this context, banking organisations are seen to be at the sharp end of global economic transformations including processes of 'deregulation' and the emergence of 'universal' banking (Canals 1997; Smith and Walter 1997); transformations in employment legislation and the emergence of flexible working patterns (Knights and Tinker (Eds) 1997); changes in the nature of consumerism (Burton 1994) and the development and widespread implementation of new technological infrastructures (Spinardi, Graham and Williams 1996). The combined result of these factors is that banks are now at the forefront of changes from what has come to be called Fordist to Post-Fordist organisational structures and exemplify the move away from the manufacture of product to the provision of knowledge. Moreover, banks are at the leading edge of institutions that are catering for and indeed encouraging the fragmentation of consumer demands. The overall effect of these multifarious changes has combined, according to many sociological observers, to make banks exemplars of 'Postmodern' organisations.

It is perhaps unsurprising therefore that these changes have been the subject of significant sociological enquiry. Findings from the banking industry have been used not so much to influence banks themselves however, as to refine and develop sociological theories of organisations and organisational behaviour. So, by way of illustration, some authors have reported on how de-regulation has played out in different countries, re-emphasising the need for sociological theory to acknowledge the diversity of culturally defined patterns of business relationships (Morgan and Knights 1997); others have examined the impact of 'organisational' cultures on organisational change (Knights and Tinker 1997); and improvements to Callon's theory of translation have also been provided through reference to change in the banking industry (Bloomfield and Vurdubakis 1997).

We now turn to say something more about a handful of these agendas – or as we prefer themes – so as to give more of a flavour of the sociology of banking in general and to highlight the theoretical goal of this research as against our own, more engaged ethnographic position (discussed in Chapter 4). The first theme (though no order of priority is meant here but simply the fact that it is the first one recalls) consists of a concern with how current banking structures reflect much larger-scale transformations, particularly globalisation, knowledge accumulation and new foundations for individual identity. For example, in *Economies of Signs and Space*, Lash and Urry (1994) advance an account of economic growth in modern industrial societies based on a process of 'reflexive accumulation' suggesting it provides a better account of contemporary socio-economic processes than other frameworks such as flexible specialisation, flexible accumulation and Post-Fordism. Lash and Urry suggest that these other approaches are characterised by a series of conceptual and empirical inadequacies and fail, for example, to recognise the importance of services. A reflexive economy, Lash and Urry argue, increasingly involves services such as banking, insurance, stockbroking and so on (as against the production of things in traditional capitalism). Information and knowledge are fundamental to economic growth in these areas. They go on to argue that other explanatory frameworks place insufficient emphasis on consumption and, relatedly, fail to understand the extent to which cultural and symbolic processes, including an important aesthetic component related to design, have permeated both production and consumption.

Lash and Urry portray the process of reflexive accumulation as having a number of characteristics, including the fact that there is an important aesthetic aspect to personal identity (this is contrasted with the purely cognitive). 'Aesthetic reflexivity' is constitutive of both production and consumption and has to do not just with the obvious areas of 'niche' marketing (e.g., of financial services to students and so on) but with the growth of individualism more generally. This embraces the notion of the 'enterprising consumer' and how this notion feeds into notions of self-identity:

> The semioticization of consumption whose increasingly symbolic nature is ever more involved in self-constructions of identity.
> (Lash and Urry 1994: 61)

Indeed, as Burton (1994) notes, one feature of financial service innovation in the 1980s was the use of market segmentation to identify the financial needs of particular population groups and create financial products to meet their perceived needs:

> ... a life cycle analysis of financial service needs would acknowledge that families and individuals at different stages in the life cycle have different financial requirements. The segment described as 'full nest 1' is one in which the youngest child is under 6 years of age. The emphasis would probably be on building up the family home, and the household is likely to be short of cash ... people within this market segment tend to be interested in newly advertised products, either home or child related.
> (Burton 1994: 37)

Lash and Urry claim that such 'economies of signs and space' do not lead inevitably and inexorably to the kind of pessimistic futures suggested by a number of writers but instead:

> ... open up possibilities for the recasting of meaning in work and in leisure.
> (Lash and Urry 1994: 3)

The increasing aestheticization of material objects in both production and consumption – seen in the increasing design component of goods – is, they suggest, evidence that those individuals subject to 'space economies' are becoming increasingly self-conscious of their identities as members of a consumer society. This is shown in the declining trust in 'expert systems' that would include, for example, those used by bank managers and financial advisers.

Despite its obscure language, Lash and Urry's work is fairly central to most sociology these days, and their analyses are taught in most undergraduate classes. But sociology is a large discipline and there are numerous other themes of research which though not so high profile, have similar concerns. For example, one concerns itself with developments and changes in the economy and its impact on the specific organisational form of banks – clearly seen in debates on Post-Fordism and Postmodern forms of organisation already mentioned, as well as theories of the 'flexible firm'. Though the notion of the 'flexible firm' and its empirical validation in relation to banks has been extensively criticised (Rajan 1987a, b), the general factors viewed as contributing to the emergence of flexible firms include such things as the weakening of the welfare state, an increasing dependence between the state and capital, the breakdown of the mass market and the need for new forms of production. These are viewed in turn as related to changes in consumption patterns and life styles and major technological innovations (Atkinson 1986; Bagguley *et al.* 1990). Within this literature there has been particular interest in the 'virtual organisation' (Davidow and Malone 1992); a form of organisation which, it is claimed, implements many of the themes mentioned in the arguments about postmodernism, evinced in the work of Lash and Urry. According to this view, virtual organisations are a solution to the problems of task and environmental uncertainty insofar as they provide the conditions of 'knowledge generation' required for organisational success in the contemporary world (Nonaka and Takeuchi 1995). These 'virtual' organisational arrangements consist of networks of workers and organisational units, linked by information technology, combining computer power with the skills of organisational staff to achieve organisational goals. The view proposes the need for organisations to encourage the development of open and creative relationships between staff (and to some degree clients) capable of sharing knowledge and expertise in 'evolving communities of practice'.

In a more general vein, Zuboff (1988) writes of new forms of organisational behaviour 'in which relationships are more intricate, collaborative and bound by mutual responsibilities of colleagues' (Zuboff 1988: 6), while Casey (1995) perceives the development of new forms of teamwork:

> in which people share knowledge, skills and resources and work cooperatively in the manufacture of their products. ... Relationship to a product, to team family members and to the company displaces

identification with occupation and its historic repository of skills, knowledges and allegiances.

(Casey 1995: 109).

Such teamworking:

less fettered by the constraints of traditional hierarchies and spheres of responsibility, engenders a heightened sense of empowerment, commitment and collective responsibility.

(Casey 1995: 45)

However, such views of organisational change and the virtual organisation need to be subjected to rigorous empirical examination. Other researchers are considerably less sanguine about the consequences of technological change and more sceptical about the likelihood of such a transformation in teamworking, skill, identification, empowerment, and so on (Kunda, 1992). As Ducatel (1992) writes:

the absence of an a priori direction in which the technology will take organisations makes the empirical investigation of how computer network technology is being implemented of the utmost importance and urgency.

(Ducatel 1992: 166)

Another major set of themes in the sociological literature evince an interest in researching particular features (as against organisational forms) of organisational behaviour as indicators of more general economic and organisational structures and changes. This is perhaps most obvious in the 'traditional' studies of those who have been primarily interested in bank workers as instantiations of 'white-collar' workers. Historically this can be seen in the early work of Lockwood (1958) and 'The Blackcoated Worker', although it is a tradition resurrected by more recent studies by Stovel *et al.* (1996) which specifically examine the 'work' of clerks (although the emphasis is primarily on pay, conditions and status rather than actual work). These studies relate descriptions of work to theories about changes in the class structure of modern capitalist society.

Essentially similar approaches are adopted by those whose interest is in aspects of 'alienation' and clerical work and in more recent studies on the career structure of bank clerks relating them to notions of social change and the concepts of 'ascribed' and 'achieved' status (Stovel *et al.* 1996). In part this is because banks have provided a rich resource for documentary research and consequently have enabled the historical examination of change. Other studies focusing on this theme include the various debates surrounding the issues of 'skill', managerial control and 'resistance' following Braverman (1974) and applied to financial service organisations in the work of Smith (1989) and Smith and Wield (1988). These and other writers have used the issue of skill related to changing organisational forms (notably flexible specialisation) to examine employment patterns within banks. Discussion of the model of the flexible firm and the extent to which it matches the reality of bank work is relevant here. This model is predicated on evidence suggesting that there are increasing numbers of part-time workers in banking. There are, however, other explanations for such employment patterns (one of the reasons for the dispute about flexible firms already mentioned). Rajan (1987b), for example, suggests that a tiered recruitment strategy and segmentation of the workforce is a product of the demise of the internal labour market; while Burton (1994) argues that increased competition between financial service organisations has meant that reskilling and enskilling (of permanent staff) has taken place. This allows banks to more effectively market their services. Furthermore, Burton's suggested explanation for the changes in employment is in terms of the 'feminisation' of the workforce. In a similar fashion, Bertrand and Noyelle (1988) present an historical account of employment in financial services linking 'deskilling' with the changing position of banks. In this view, the 1960s and 1970s were periods of expansion for banks who pursued a Tayloristic approach of deskilling. Increased competition in the 1980s, however, resulted in an emphasis on qualitative growth and increase in workforce skills especially in sales and marketing, what Burton (1994) calls 'turning tellers into sellers'. Any standard interpretation of employment in financial services in terms of straightforward 'deskilling' is, consequently, complicated by the increase in the numbers of part-time workers who are usually excluded from more highly skilled positions.

Another set of related themes may be distinguished by reference to a major concern with the consumption of financial services as opposed to their production (Urry 1990). Here the interest lies in developments in the relationship between organisations, economic change and the consumer and can, for example, be seen in the already-discussed work of Lash and Urry (1994) on aesthetic reflexivity and, more obviously and specifically related to financial services, in the research of Burton (1994). One other (perhaps bizarre) valuable and informative addition to this category would be Hochschild's (1983) work on debt collectors (see also Rafaeli and Sutton 1989, 1990, 1991). In this literature the argument is put forward that banks have become more consumer oriented. This begs a whole host of questions about the relationship between producers and consumers, and whether we are witnessing the arrival of 'new times' with an emphasis on individualism and consumer choice. As Urry puts it:

> consumption rather than production is dominant as consumer expenditure further increases as a proportion of national income; new forms of credit permitting consumer expenditure to rise, so producing high levels of indebtedness; much greater differentiation of purchasing

patterns by different market segments; greater volatility of consumer preferences; the growth of consumers; movement and the ... reaction of consumers against being part of a 'mass' and the need for producers to be much more consumer driven, especially in the case of service industries and those publicly owned; the development of many more products each of which has a shorter life.

(Urry 1990: 277)

Nevertheless whether consumer sovereignty actually exists is a matter of considerable debate (see, e.g., Keat 1991) since clearly producers attempt to shape and control consumer choice through marketing and advertising. In a similar fashion, whether financial-service organisations have become more consumer orientated is also debatable. Changes in the consumption of financial services are the product of a range of complex social, economic and political processes. Financial-service producers have also gone to considerable lengths to retain existing and attract new customers:

There has evidently been a shift from organisational cultures which were conservative, reactive and cautious, and where the main element of the job was administration. Contemporary financial service personnel are required to be proactive, entrepreneurial and possess a high level of interpersonal skills and marketing expertise.

(Burton 1994: 5)

Meanwhile, the creation of a host of regulatory bodies and the growth of various consumer groups – such as 'Which Watchdog?' in the UK – as well as daily newspaper financial columns on financial services reflects the fact that there is now a critical assessment of financial-service institutions and their products; at least in the mass media. The implications of this are yet to be fully reported.

A final theme of research worth mentioning – though we could add extensively to the list we have provided – focuses principally on the relationship between Information Technology (IT), the economy and organisational change in banks. Since this relationship is central to our empirical chapters where we will discuss the nature of this relationship in detail, it is worth mentioning the general character of this research now. There are a number of different yet interlinked approaches to IT and banking organisations. Some are primarily interested in the role of IT (in various forms) in producing or enhancing global economic and social change; that is, for example, in producing an 'information society' (Webster 1995). The work of Bilderbeeck and Buitelaar (1992) presents financial-service organisations as important exemplars of organisations at the forefront of IT implementation and innovation, an approach that perhaps reaches its apogee in the futuristic prognostications of Sweet (1997) and Angel (1997) with their ideas on 'off-planet' banking. Other approaches have a more 'down-to-earth' focus on the impact of IT on specific aspects of work, working life and behaviour (Cressey and Scott 1994; Smith and Wield 1988; Fincham 1998). Central to these approaches is the assertion that changes in the nature of work in mature industrial societies have been increasingly intertwined with the deployment of IT. Information Technology, especially systems that can facilitate groupworking, coordination and communication of decision making, is seen as a key element in the change to more flexible and responsive forms of organisation. According to this view, collaborative work, a central feature of distributed organisations, has increasingly moved from a 'physical' to an electronic basis with the advent of widespread distributed computing (Robins 1992). Such developments are highlighted by the introduction within organisations of e-mail, desktop video-conferencing systems and the expansion and use of databases of electronic documents running across internationally distributed electronic networks. The projected development of virtual reality environments within banking is also creating some excitement (Rheingold 1992).

Although sometimes – if not always – the source of considerable imaginative hype, most if not all of this research places tremendous emphasis on IT in supporting new organisational forms. Given the importance of IT in current banking, we shall discuss much of this research in later chapters. At this point, however, what is important to note about this research is that, like much of the research on the new aesthetics of the postmodern society and the new forms of consumer identity discussed earlier, it is remarkably lacking in empirical detail. It is driven not by a concern with specifying what the role of technology may be (or could be) in practice or even with the close examination of technology use, since the main purpose of the research is to refer to technology and associated changes to develop broad and often generalising arguments about the role of technology in any organisation. By way of further illustration, analyses of IT and the labour process have generally been strongly theoretical as well. This leads to what Button (1993) calls 'the case of the disappearing technology'; that is, to a view that does not provide any information about what technology use involves. The consequence of this is that such research, and indeed sociological research on banking in general – is irrelevant to the needs of those within banks who are subject to or wishing to manage the processes of organisational and technological change. In a phrase, banks are the subject of sociological inquiries but are not in any practical or real way guided by it.

Financial services and more engaged sociology: CSCW

An altogether separate set of approaches to understanding features of the work of banks has emerged from an entirely different tradition, that of the aforementioned computer supported co-operative work (CSCW). CSCW's focus on 'design' has been predicated on technology and organisation being treated as 'encountered' phenomena implicated in the 'doing' of work tasks. While (arguably) sharing a common interest and a common focus on design there is little in the way of a common approach to research within CSCW, sociological or otherwise. Even within those areas within CSCW that are sociological, there is some diversity too. This is reflected in a number of very different views to understanding work within financial-service organisations.

Within the 'Lancastrian School', for example (Harper, 1997), the need to increase the utility of fieldwork-based approaches and especially ethnography has motivated a range of very different developments. One particular concern has been to investigate how the results of such studies might be structured for presentation in a manner which makes them more 'digestible' in a commercial context. Those interested in organisational re-design are frequently primarily interested in rapidly and succinctly ascertaining aspects of organisational work or processes that are 'useful or 'problematic'. They also need practical policy recommendations – as reflected in the statement reported in Blythin *et al.* (1997):

> Despite the importance of the fieldwork study the appropriate presentation of the materials to those responsible for managing the Centre was key. Because the study was about the work as actually done it was able to use presentational materials which resonated with the practical experience of the managers who were the group to convince about the nature of their problems. Once they could see them through the fieldwork results, they could then better also see what sorts of things needed to be changed and improved by better communication. They came to 'own' the problems and take steps to share them as a means of coming to an agreed solution.
>
> (Blythin *et al.* 1997: 47)

These practical methods of information exchange are familiar to all interdisciplinary research enterprises, of course.

Nonetheless, over a number of years a set of analytic foci have developed within this sociologically informed empirical work, including the work of the Lancastrians. These foci have included a concern with 'distributed co-ordination' and 'plans and procedures'. These have evolved to help organise and present the materials that ethnography in particular can provide and thereby go some way to addressing this question of how to communicate the resulting materials. They have also helped ensure the development of a suitable concern within the fieldwork activities that allows the practical engagement we have spoken of (in the case of CSCW this engagement is addressed to technology design, of course). Since some of these foci will run through later chapters, it is worth elaborating at least these two now.

Distributed co-ordination refers to the various ways in which the co-ordination of people and tasks is accomplished as a routine feature of 'real world, real time' work. Such co-ordination does not consist in any one feature of the work but is deeply and inseparably implicated in the procedural details of all work activities. Much of this co-ordination work consists of distributing relevant information to concerned parties and keeping this flow of information going as a routine state of affairs. This is especially relevant to many aspects of work in banks which are explicitly concerned with co-ordinating interdependencies of various kinds – the transferring of funds between various accounts, the creation of customer notes of relevance to different experts within a bank, and so on.

Plans and procedures is a label for a concern with how rules and regulations get exercised and oriented to in specific settings. There are, of course, a wide range of formal procedures in banks which include, for example, 'How to Sanction a Loan' and 'How to Return a Cheque'. The step-by-step processes for the accomplishment of such tasks is contained in widely available manuals. The research undertaken within this analytic focus is concerned with how they are used as co-ordinating mechanisms within socially organised 'real world, real time' work activities.[1] The construction and use of plans in such activities typically involve the supposition that 'practically' and 'characteristically' plans are 'recipient designed'; that is, spelt out to an extent to which those who are to follow them are, for example, familiar with the circumstances in which they are to follow them, sufficiently trained in the tasks involved, and a host of other possible considerations.[2] By placing plans, procedures and decision making within its social and organisational context, they come to be seen as elements which enable workers to make sense of their own work and that of others and to come to a decision about future courses of action. What this emphasises is the importance of seeing how and in what ways plans and procedures are interwoven into a highly variegated set of phenomena that make up the social organisation of work.

---

1 It is important to point out here that the research makes no assumptions that all the items in the 'variegated collection of phenomena' are used in the same way – it may also be important to note that some of these items, for example, certain of the action sheets, are used to overcome some of the problems emanating from the fact that some banks' computer systems do not operate in 'real time'.
2 The making of plans does not indicate any expectation that the course of actions which they specify will, of necessity, follow through. It is quite clear, to anyone observing bank lending that relevant staff consider that they have flexibility to depart from the regulations in order to develop issues that arise in the course of the lending interview and because of the 'customer-facing' nature of their work. Indeed, the point of plans is often to direct courses of action to maximise the chances that these courses of action will ensue despite the contingencies which can arise.

CONCLUSION

These remarks are simply intended to give a flavour of how distinct the approach to empirical phenomena that has emerged in CSCW is from the extant sociological literature on banking. But for the implications of our arguments to be fully understood, and then in turn for the output of the deriving arguments to have impact in practical ways, will require that they be placed in a broader context. Here it is not only matters of analytic attention that is relevant. In addition, for the research we outline to have an impact will require that those already well ensconced in terms of delivering contributions to management of change process to allow another view, another voice if you like, into the relevant discourses and discussions. There is likely to be some resistance here as well as suspicion. This will arise in part because of a natural desire for self-interest, and partly because of a more objective assessment of the historical value or sociology, especially when compared against the promissory notes that have been endlessly proffered by sociologists in the past. Of course, one of the goals of this book is to go over some of the reasons why we believe that a new kind of sociology – a post-disciplinary one as we have put it – can deliver the goods that previous sociology has failed to do.

Even so, we have to be careful to control expectations here: for when we highlight and explain the weaknesses in the kinds of approaches typically turned to in change management we will not be wanting to say that these approaches are without merit. As we have already noted, it is rather that they do not do all that is necessary. And it can be reasonably asked: What approach ever does? It is in full awareness of this oft-forgotten fact that the modesty of our ambitions needs to be understood. For we are wanting to be modest in the sense that the kind of sociologically informed approach we develop should be viewed as a supplement to more mainstream contributors to change management. It does not replace them or provide a competitor.

In any case, more than a book will be required to generate the substantive shift in either sociology or the form of its contribution to organisational change. The kind of empirical research we think is worth undertaking requires a subtlety of understanding in its undertaking that is all too often lacking on the part of sociologists trained to think on the large scale and in broad brushstrokes. Those participating in organisational change processes are often working under extreme pressure and here too subtlety and refinement are too easily lost. For these individuals, tools that enable rapid navigation through large volumes of material are more desirable than those which provide access to details. But these factors notwithstanding, we hope to show in what follows that a sociologically influenced approach to empirical phenomena can offer considerable insights, so much so that ensuring that the time and the subtlety of mind required is provided. We are not alone in this – colleagues in various institutions in

Europe and North America are convinced of the same and their work too is beginning to see the light of day. But we do not want ours to be a closed community – we want and indeed are motivated by a desire to get those who have the training, the instinct and the ambition, to undertake what we have been doing for the past decade. The rewards are much greater than can be achieved with the publishing of another article in a journal or another soon-to-be-forgotten theoretical monograph: the rewards are seen when those whose business it is to change their work places take heed of what has been said.

Part I

2 Organisational studies and empirical description

INTRODUCTION

Much of the material in this book reports work we have conducted in various financial retail-service organisations over a number of years. It is our hope that the results of these 'organisational ethnographies' will be of interest in themselves. Nevertheless, the retail financial-services sector itself is not our primary subject. Our interest is the nature of enquiry in the sociological and more generally the human sciences, and the purposes to which it can be put. The human sciences, and our particular discipline, sociology, have had an input into a whole variety of human endeavours and experiences, and have done so for the most part in a particular way. Sociology especially has sought, broadly speaking, to explain human conduct using a range of theoretical models, and to critique what it sees as the foundations of this conduct. Such foundations may be found in gender division, hierarchical institutions, various hidden-power formations, and so forth. Our task in this chapter is not to resolve the various debates surrounding discussion of these foundations, so much as to inquire into the practical implications these approaches may have for the management of change in organisations. Doing so will make many of the debates seem irrelevant, at least to our concerns. This may seem a curious thing to say at the outset, but by the time we have concluded our discussion we hope it will be clear that these debates are primarily about competing theories of organisation. We will suggest that most of these theories offer little guidance on how to investigate and analyse organisational behaviour with the concerns we have in mind.

This is not to say that such sociological theorising is without its merit, far from it. It is wholly appropriate in a large and complex discipline like sociology. Nor is it such an extreme view as it might first appear. All we are wanting to argue is that the primary goal of most inquiries into organisations consists of using empirical materials to refine and develop theory. Unsurprisingly, this distracts attention from the problem of how to capture and present empirical materials for those less interested in theory. One by-product of this is that such materials are more or less unsuitable for use in management change activities.

Besides, before we can turn to outline our own approach to empirical investigation, it is necessary to outline the kind of theory-driven knowledge of organisation we are referring to. This will allow us to place our own programme of research into a broader context. Our purpose will not be to provide a comprehensive review of such thinking but to summarise what we feel are its salient features. We will begin by sketching some of the early functional approaches to organisations mainly motivated by a desire to create typologies. We will note what implications these approaches have for understanding technology and how one paradox is that they tend to make human action seem very mechanical, almost like a technology itself. We will then review the slightly different programme of functionalism which focuses on action in organisation, rather than organisational structure. Here the concern is with psychology, and the relationship between the psychology of organisational actors and the achievement of organisational goals, suitable levels of motivation, and so forth. We then remark on some of the current perspectives in the sociology of organisations, which try and correct what sociologists see as the inappropriateness of psychological as against sociological factors in the explanations of the construction of identity.

We will then take a different tack in our discussions and ask what purposes have motivated this literature. We will be primarily concerned with what motivates current sociological approaches. We will start this section by going back to the early 1970s to the work of David Silverman, and then trace some strands of continuity between this and the more recently emerged concern with sense making in organisations in the work of Weick. We will suggest that both Silverman's and Weick's work is typical of the bulk of current sociological approaches insofar as it is concerned with the structure-agency debate. That is to say, there is an interest in explaining, theoretically, the relationship between the individual and organisation – classically if crudely characterised as a conflict between freedom and restraint, between rules and autonomy. This conflict (or dichotomy), we will suggest, is paralleled in the concerns of the psychological research will have reviewed, as well as in early functionalism. We will suggest that if one looks at all of this together, one can see that this research – the bulk of organisational studies – is primarily focused on theoretical explanation rather than, say, empirical description. We will ask whether the research justifies itself in terms of empirical description and whether the same (i.e., those descriptions) could be used to support more pragmatic and practical contributions to organisational life, for example through change management. We will be negative in our conclusions.

Nonetheless, it should be noted at the outset that the research we will have reviewed is not by any means all that there is within organisational studies and perhaps more importantly leaves aside those approaches which are more design oriented, including Business Process Re-engineering. Since these are often important in current change programmes, the next chapter will be dedicated to their investigation. Only then will we have concluded describing the context in which our own approach exists.

ORGANISATIONAL STUDIES

Our goal then may seem rather broad, although as we say, our argument is not as radical as it might appear. Our concern is to consider the degree to which, in the context of organisational studies, we can discern what the 'grounding' of candidate theories might be, and if any 'real world' consequences are entailed by such theorising. We are concerned especially to identify what a description of being a member of an organisation (such as a bank) would be. We will want to seek a description which provides an adequate sense of the experience that is constitutive of being, say, a cashier, a sales representative or an individual who undertakes the processing tasks behind the scenes in banks, often called 'waste' activities or 'back office' work. We will be concerned too with descriptions of more technologically oriented work as well as the work of senior managers within such organisations. Our view is that change management needs adequate descriptions of any and all jobs in any organisation. The kinds of phrases that typically get used to convey or label such descriptions are, unfortunately, rather awkward; the 'lived experience' is perhaps one of the most popular. But what such descriptions should say is something about what 'doing a job of work' is like without losing sight of the work in question for the sake of theory. Perhaps the most striking feature of the organisational literature is how little understanding of these 'experiential' aspects it confers, and this holds true regardless of the theoretical stance in question. It seems to us that reasons for this lie in the purposes to which the research in question is put to. By and large, these purposes have to do with elaborating or refining theoretical discussions.

Although it might seem the wrong place to start, the reader can get a hint of what we will be wanting to conclude by having his or her attention drawn to the fact that current organisational literature is replete with competing theories. One writer, Peter Manning, has summed this up:

> Organizational analysis faces a turning point as the now-tired functionalism, including the systems theory and organic models of another generation, seems exhausted. In functionalism, systems theory, Marxism, structuralism and semiotic-influenced work, system and structure precede content and pattern agency. These outlines of the possible seem blurred now, and 'exhaustion' is perhaps less accurate than desuetude. A cursory examination of research in organizational analysis suggests a proliferation of new journals with a continental flair, combining ethnography and case studies with a dash of semiotics and poststructuralism. If an intellectual centre now exists, it is loosely

articulated. ... These versions of organizational analysis have not been widely accepted. ... Several reasons for this can be noted. Some are a cluster of critiques, shaping an anti-theory of sorts. They draw on unfamiliar and abstract models (structuralism, semiotics, population biology), cite difficult (perhaps even unread) sources (Derrida, Lyotard, Kristeva, Baudrillard) and walk the blurred line between organizing, a focus on meaning creation and ordering, and organization as a product and determinant. Some argue from philosophical premises free of empirical data.

(Manning 1997: 139)

Now it is not our business to offer a full account as to why this might be so. Our concern is, rather, to briefly characterise the developments that have led to this situation. This will require us to navigate our way through a vast literature. The map necessary for this will need to be based on some general distinctions, simply because the mass of literature would look incoherent without them. As it happens, in many instances stronger claims are made on the basis of such distinctions than one might associate with the simple use of a map. For example, much of organisational writing characterises different approaches according to sets of assumptions about knowledge, sociological auspices and intellectual stance. This holds true for Burrell and Morgan (1979), two of the most cited researchers in this area. According to these authors, the variations in question are such that the word 'paradigm' can be used to categorise them.

More specifically, Burrell and Morgan argue that there are basically two dimensions which intersect in organisational theorising. On the one hand, there is the sociology of 'regulation' as against the sociology of 'social change'; and on the other, 'subjective' against 'objective' sociology. From the four spaces that occur in such a matrix, they argue that there are four distinct paradigms in the study or theory of organisations; namely: functionalist, interpretive, radical humanist and radical structuralist.

The specifics of this particular matrix need not concern us, though what does are the consequences that follow from this rather Kuhnian way of conceiving intellectual endeavour. Two especially are worth a mention:

(Each) paradigm (has) an underlying unity in terms of its basic and often 'taken for granted' assumptions, which separate a group of theorists in a very fundamental way from theorists located in other paradigms. The unity of the paradigm thus derives from reference to alternative views of reality which lie outside its boundaries and which may not be necessarily even be recognised as existing.

(*ibid.*: 23–4)

one point is worthy of further emphasis. This relates to the fact that the four paradigms are mutually exclusive. They offer different views of social reality, and to understand the nature of all four is to understand four different views of (organisations). They offer different ways of seeing. A synthesis is not possible.

(*ibid.*: 25)

From this view, the history of organisational theory consists of a debate across a set of mutually exclusive assumptions.

By way of an aside, whether this 'strong' paradigmatic version is adequate is open to question. For one thing, it is doubtful whether paradigms are radically incommensurable much of the time, and for another, it is doubtful whether there is unity of perspectives within particular paradigms in quite the way that Burrell and Morgan argue. Thirdly, their positioning of particular perspectives, notably ethnomethodology, is fundamentally mistaken.

Be that as it may, the paradigm matrix does serve one important function, though it is seldom made explicit by Burrell and Morgan themselves. Specifically, it is a matrix structured according to analytic purpose. Whereas the distinction between, for example, 'objective' and 'subjective' approaches is represented as a struggle between those who seek to explain the form of organisations in terms of efficiency and effectiveness (the objectivists), and those who seek to understand the influence of 'culture' (the subjectivists), Burrell and Morgan's typology also serves to make explicit the different purposes organisational analysis might serve. This is what interests us. Some of these purposes are moral and some are political. But rarely do these purposes lead to any practical implications for organisations. Or rather we should be more precise: though some of these could (e.g., some of the early scientific management work) by and large they are not and the practical implications are either disregarded or simply neglected. Burrell and Morgan's account of certain 'functionalist' explanations can be used to demonstrate this. It is to that we shall now turn.

Functionalism and the creation of typologies

Burrell and Morgan characterise two broad forms of functionalism, the first being a set of approaches which attempt to typologise organisational structures and practices and the second focusing on the relationship between structure and such things as individual psychology. In more detail, the first of these entails analysis of how organisational forms are functionally related to various endogenous factors, such as other organisations or social processes. Doing so relies on assumptions about the dependence and independence of analytically separable phenomena. The primary axis along which accounts of this kind are distinguished is largely to do with whether these variables are internal or external to the organisation.

The classic accounts of this functional approach to organisations include Taylorism (Taylor 1947; Fayol 1949), which treats management as the key variable in determining organisational efficiency; the goal-oriented explanations of organisational action (Parsons 1960; Blau and Scott 1963); the compliance or control models of organisation (Katz and Kahn 1966; Etzioni 1970); and the contingency approaches (Burns and Stalker 1961; Lawrence and Lorsch 1967; Blau *et al.* 1976). There are also the Aston studies (Pugh and Hickson 1976; Pugh and Hining 1976; Pugh and Payne 1977). In the latter, discussions surround the relative importance of factors such as technology, size and specialisation. One notable treatment of technology in this vein was in the research of Joan Woodward; still referred to over 30 years after its publication (1965). Of more interest to us, however, was the work originating in the late 1950s with such writers as W. F. Whyte (1959), Walker and Guest (1952) and Sayles (1958). These researchers sought to develop what they saw as the implications of the human-relations school (which Burrell and Morgan view as functionalist) by analysing the impact of technology on the workgroup in terms not only of work behaviour but also in terms of sentiment and work satisfaction.

We need not concern ourselves with the deterministic consequences of this form of argument (but see Silverman, 1970, pp. 100–3), but wish to note that this kind of research took for granted the fact that technology, when implemented, would simply work. The nature of that work, that is, what people did with technology, was left aside as were questions about how the technology was made to 'fit into' processes and contexts.

A similar concern with typology and technology, combined with a curious disregard for what using technology actually involved, was socio-technical Systems Theory, long associated with the Tavistock Institute. In essence, this was intended as corrective to what was viewed as the excessive determinism in the work of Whyte and others. Here, researchers such as Argyris (1965), Emery and Trist (1965, 1972), Trist and Bamforth (1951), Rice (1958), Thorsrud *et al.* (1976) developed what are sometimes called motivational accounts which incorporate not only psychological but social-psychological factors affecting the relationship between small-group behaviours and changing technologies, for instance in coal mines. This body of work has been hugely influential, largely through the auspices of the charismatic Enid Mumford. There is also the related 'Participative Design' movement in Scandinavia and the USA (we will discuss this movement further in the next chapter). Shulman (1995) provides a useful overview of the assumptions built into Socio-technical Systems work and points out one of its peculiar paradoxes. A paradox in the sense that if we are suggesting that how technology actually gets used as part of a day's work gets lost from view in much of this work, then at the same time the practices and processes of those individuals who use technology comes to be treated as if it were a technology of sorts itself. He points out:

> firstly, their roles in effecting group performances are claimed to be of increasing importance, yet they are little understood; and secondly, by

focussing on the question of what are the relationships between good work group performance and information technology, it becomes apparent that the answers rely on our underlying assumptions about communication within the organizations in which these work groups are partially embedded. By reflecting on these assumptions, a more informed view of work group performance emerges.

(*ibid*.: 357)

He sums up the direction of research in this area as follows:

some of the problematics ... can be associated with the proclivity of researchers to examine human work groups as if they were technology.

(*ibid*.: 369–70)

So, despite the fact that the Socio-technical Systems approach emphasises the role of technology in work, little attention is paid to the way in which technology relates to workgroup performance.

There are various accounts offered for this. According to Polley and van Dyne (1994) there is an excessive emphasis on motivational and training factors. In any case, to our mind, though attaining 'good workgroup performance' may well be a laudable goal in Socio-technical Systems research, the evidence concerning what 'good' means to the groups themselves or, say, from the perspectives of the managers of these groups would appear hard to come by. Similarly, understanding how workgroups are in practice constituted, and how they relate to wider organisational concerns, is not substantially dealt with. Of particular interest – the relevance of which will become clearer in later chapters – is the fact what it means to 'co-operate' and 'co-ordinate' a workgroup requires a much more detailed description and explication than is provided in Socio-technical Systems research.[3]

This literature, then, has the great merit of pointing out how technology and organisational work are linked. Nevertheless, the absence of empirical detail has at least one unfortunate consequence, and that is it leads to a presumption that the introduction of new technology *tout court* has effects. To be clear, what we are alluding to is not that a variety of 'technical'

---

3 Shulman makes the point (drawing substantially on Sless 1981) that much of this literature relies on an uncritical conflation of information and communication. Information is held to be a property of the 'physical' world and is entity-like. Communication is a property of the social world, and is meaning-dependent. A critical point in Sless' argument is that meaning is indeterminate. The consequences are that: 'It is logically impossible to establish foundations for, and derive predictable long term generalisations from, anything as inherently unstable as human social life ... This then is the real key failure of past research on information technology ... The past research attempted to predict the impact of technology on work group activity, when that activity itself is inherently unstable.' (p. 369)

determinism needs to be replaced with a radical 'social' determinism. We are wanting to point out that long before one can begin to consider what kinds of effects technology might have, one would want to examine the work to be done in making the technology work. This is absent in this research.

Other forms of functionalism

Our remarks on those studies expressly focused on technology and organisations is intended in the main to suggest that studies concerned with the organisational impact of technology are for the most part consistent with what Burrell and Morgan regard as functionalist theory. Of course, it would be wrong to assert that what Burrell and Morgan call functionalist approaches to organisations are the only strand of organisational research that can be described in functionalist terms. What Silverman terms 'organizational psychology' for example, has been a respectable counter-tradition to main functionalist approaches represented in the work mentioned above. This has certainly been so since the earliest days of organisational research; even as far back as the famous Hawthorne experiments conducted by Roethlisberger and Dickson.

Whatever the intellectual auspices of the organisational psychology tradition, the fact that they seek to provide 'motivational' accounts is unarguable. By motivational is meant that they are concerned with what these days is called 'agency'. Burrell and Morgan are particularly interested in this, since they view a concern with agency as one of the issues that differentiate paradigms. According to them, a concern with agency or, in their terms, the 'action frame of reference' is not an alternative to functionalist theory. It is a part of it. Hence, rather than the Human Relations school providing, let us say, a radical and comprehensive critique of Taylorism, it simply offers a slightly different approach; differences which are largely to do with some variation in theoretical assumption. According to Burrell and Morgan, 'The main difference between Taylorism and the work of the early (organisational) psychologists (such as the Human Relations school) is thus not so much one of principle as of detail' (p. 130).

Key to the claim that these approaches are not so different is the argument that such studies, though appearing radical because of their concern with action or agency, actually function to serve management interests as much as any other forms of functionalism. This is confirmed by Mitchell and Larson (quoted in Chanlat 1994), who suggest that organisational psychology:

> is a field whose aim is to develop a better understanding of human behaviour, and then use this knowledge to make people more productive and more satisfied within their organizations.
>
> (Chanlat 1994: 156)

Irrespective of what lay behind this research – which we shall be coming back to – this research did lay down a marker for the study of social rather than material need and its relationship to organisational behaviour. For Burrell and Morgan the Hawthorne studies shifted functional explanation from *'the narrowly behavioural and deterministic approach ... towards a mechanical equilibrium systems model'* (p. 132).

Be that as it may, what is more fundamental is this question of ultimate purposes. For the most part, these management purposes are portrayed very one-sidedly in the so-called 'critical' literature. Such literature focuses on the political and moral assumptions underscoring research, and asks whether research should accept any assumption that, for example, hierarchical organisations are acceptable in the first place, and thus whether management interests should be adopted.

Our own response to these critical perspectives is actually to note that irrespective of the specifics of these particular functionalist accounts, what they are first and foremost is largely pragmatic. Their 'business', so to speak, is the business of seeking more effective performance. Now, we claim no originality in pointing this out, but would suggest that when it comes to critique, such research ought to be judged on its own merits rather than any grand philosophical or moral code that critics wish to apply. Such research should be judged according to whether that research achieved what it set out to achieve. Many commentators have pointed out that supporting evidence is often contradictory, ambiguous and sketchy, including Burrell and Morgan, though few have recognised what we see as the fundamental difference between assessing research in its own terms as against assessing it against external criteria.

One exception is Charles Perrow. Though we are not providing a full overview of organisational studies, no review could be adequate without discussion of Perrow. His work is remarkable in a number of ways, not least because he brings a laconic humour to a typically dry and rather charmless intellectual domain. Of greater importance, he offers a useful corrective to those who try to understand organisational studies through the use of paradigms and, furthermore, restates the importance of understanding what the intentions and goals of any research programme in organisational studies might be. He did this in 1970, and his work came to be seen as something of a revolutionary defence of functionalist perspectives – revolutionary because, at that time, critical views were very much in the ascendancy and any mention of functionalism was usually linked with disdain and castigation.

Perrow sought to revitalise functional approaches by providing a distinctive view of complex organisations. Perrow raised the following problem for the anti-functionalist 'people' perspective which had not hitherto been fully addressed:

> one of the enduring truisms of organizational analysis is that organizations are, after all, made up of people. Such a statement usually

brings about a sagacious nodding of heads and a comfortable feeling of being on solid ground. But it is also true that organizations are inanimate things – they are filing cabinets, typewriters, machinery, records, mailing lists, or goods and services. This observation usually elicits no resounding thump on the table. Still, it raises a good question.

(Perrow 1970: 2–3)

This is indeed a question that we ourselves take up in later chapters, but we bring Perrow into our discussion for another set of remarks he makes. For Perrow pointed out that the scorn heaped upon the functionalist Scientific Management approach was – and still is it must be said – typically based on an indifference to what was actually said. Hence:

in the 1920s and 1930s, the principles being enunciated by the management school were less obvious. Indeed, many of them are still violated in organizations today. Scientific Management theorists prescribed a span of control of about five ... but one finds twenty men reporting to a company president or the administrative head of an agency. They advocated unity of command, but we find units being given contradictory orders by two or three different groups above them. They developed the idea that managers should only deal with exceptions and planning, not with daily routines, but many organizations do not distinguish between routine administration and long-range policy formation.

(*ibid.*: 15)

and

More important, they insisted that an organization cannot be designed on the basis of the kinds of informal relations that grow up in an organization. Rather, they held that the design must minimise the opportunity for unfortunate and uncontrollable informal relations, leaving room only for the necessary ones. Their view of man was simplistic, but in laying out general principles ... their simple views were probably adequate to the task.

(*ibid.*: 19)

Perrow is drawing attention to the pragmatic purposes of this approach; the importance of which we have already noted. Following from a discussion of Burns and Stalker, he remarks:

One of the constant complaints of the supervisors and engineers in the firm I studied was that when something went wrong on the production line, as it did quite frequently, they had no way of knowing just where the problem was. Sometimes sheer intuition on the part of a foreman or engineer was necessary to correct the problem.

(*ibid.*: 46)

and

In this era of increasing computerization, production control measures, and time-study experts, the temptation to 'rationalize' production is great. No doubt a great many firms need greater rationalization of their production methods and organizational structures. However ... in some technological situations, the tight bureaucratic structure ... might be quite inappropriate.

(*ibid.*: 47)

Perrow goes on to recognise that one of the advantages of a specifically functional analysis is that it offers a 'convenient tool' for analysing differences between organisations; differences as regards such things as the scope of management responsibility, complexity of decision making, and such like. These are the kinds of things that Scientific Management wanted to address. However, though we think very highly of Perrow's work, we want to note that just like the majority of functionalist researchers, Perrow does not say much about what kind of data would be appropriate for giving a detailed understanding of what these differences might look like. There is no description of the practical actions that are undertaken in different organisational contexts for example, the descriptions of the kinds of lived experiences we mentioned earlier. Nonetheless, Perrow does draw attention to the need to understand what the purposes behind some programme of inquiries might be. As we shall see, if the practical and pragmatic concerns of the early functionalist have been largely forgotten, then today such pragmatism is largely absent altogether from a great deal of organisational research.

Functionalism, psychology and organisational behaviour

A second major grouping of functionalism can be identified by its concern with psychology or motivational factors – at least according to Burrell and Morgan. Burrell and Morgan have this view despite the fact that there remains a view in sociology that functional accounts which concern themselves with motivation are somehow vastly different or at least incompatible with those which focus on functional structure (such as Taylorism). Yet it is social psychology that has produced some of the more elaborate accounts of what this relationship might be – so elaborate that at first reading one might be persuaded that they have been solved.

In broad terms, such social psychological research assumes that certain 'wants' or 'needs' can be imputed to an individual, and analysis can then concentrate on the gap between those needs, emotions and cognitive state at work. This in turn can be linked to organisational structure, goals, and so forth. Over the years the complexity of the relationships between these factors has been developed. For example, early research in this vein (Morse 1953), suggested that the notion of work 'satisfaction' in Taylor's scientific management did not directly associate with reward, but to the degree to which reward associated with 'want'. Further research looked into the problematic relationship between 'intrinsic' and 'extrinsic' factors. Work such as that of Maslow's (1943) on the 'hierarchy of needs' was clearly of this kind, as indeed were subsequent correctives such as that of Hertzberg (1968), distinguishing between motivation and hygiene. According to this view, needs and wants are internally related; the satisfaction of lower level needs leads to the desire for higher level needs to be satisfied. All of this is dependent upon mental structure.

Even from an early stage, the task in this social psychological research was to relate needs – whatever they might be and however understood – to organisational effectiveness. Hence, Mcgregor (1966) specifically contrasted the assumptions contained in management views in his famous Theory X and Theory Y distinction, the point being that these assumptions are motivational assumptions. Others, such as Argyris (1957), developed a 'maturation' model of the personality and related it to the problem of interpersonal competence in organisations and tensions in organisational goals. Their model draws heavily on notions of pathology and 'health' in the personality.

Key to all of this research is the assumption that the psychological state of individual members of organisations is viewed as the primary factor in explaining behaviour. It should be pointed out that this remains true even when more complex and subtle models are deployed, as with attempts to relate personality and 'trait' (e.g., Mount *et al.* 1994), or emotion to behaviour (e.g., Warr 1994).

Perhaps the most fully-fledged version of such motivational accounts is the 'job design' or 'workload' perspective associated with, amongst others, Vroom (1964), Porter and Lawler (1968) and Lawler (1973). This was initially developed for application to industrial contexts. In the work of Lawler, for example, the intrinsic rewards in task performance were viewed as enhancing employee motivation and thus productivity. Such analysis aimed to investigate how effective human operators are subject to a range of working conditions, and argue that using typologies such as Hackman and Oldman's (1976) Job Characteristics model, should make it possible to optimise work satisfaction, and thereby performance. In such accounts, 'psychological states' such as 'experienced meaningfulness of the work', 'experienced responsibility for work outcomes' and 'knowledge of results' provide 'core job' characteristics such as 'skill variety', 'task identity', 'task significance', 'autonomy' and 'feedback from job'. In turn, these dimensions are predictive of job satisfaction, intrinsic motivation and quality of work.

In recent years, there has been a decline in work of this kind, perhaps because, as Handy suggests:

> If we could understand, and then could predict, the ways in which individuals were motivated we could influence them by changing the components of that motivation process. Is that manipulation – or management? ... Early work on motivation was indeed concerned to find ways by which the individual could be 'motivated' to apply more effort and talent ... we should be relieved that no guaranteed formula of motivation was found.
>
> (Handy 1993: 29–30)

It may be that, as Katzell and Thompson have pointed out, theories of work motivation are overly simplistic (quoted in Nord and Fox 1995). Hence, Schein (1992) refers to the complex assumption, wherein there is no unique role for the traditional industrial/organisational psychologist, but I see a great potential for the psychologist to work as a team member with colleagues who are ethnographically oriented. In other words, and with deceptive simplicity, in recent years authors like Schein have suggested that the field of organisational behaviour needs to discover 'context'. This means that motivational accounts need to link the psychology of the individual to the structure of the organisation through an analysis of symbols, rules and social construction (Wilpert 1995). There is obviously an extensive programme of research implied here, since the relationship of such things vary considerably from one context to another, as Karpik pointed out as long ago as 1968 (Karpik 1968)

A sociological response

Sociological responses to these developments have been provided by many authors, including Thompson and McHugh (1990). The latter argue that the somewhat general typifications of organisational psychology have been turned into measurement tools that relate motivation to organisational efficiency. This 'prescriptive' turn as they put it, explicitly rendered into the 'job design' perspective just mentioned, is founded on some problematic assumptions. They argue that the most telling is the assumption that motivation is an 'internal', or cognitive state, rather than a social one. They further assert that programmes such as Total Quality Management (TQM) are heavily influenced by these assumptions, in that they are geared to the integration of individual and organisational goals (*ibid.*: 279). For Thompson and McHugh, organisational psychology's move towards management purposes justifies a move to sociological accounts and away from psychological ones; after all efficiency, improved productivity are, they claim, sociological phenomena, not psychological ones. Nonetheless, they do not propose to disregard the importance of psychology in organisations so much as to present its importance in a different way. They have in mind analysis which centres on the problem of identity – a psychological phenomena if ever there was one – but give this a sociological slant by emphasising the need to focus on 'the reproduction and transformation of those identities in the context of work organisations' (*ibid.*: 286–7).

Citing Weigert *et al* (1986), they provide a definition of identity as produced by the more 'helpful' forms of social psychology:

> identity is a definition that transforms a mere biological individual into a human person. It is a definition that emerges from and is sustained by the cultural meanings of social relationships activated in interaction.
> (Thompson and McHugh, 1990: 288)

The 'sociological' rendering of behaviour through notions of 'identity' is, in effect, a vehicle for critical renderings of motive as social constructions. They argue that:

> new and theoretical knowledge often becomes part of the repertoire of the science of organisational behaviour, functioning as technologies of regulation which are used to control and discipline employees.
> (*ibid.*: 297)

That is to say, that theories of organisation come to inform and help create the identities people have within organisational settings (*ibid.*: 297). Thus research should look less at cognitive processes of emotional need and more at the discourses and ideologies that surround people (Knights *et al.* 1985).

When Burrell and Morgan wrote their text (1979), they were unable to find a substantial body of literature in this area, but pointed to what was then a relatively small corpus. They would be no doubt gratified by the subsequent rapid expansion of the 'critical' literature on organisations, such as Thomson and McHugh's. The 'new' organisational studies have been strongly influenced by at least two sources. First, Marxism and theories of the labour process derived from the radical 'continental' literature associated with 'critical theory' and the Frankfurt school (see Braverman 1974). And second, postmodernism, often associated with French thinkers such as Foucault, Lyotard and Derrida.

The issue of power is not of course new, and was raised some time ago by writers such as Blau and Schoenherr (1971) and Etzioni (1961). The development of a critical perspective, however, with a specific interest in power, resistance and subordination has come to look more like a defining feature of contemporary sociological analysis of organisations (perhaps best exemplified by Clegg and Dunkerley 1980; see also Edwards 1979; Carchedi 1977). It is paralleled by feminist research in this area (see for instance Cockburn 1983). Separate from it, but nevertheless related through the critical stance it takes, is the growing body of work on regulation, globalization and the Post-Fordist mode of production (see, e.g., Piore and Sabel 1984). Such critical analysis emphasises the role of ideology, discourse (or textuality) and power in the contingent construction of the 'self' and 'identities' in organisations. A flavour of their concerns can be gleaned from Clegg:

> After Foucault, one might see organizations as discursive locales of competing calculations. Places where talk gets done, texts produced, disciplines situated, practices accomplished, subjectivities formed, organizational rationality fabricated from distinct auspices of power and knowledge.
>
> (Clegg 1994: 3)

In these accounts, the contingent nature of the 'self' and its subjugation in regimes of power and knowledge is appropriated for organisational analysis. These conceptions of 'subjectivity' are evident in the work of, for instance, Miller (1987), Rose (1990), Miller and Rose (1988), Morgan and Knights (1997).

REVISITING THE AUSPICES OF ORGANISATIONAL STUDIES

The important point about such critical sociological views is that the empirical arguments may not be the main issue (i.e., we do not think that questions to do with whether it is discourse or emotion that needs to be understood are important). We think that there might be contentious assumptions about the relationship between identity and its relationship to organisation. These underscore all such views. It is these we think are worthy of investigation. We have in mind assumptions about a perceived conflict or tension between agency and structure, between the individual in an organisation and the organisation itself.

To an extent at least, this problematic has allowed a convenient division of labour between sociology and social psychology, albeit one that is constantly traduced. More importantly, within sociology, attempts to solve this problem, to meld the individual to the structure and vice versa go back some way. Mills and Murgatroyd (1991), for example, point out that the 1970s saw in the work of David Silverman (and others) a head-on challenge to organisational theory insofar as there was an attempt to better understand and account for the role of individuals within organisations without abandoning the importance of structure of organisations. The latter was taken from functionalism. Unquestionably, these insights had some considerable influence. This led to new attempts to analyse organisational behaviour in terms of symbolism and rules rather than through reference to motivation associated with organisational studies of culture. Mills and Murgatroyd refer to these paradigmatic 'fragmentations' to argue:

> it makes sense to us that organizations can appear to confront people as an objective entity, as something external to them. It also makes sense to us that organizations are human creations, moulded out of the interactions of people. It does not make sense to us to focus, as so many studies of organizations have done, exclusively on one or the other of these two features.
>
> (Mills and Murgatroyd 1991: 1)

The themes displayed in the resulting research remained much the same as prior to Silverman and others, however. Studies of organisational change looked pretty much the same as before, as did investigations into environments and boundaries, gender and power, as well as the time-honoured research into organisational conflict. What distinguished research post-Silverman was the idea of 'truce'. According to this view, there is a stand-off between the imposition of a rule and the means by which individuals negotiate them. This:

> does much to reconcile some competing themes in our understanding of organisational action (in that a truce) permits the examination of practice – the difference between the formal organisation and the organisation in action.
>
> (*ibid.*: 61).

The 'formal' and the 'informal' then stand proxy for structure and agency, and linking the two remains the task.

The origins of much of this work can be seen in David Silverman's book *The Theory of Organizations* (1970). At the time, this was regarded as a radical departure for organisational analysis. It relocated the sociological problem of the organisation within a paradigm of 'meaning'. More specifically, Silverman identified a number of problems associated with organisational theory. He asked, for example, in what sense institutions could be said to be the embodiments of 'meaning', and hence how could organisations be said to have goals? Previously, the idea of organisational goals had been unproblematic, or at least theoretically so (see Etzioni 1961; Miller and Rice 1967; Simon 1964). The problem of fitting these ideal-typical formulations to empirical reality meant that theorising became more middle-range. That is to say, they became concerned with typologies which reflected some of the differences seen in practice. This opened up what has come to be termed 'contingency theory'; theory which rests on the notion that organisations will vary in their structure according to the impact of different environmental factors. It also opened up the possibility of new ways of understanding the relationship between the individual and the organisation, particularly in reference to how individuals contract and perceive the organisational situation in which they find themselves.

Sense-making in organisations

Perhaps the most interesting recent development in this regard is the concern for decision-making as a 'sense-making' activity. This concept has become closely associated with Weick and his book *Sense Making in Organizations* (1995). Here Weick claims to dispose of the classic antipathies between the 'formal' and 'informal' structures of the organisation by providing what he calls an integrationist position. This involves making intersubjectivity the product of sense-making. This in turn provides a solution to the structure as against agency debate. Weick seeks to characterise sense-making as a unifying principle, one which underpins the way in which organisational members encounter organisational structures and proceed to act on the way in which they interpret them. Weick argues that sense-making is occasioned, rather than being an ordinary part of being in the world. It is characterised by various features, which include the fact that it is grounded in identity construction, is retrospective, is social, ongoing, focused on by enacted cues, and driven by plausibility rather than accuracy.

He goes on to refer to the relationship between information technology and sense-making, asserting:

> what is emerging as a growing issue for sense making is the disparity between the speed and complexity of information technology and the ability of humans to comprehend the outputs of technology. These disparities create the conditions for increased arousal.
>
> (*ibid.*: 175)

Such an account allows Weick to make arguments concerning 'pre-structuring':

> I mention this to illustrate the kind of comparative work that needs to be done more systematically if we are to grasp what is lost and what is gained when information technology prestructures what people come to treat as their world. At a minimum, information technology tightens the coupling between events ... which increases the likelihood that interactive complexity and normal accidents ... will be more pervasive.
>
> (*ibid.*: 179)

Thus, it appears 'sense-making' is specifically associated with 'problem solving'. It has to do with the anomalies, difficulties and the strangeness of new encounters.

This version of sense-making relies on a distinction between it and the 'taken for granted'. That is, people seemingly do not 'make sense' of the world on occasions when they take it for granted, a cognitive space is opened, a threshold. This can be seen in discussion of, for instance Czarniawska-Joerges (1992) assertions concerning the degree to which organisational life is taken for granted to a lesser degree than is everyday life. Weick uncritically accepts this; thus for us it is a rather strange proposition. He quotes approvingly the suggestion that 'the job itself' is taken much more for granted than the organisation itself (*ibid*.: 212).

There is much in Weick's work that one can take no exception to, and the consistent emphasis on sense-making as an activity is to be applauded. Nonetheless and as we have hinted, there are problems. First, there is an uneasy alliance between sociological concerns with activity and some standard conceptions of cognition evident in Weick's arguments. For instance, according to Weick 'intentional sense-making' is triggered by a 'failure to confirm one's self'. Thus the sociological task (as such it is according to Weick) of sense-making is coined with the cognitive or psychological needs of the self. Similarly, the use of terms such as 'arousal' to explain how an individual joins a stream of activity, and the 'simple, familiar structures' that act as cues for individuals all resonate tacit cognitivism.[4]

Second, it is difficult to see in what sense organisational life is not 'everyday'. After all, encounters with organisational reality are replete with the 'taken for granted'. That interpretative occasions may arise as a result of certain kinds of problem or 'trouble' is in all likelihood true, and we will ourselves provide a number of examples, but how one would demonstrate that this is not the case elsewhere remains a mystery. Third, how does one distinguish between the 'job' and 'organisational life', unless one wants to take a narrow and thoroughly cognitivist position on the job as a set of 'tasks'? After all, 'doing a job' hardly entails bracketing what one knows about the organisation. Doing it competently, rather, may well involve deploying all sorts of 'known' features of the organisation.

Cognitivism aside, a fourth and greater problem with Weick's work is that he wants to treat sense-making as a micro-sociological resource *vis-à-vis* macro-sociological phenomena. That is to say, he views sense-making as a building block which eventually enables the grounding of organisational structure. Sense-making is the task of the individual; the resources available for this are provided by the organisational structure. This tendency is apparent when Weick distinguishes three levels of sense-making above that of the individual. These are the intersubjective, the generic subjective and the extra-subjective. The first refers to contexts in which the self is transformed from 'I' to 'we'. The level above is that of social structure, and

---

4 *See* Chapter 2 of Weick (1995) for these and other examples.

here selves are left behind, and some automatic rule following presence (or absence) is all that is required.[5] The third, extrasubjectivity, is at the level of culture. This is a level of symbolic reality – the world of 'pure meanings'. 'Sense-making' for Weick, then, is a linking device – linking the individual to organisational structure. With this concept, a structure of levels for sense-making can be generated, a structure which incorporates for Weick such notions as 'ideology', 'paradigm' and 'tradition' as part of its 'substance', and thus deals in the currency of beliefs, attitudes, or even the 'premise controls' mentioned by Perrow decades before (1970). Subtly, then, what looks like a new approach turns out to have the same concerns for structure and agency that sociology has had for decades. 'Rule' and 'Sense-making' here exist in an analytically distinct, and inverse relationship.

But fifth, and perhaps the biggest question of all for this kind of approach, is the kind of empirical test that would be both appropriate and adequate. Weick alludes to this when he refers to and rebuts the criticism that there is little empirical work in his book (Weick 1995: 169). For Weick, criticism of this kind is misguided; in part it stems from the inability to see 'qualitative research' as evidence. He makes some suggestions concerning the 'content and craft' of such research in this context. Organisations are conceptualised as:

> the generic subjectivity of interlocking routines, the intersubjectivity of mutually reinforcing interpretations, and the movement back and forth between these two forms by means of continuous communication.
>
> (*ibid*.: 170)

What makes organisations unique is the pressure towards generic subjectivity in the interest of premise control and interchangeability of people (*ibid*.: 170). Weick identifies a number of candidate methodologies for doing 'sense-making' analysis, including naturalistic enquiry, critical incident timelines, case scenarios, interviews, work diaries, participative observation. They share features such as a concern for 'situatedness', close observation of what people do and say, observing patterns rather than hypothesis testing, meaning rather than frequency count. What they share, in other words, is a conventional sociological take on 'qualitative' analysis. None of them, in and of themselves, could be objectionable to anyone undertaking an organisational ethnography. But underneath them still remains what we believe is a concern with theory, not description.

---

5 The notion of rule-following has generated immense confusion, and no doubt will continue to do so. For ethnomethodology, rule-following is a term which refers to the way in which members manifestly orient to rules. There is no implication that rules have causal properties in such a formulation. The distinction is best formulated in Wittgenstein's famous dictum that 'no rule dictates its own application'.

CONCLUSION

Along with the critical approaches we have all too briefly mentioned, we see two features in the work of Weick that need to be thought about. First, we can discern an attempt to maintain the structure/agency problematic through careful analysis of behavioural patterns such that those patterns become evidence of a structure. Such a view relies in Weick's case on problematic assumptions about 'mental' states such as arousal. Second, and in our view the most striking feature of these broad stances on the action approach to organisations, is the absence of substantial detail concerning work. On the face of it that may seem a rather surprising statement; though nevertheless, we think, an entirely justifiable one. The reason for this has to do precisely with the concerns of organisational studies at large.

We have seen that since critical organisational studies are in large part interested in exposing the assumptions contained in other views of the world (in the ideologies and discourses sustained and reproduced by power groups within organisations), it is hardly surprising that studies of 'work' under the auspices of critical research are in fact studies of these relations. In other words, when Morgan (1990) says:

> organizations consist of sets of disciplined relationships in which individuals perform tasks assigned to them. The nature of those tasks, the manner in which people are persuaded to fulfil them and the mechanisms of control over them is the main subject.
>
> (Morgan 1990: 17)

few would see any irony. We do.

Long ago the somewhat obtuse writer Harold Garfinkel observed that the sociology of work contained a 'missing what'. By this he meant that however hard one looks, one will not find much information about the work that is the purported subject of sociological investigations of work. Our view, like Garfinkel's, is that the phenomenon of organisational work is itself worthy of investigation. The point of our review of the research into organisational life is that it shows how little one will find out about what goes on in organisations. It shows too how much elaboration of theoretical and conceptual concerns is undertaken. We have seen this has become increasingly the case with the spread of more critical approaches to organisational studies, which have amongst other things ignored and written out of history the very pragmatic purposes of the early functionalists. These critical approaches have themselves been criticised by those like Weick who have wanted to bring a phenomenological slant to organisational research. But even here, the preoccupation still ends up being the production of ever more elaborate theory. Weick tries to build a bridge between sense-making on the part of the actor and the resources for this provided by the organisational 'context'. In this his work is like that of the critical approaches, haunted not by the need to describe and detail activities in organisational settings, but to solve that interminable riddle of the tension between the freedom of the actor on the one hand and the restraints imposed by the organisation on the other; between rules and freedom, between the world as constructed through individual perception and the world as a set of constraints that impose meaning.

3 Approaches to the management of change

INTRODUCTION

Our argument in the preceding chapter has been that organisational research has been haunted by the concerns of theory and this has obscured the problems of empirical description and data gathering. This concern with theory has been curiously unprofitable, and the falling into disuse of many theories may have as much to do with a failure of theory in general as with any particular version. It would seem that no candidate theoretical stance can make a contribution that gains general approval, and that there is little agreement even on what the purposes of theoretical work on organisations might be. As we have argued, even 'new' approaches (those largely predicated on the structure/agency problematic), do not offer a way out of this impasse. The great mystery, at least for those who believe in the value of theory, is how it is that at just such a time more prescriptive and less theoretical work on organisations – what is normally referred to as 'change management' – is, far from being ignored, more common than ever before. Change-management programmes are both seemingly universal and extraordinarily powerful, in the sense that the willingness of managers to employ consultants with the required knowledge and skills is obvious. One possible reason for this is quite simply that theorising about the organisation turns out to be significantly less interesting or valuable from a management point of view than the simple act of prescribing.

In suggesting that much, we are in no way subscribing to the various change-management fashions. Nevertheless, and disregarding what is or is not in fashion, change-management approaches are interesting for two reasons. First, sociologists who, like ourselves, have or are about to embark on ethnographic studies of organisations would find it hard to locate any organisation where change management was not an explicit part of the organisation's concerns. Indeed it has been in each of the organisations we discuss in later chapters. Second, and no less important, change-management approaches include, obviously, a concern with specifying the process(es) of change. But they also include a concern with specifying what we would call data-capture methodologies. We have in mind methods that deal with the problems of defining data; agreeing, empirically, what role technology currently has and hence what role it might have in the future; as well as techniques for describing the various form work activities take. We investigate three particular approaches to change, namely Business Process Re-engineering, Participative Design and Soft Systems Methodology, and ask how they answer these sorts of questions.

Of course, each of these approaches is quite different so it may seem unfair to bundle them together. Moreover, the latter two – Participative Design and Soft Systems – are more especially concerned with technology design than the first, leading to the scope of the questionings undertaken under their auspices being somewhat different. But these differences notwithstanding, our concern will be to suggest that each still suffers from a certain negligence when it comes to dealing with specific aspects of organisational action and context. This does not invalidate the need or even the utility of these approaches but points towards the need to supplement them. Such a supplement is offered by our own ethnographic approach outlined in the next chapter.

More specifically, we commence our discussions with Business Process Re-engineering (or BPR). Though this is not by any means the most common approach to change (there being simply too many approaches around for any one to dominate), it is certainly the most famous. More importantly, it is self-confessedly the most 'radical', systematic and far-reaching of the change-management techniques now available.[6] Most notably, and unlike the mainstream of organisational theory, it brings technology to the foreground and explicitly engages with the affordances and constraints that technology brings. Our interest is also driven by what we see as its flaws, which have to do, broadly speaking, with the compromises it has to make in its concerns. These relate to the need, on the one hand, to offer practical guides for managers concerned with the organisation from the top down, and on the other, with descriptions of tasks and processes. By necessity, these lack the kind of rich descriptions we think are important in change management.

We will then turn to brief mention of Participative Design and associated approaches, and explicate how certain political assumptions underscoring these perspectives lead to an emphasis on capturing the 'views of the users'. Though this has important advantages over other approaches, it can and often does lead to misunderstandings as between what users said they want and what they get, as well as poor characterisations of the complex interplay of technology, process and action. Such complexities are sought by Soft Systems Methodology, a review of which will follow. This approach

---

[6] Proponents of BPR can make some startling claims. Jacobson *et al.* (1995) for instance point out, 'There are estimates that 50 to 70% of companies that try it fail. I think the risk of failure is even higher' (1995, p. x, Preface). They are, of course, implying very high risk but even higher reward. In other words, the word radical here has a surgical sense.

provides perhaps the most elaborate representations of organisations, allowing as it does equal status to a host of diverse information resources and process goals in its organisational maps. Nonetheless, it displays little concern with descriptions of task or activities, tending to gloss over these despite the fact that its techniques for representing organisations are, as we say, comprehensive.

We will then turn to review the relationship between these three approaches and understanding of the role of technology in organisations, and explain how their emergence was in part a response to the now well documented 'technology paradox'. This is a label for the failure of information technologies to deliver the improvements they had been predicated to achieve. This has led to a recognition that such improvements are more likely to be delivered if technology is more closely bound with processes, through the use of Soft Systems Methodology, for example; are designed in such a fashion as to be more acceptable to users with Participative Design approaches; or are introduced in relationship to the overall functioning of an organisation's processes and value chains as with BPR. We will suggest that, though these approaches were developed with the goal of reducing the technology paradox in these ways, they too have certain deficiencies – some of which we have already alluded to – and this is necessitating a turn to additional, more detailed approaches to data capture.

APPROACHES TO CHANGE

Business Process Re-engineering

In treating BPR as an identifiable and separable form, we do no justice to a complex and sophisticated set of techniques and procedures. Nor can we engage with BPR as a practice, simply because we are unfamiliar, except on a fairly superficial level, with the actual practices of consultants working in the field. We rely on the literature for our picture. There is by now a substantial literature on BPR (see, e.g., Hammer and Champy 1993; Harrington 1991; Davenport 1993; Jacobson *et al.* 1995). So we do not propose to re-invent the wheel by elaborating its practices unnecessarily.

Our primary purpose, as should be clear, is to consider the degree to which, if at all, BPR's systematic approach to work, organisations and IT systems provides an effective solution to the problem of organisational change. In examining the methodological presuppositions of BPR, therefore, we are not seeking to make, let us say a moral point about downsizing, etc., but attempting to assess whether BPR can and does live up to its radical promise in terms of delivering all the materials that are required to achieve change.

The first point we wish to raise relates to the underpinnings of BPR – what commentators like Burrell and Morgan might call its ontological stance.

This has to do with the apparent parturition of organisational studies along a divide which we have not previously mentioned. This new division is between what one might think of as sociologically informed organisational research such as Participative Design, and more economic stances in BPR. We use the term economistic because its conventional alternative, 'rationalism', though a valid description of what stands behind much economic theory, tends to be used as a gloss when applied to change-management techniques. It is clear, not to say blindingly obvious, that the importance of 'value chains' and associated concepts in change-management literatures, along with the centrality of measurement, has much to do with economic thinking as opposed to sociological thinking. It is not so clear, taking a quote from an orthodox and by now fairly elderly text on value analysis that 'rationalism' does adequately describe the analytic stance of BPR and associated approaches. Hence:

> Value analysis is a problem-solving system implemented by the use of a specific set of techniques, a body of knowledge, and a group of learned skills. It is an organized creative approach that has for its purpose the efficient identification of unnecessary cost, i.e., cost that provides neither quality nor appearance nor customer features (...). It focuses engineering, manufacturing and purchasing attention on one objective – equivalent performance for lower cost.
>
> (Miles 1972: 3)

This stance shows itself in a number of ways. First, this economist stance can be seen to have considerable pedigree. Indeed, it is hardly a revelation that elements of BPR have been around for some time. They can be discerned in literature on 'value' and 'quality' going back some time. The more cynical might be forgiven for feeling that what has been re-engineered is the wheel.

Even so, amongst its distinctive features, and one which perhaps explains its attractiveness (as well as saying much about its dangers) is its claim to socio-technical systematicity. Leaving aside all this means for the moment, one thing this systematicity does entail (or perhaps we should say necessitate) is effective measurement. This is why technology is so central in the BPR literature. Although BPR can be variously characterised as a recipe for fundamental change[7] or as a more modest and progressive refinement of business objectives in terms of core processes (Harrington 1991), the role of IT is almost universally seen as critical. In particular, IT is significant because it is capable of magnifying the accuracy and the scope of measurement. Thus:

---

7 For instance by Hammer in his famous injunction to stop 'paving over the cowpath'.

> Measurements are key. If you cannot measure it, you cannot control it. If you cannot control it you cannot manage it. If you cannot manage it you cannot improve it.
>
> (Harrington 1991: 82)

Nevertheless, despite placing IT at the centre of the change-management process, BPR is predicated on the recognition that traditional design has, in many instances, failed to produce the productivity gains anticipated for business, especially in its 'white collar' sectors. That is, whilst being fundamentally a method for changing the organisation, implicitly at least, BPR problematises and challenges orthodox approaches to systems design. BPR proponents create a distance from the modelling activities associated with traditional design by arguing that:

> all these techniques come from the computer world. It is as though we learned to think in a way that works for computer systems, and we realized we could apply the same way of thinking to describe an organization ... we find this unacceptable ... we shall introduce ... the basis for a modelling technique for people, not machines.
>
> (Jacobson *et al.* 1995: 36)

The distinction between BPR and traditional approaches to design is further established by an argument which underlines the difference between 'what actually happens now' and what procedures (or processes) may be in specifications. Whereas certain approaches as structured design have to a greater or lesser extent reduced the difference between the actual and the ideal (see Yourdon and Constantine 1979; Benyon 1992a, 1992b), BPR wants to re-establish the problematic relationship between the two, something that ethnographers have also tried to do (Randall *et al.* 1992). In other words, like ethnography, BPR is interested in the gap between actual practice and idealised conceptions of practice. Thus, Davenport argues that BPR:

> implies a strong emphasis on *how* work is done within an organisation, in contrast to a product focus's emphasis on *what*.
>
> (Davenport 1993: 5)

Harrington (1991) provides a description of the appropriate methods for understanding actual work. Key are 'process walk-throughs'; this is a principle method for understanding how work is done. Stowell (1991) explains:

> One of the key activities in the walk-through process is to observe the activity being performed. Immediately after the interview, the interviewer and the interviewee should go to the work area to observe the activity discussed in the interview. Observing the individual tasks being performed will stimulate additional questions. As Dr H. James

Harrington puts it, 'You never really understand the activity until you do it yourself. If that isn't possible, the next best alternative is to observe the activity while it is being performed, and ask a lot of questions.
(Stowell 1991: 266)

Such insights would, at first glance, seem modest and somewhat unoriginal were it not for the extra dimension which BPR seems to provide, that of socio-technical systematicity. That is, in its 'problem specifications' and its solutions, the focus (in theory at least) is on comparison between the formal process and actual practice; the differences in the way employees perform tasks, the relevance of training requirements, the existence of process problems and 'roadblocks', and so on.

Moreover, analysts such as Harrington recognise, as do ethnographers of the organisation, that not only are process specifications and the organisational activity in question not the same thing, but that deviation from specifications is explicable by a whole range of factors, including the possibility that there may be potentially positive reasons why specifications are not being followed since, and for example, individuals may have found that goals are more effectively attained if they are bypassed. Bypassing specifications may also compensate for problems. In particular, BPR stresses the role of 'chronic' problems in working life, especially so given that chronic problems are often difficult to see. One reason for this is that methods for completing processes often adapt to chronic problems. People often find ways round persistent obstructions and this can disguise what the problems may have been in the first place without necessarily removing them.

The systematicity that BPR offers may appear doubly attractive because it addresses both the weaknesses of traditional IT design and the glosses on organisational context provided by, for instance, the 'job design' movement. By way of example, an adequate picture of what is going on in the organisation and how to transform it requires, for Davenport, a holistic approach which encompasses not only every dimension of an organisation's activities, but also a method for designing the future. Thus:

> The term process innovation encompasses the envisioning of new work strategies, the actual process design activity, and the implementation of the change in all its complex technological, human, and organizational dimensions.
> (Davenport 1993: 2)

That is, BPR promises a complete understanding of how the organisation currently functions and what has to be done in both work and technological terms to provide radical success in redesign. Nevertheless, asserting that one has provided an 'all singing, all dancing' solution to problems raised is a long way from demonstrating that the assertion is valid. Merely because a system is offered which claims to deal with problems of appropriate technology as well as appropriate organisational structure does not make it so.

BPR's approach, then, consists of conceptualising what goes on in organisations as a matter of understanding and defining 'processes'. These processes, whether specified in rules or developed to solve problems by workers themselves, are unequivocally defined according to their measurable relationship to the customer. Thus, Harrington[8] describes a process as:

> any activity or group of activities that takes an input, adds value to it, and provides an output to an internal or external customer. Processes use an organization's resources to provide definitive results.
>
> (Harrington 1991: 9)

A business process in turn is defined as:

> All service processes and processes that support production processes. A business process consists of any logically related tasks that use the resources of the organization to provide defined results in support of the organization's objectives.
>
> (*ibid.*: 9)

This is the way BPR makes use of an economistic perspective on organisational goals, but orients that perspective to a set of explicit change-management objectives, such as improving effectiveness, efficiency, and adaptability. The analytic work involves identifying a set of defined tasks which are to do with meeting organisational objectives, and which are construed in terms such as determining where the process boundaries will be, and what the inputs and outputs to the process are. Key aspects of this work might include identifying suppliers to and customers of the process identified, along with who is performing the key operations. Thus, determining process boundaries has to do with 'identifying the ownership of the process and where it begins and ends', with a view to assessing the strategic relevance of each process.[9]

As one might expect from a largely top-down methodology, the point of investigating how operations are performed is to establish the 'health' or

---

8 We cite Harrington more than other proponents of BPR not out of any conviction that his work is the 'best' or even the most 'typical' of the field, but because in our view he spells out the method in rather more detail than most.

9 It would, therefore, be a mistake to view BPR as a *naive* reformulation of Taylorist principles for the white collar world. Although aspects of BPR are unmistakably Taylorist in their force, the method recognises that 'informal' aspects of organization may impinge on the success or failure of objectives. Thus and for instance, Harrington refers to the problem of qualifying the 'culture and politics' surrounding the process.

otherwise of the processes in terms of the business objectives of the organisation. A sample method advocated by Harrington for doing precisely that involves identifying 'multiple buffers', which produces the 'queueing up' of stages. Indeed, a recurring theme in BPR is the distinction between the logical connection between activity, which tends to be horizontal, and the vertical connections of the organisation. It is this distinction, perhaps more than any other, which has informed the developing interest in workflow. Workflow is defined in BPR as the method for transforming input into output, and is one of the primary characteristics of a process, and in many respects is the key to understanding what is distinctive about BPR.

There is, of course, much more we could say about BPR but, in summary, the analytic force of BPR lies in its interest to use direct observation of current practice to identify, from the top down, what is wrong with specified business goals and the means for pursuing them. Further, its conception of what is wrong is defined in terms of measurable obstructions to efficiency with a view to producing alternative structures in which those obstructions have been eradicated. These obstructions may, of course, be of more than one kind and may include, for example, the generation of error, the existence of 'poor quality' costs (waste) and 'multiple buffers'. In any event, the presupposition is that analysing current work can unproblematically lead us to conclusions concerning what it is that causes 'problems' to arise. The presumption is that measurable benefits will be obtained precisely from the identification, measurement, and respecification of process. These benefits – and we highlight them only to provide a flavour of the direction in which this kind of analysis takes us – conventionally include the elimination of duplication, error proofing, automation and standardisation.

Participative Design

As we noted at the outset of our discussion of BPR, the economistic underpinnings of the approach are one of its defining characteristics. There are numerous alternatives in the change literature, of course. These alternatives are typically viewed as being 'non-rationalist' in one way or another. Depending on the perspective adopted, they can be held to include the 'job design' approach, the 'Socio-technical Systems' literature, and substantial parts of organisational psychology. Though in the (theory-driven) organisational literature discussed in the previous chapter, there is little discussion of it, there have been considerable developments in the approaches oriented to what one may call the 'design' discourse. These developments include, for instance, contemporary offshoots from Socio-technical Systems work such as the mainly Scandinavian 'Participative Design' movement. In addition, revisions to the orthodoxies of cognitive psychology including 'Distributed Cognition' (Hutchins 1995)[10] and the more humanistic psychology of 'Activity Theory', developed from Vygotskian perspectives, are becoming equally well known.[11] Even 'Grounded Theory' (Glaser and Strauss 1967) can be and (occasionally) is used as support for a perspective on the design process.[12] Be that as it may, we cannot review these different and often competing perspectives in any detail. Rather, and in keeping with our earlier arguments, it is the status of empirical work as it relates to theory and/or methodology in some of these approaches that concerns us.

What makes these perspectives interesting is their common concern for conceptualisation, and in particular conceptualisation of the 'user'. This points towards the problem of knowledge elicitation. In their distinctive ways, these approaches attempt to get to grips with the way in which users are members of organisations by getting those users to speak about that relationship. Our point will be that assuming that 'asking users' is the best way to find out what is needed, though often times very valuable, does not provide everything that is necessary to understand the work in question.

We should be clear, however, and state that it should not be presumed that the 'user as resource' is necessarily a founding principle. At least one of these perspectives, Participative Design, is for instance overtly political. While issues like how to design jobs using notions of job satisfaction owe much to the pioneering work of Mumford (1983), Participative Design has a much more open stance on the user's role. Mumford's original work was in the Socio-technical Systems tradition, and emphasised concepts such as knowledge, psychological efficiency and task structure 'fit'. These related to the effectiveness of systems. Versions of Participative Design take the argument more than a little further by arguing that conceiving of the design problem in these terms results in users being seen as individuals, and their role as, in effect, being sources of information for the designer. Users here are recognised as being rather more complex than Mumford's type of analysis would have it. Thus:

> By viewing the people who use computers as competent in their field of work, we find that the workplace takes on the appearance of a rich

---

10 For Hutchins, the marginalisation of culture by cognitive science has had reductionist effects, and has led to ignorance of context, or 'situatedness'. Hence, 'The early researchers in cognitive science placed a bet that the modularity of human cognition would be such that culture, context, and history could be safely ignored at the outset, and then integrated later. The bet did not pay off. These things are fundamental aspects of human cognition and cannot be comfortably integrated into a perspective that privileges abstract properties of individual minds' (Hutchins 1995: 354).

11 Activity theory has been of powerful interest in Computer Supported Co-operative Learning (CSCL) and to some degree in CSCW itself. (See Kuuti and Arvonen 1994; Bardram 1997.)

12 Examples of their influence include the work of Fitzgerald et al. (1996) in their study of the work of system administrators, and Grinter, who has used insights from Glaser and Strauss in her study of the development of a workflow system (1997).

tapestry, deeply woven with much intricacy and skill ... [there is a need to] ... take work practice seriously [and to recognise that] ... we are dealing with human actors, not cut and dried human factors ... work tasks must be seen in their context, and are therefore situated actions ... work is fundamentally social, involving extensive co-operation and communication.

(Greenbaum and Kyng 1991: 4)

That is, the culture and work practices of people are seen as deeply relevant to design. In this respect, articulating culture and practices through getting the users into a central place for understanding process and technology is the methodological crux of Participative Design.

The general argument for this approach is that it improves the knowledge base on which systems design is based; it enables people (users) to develop realistic expectations, and thus reduces resistance to change; and it increases workplace democracy by giving individuals the right to participate.

The more radical variant of Participative Design usually called the Collective Resources Approach (CRA) relates most closely to explicit political claims. In particular, it takes seriously Braverman's (1974) scepticism over humanism in the workplace when he asserted that job-design proponents were the 'maintenance crew' for human machinery. The criticism was that Socio-technical Systems approaches were merely a means to integrate behavioural aspects (i.e., work) into the design process, but that it did not take into account other aspects of the organisation, not least the existence of power structures. Thus, Nurminen argues:

> [early Participative Design work] never documented radically new system concepts, perhaps due to the local scope of the projects and the action research character. Participative Design is a (skew) concept because it tells, for example, that participation is something extra ... thus the design process essentially takes place somewhere else by someone else.

Hence, CRA involved attempts to treat the organisation as a normative structure, and the technical systems as part of this normative structure.

Participative Design in general, CRA included, relates to the practice of fieldwork in some interesting ways. In early work, it implied that fieldwork of the type associated with ethnography would not be necessary, in that evolving 'good practice' would appear to obviate the need for rigorous observation. Latterly, however, various Participative Design projects have moved to incorporate some element of fieldwork. Kensing *et al.* for instance, suggest that their motivation in taking an ethnographic stance along with more orthodox Participative Design strategies was based on two relevant features of the design process; namely that users often do not get what (they thought) they asked for and second, there is a need for a more flexible approach to system design. Their work is the exception to the rule, however. Workshops which involve with collaborative scenario building, storyboarding and other techniques are used to create consensus remain the norm. Direct observation of work, if it is done, is left as a residual concern, if undertaken at all. This neglect, we will suggest, is one reason why Participative Design tends to provide over-simple solutions to the complexities of organisational and technological change.

Soft Systems Methodology

An approach which sets out to deal with precisely such complexities is Soft Systems Methodology (SSM), associated with Checkland and Scholes. This is perhaps the best known 'humanistic' stance in the British context.[13] It grew out of the inability of previous tools to cope with what Checkland and Scholes (1989) call 'messy, complex problems'.

More specifically, they see their method as being designed to address a flaw in engineering methods. In their view, engineering is a 'how to' or 'constructive' discipline in which the task is to move from a statement of purpose (or requirements) through to a product which reflects those requirements. Checkland and Scholes point out that, in the real world, requirements, needs, purposes, do not actually come ready made. Many problems are ill-defined or poorly specified. SSM recognises that the very step of identifying and defining a system is problematic in almost all cases. Prior research had demonstrated that formal models of decision making ignored complexity, so SSM was explicitly developed to try and retain systems thinking, yet develop it by providing tools for understanding it, and especially 'viewpoints'. Hence, the view that design is to do with finding solutions to problems is challenged by SSM by its emphasis on deciding what kind of problems they might be in the first place.

Using general systems theory as background, and drawing on their 'emergent' character, Checkland and Scholes make the point that 'human activity systems' are unique insofar as human activity is purposeful. In this respect, SSM draws on some of the assumptions contained in interactionist sociologies (and indeed many of its behavioural concepts are redolent of that type of sociology). Basically, they want to suggest that an effective management science relies on a model of action which is iterative. That is, intentions are based on knowledge, but action creates new knowledge, or experience, which in turn creates new intentions. In other words, organisational learning is central to the issues at the heart of management and hence to the management of change too.

---

13 In passing, it is worth noting that SSM was not in origin a method for aiding the design of computer systems, although it has been increasingly treated as such in a number of evolutions since then. In this regard, it is an excellent example of the way in which the design discourse has coalesced.

Systems analysis, they argue, has to both represent complexity and provide for an orderly representation. That is, the relationship between the theoretical model and real-world complexity is precisely SSM's concern. From their early 'seven steps' model through to the more sophisticated view proposed later, system concepts are supposed to be used to enable the people in the system to learn how to take appropriate action. In the later version, various streams of enquiry are described and analysed, broadly divided into the 'logical' and the 'cultural'. Through the process of naming, selecting and modelling relevant systems, and providing root definitions via a particular mnemonic (the so-called CATWOE mnemonic (customers, actors, transformation, Weltanschauung, owners, environment), transformations can be expressed in a systematic way. In turn, these modelling activities can be used as a framework for comparison with the real world. Here, 'rich pictures' can help structure analysis and debate about the problem situation by filtering through a range of world-views. Other methods by which this can be done include informal discussion, formal questioning, scenario writing and further modelling of the real world using the concepts evolved. Like Participative Design, analysis of the intervention also forms part of the work. Crucially, 'social system' analysis, whereby roles, norms, values and beliefs are elaborated, and additionally 'political analysis' whereby lines of command, formal and informal, are identified are further stages in this collaborative analysis.

Checkland and Scholes see SSM as being part of the tradition of 'human-centred design' associated with Participative Design, and make a contrast between this view which treats information as human symbol, rather than information as data. Traditional information theory (e.g., as represented in the work of Norbert Wiener) treats information as a 'message' which is 'encoded' into a 'signal' which is then 'decoded'. It is a highly mathematical and statistical approach which enables measurement of what is being transmitted. However, it generates little understanding of the interpretation of what is being transmitted. That is, an information system involves both data manipulation and meaning attribution. The boundaries of an information system will have to include human action. As Checkland says:

> Of course, the designers of the data manipulating machine will have in mind a particular set of meaning attributions and will hope that the manipulated data will always be interpreted as particular information – but they cannot guarantee that, since users are ultimately autonomous.
> (Checkland 1981)

Checkland argues that a 'truly relevant' system can only evolve through agreement, echoing in outline the sentiments of Participative Design. He gives recommendations concerning what to ask when deriving an information-systems model. These include two sets of questions relating, broadly speaking, to inputs and outputs. As regards the first, Checkland advises that questions should include inquiries into what kind of information would have to be available to enable someone to do an activity. Following on from that, investigations should seek to identify what source that information would be obtained from and in what form. Frequency too is an issue. On the output side, questions should include asking what information would be generated doing the activity in question, to whom it should go, in what form and again how frequently.

The general principle then upon which SSM as a design resource can be used is as follows:

> SSM enrich(es) those poverty-stricken stages of systems analysis and design methodologies in which information requirements analysis is assumed to be straightforward, or organisations are naively documented as a set of unproblematical entities and functions.
>
> (Checkland 1981)

CONCLUSION: THE PRODUCTIVITY PARADOX

Approaches such as SSM and Participative Design emerged during a time when the role of technology in organisations was being – and indeed continues to be – viewed in increasingly negative terms. The 'productivity paradox', as it has come to be called, refers to doubts about the added value accruing from new technology, particularly in white-collar environments where it is increasingly prevalent (Landauer 1997). It has been claimed that innovation has had little – if any – positive effect on productivity, at least in some areas of automation. There has also been an increased concern with the measurement of the return on new systems, manifested in a developing critique of office automation systems, wherein the difficulty of measuring the gains in efficiency and effectiveness associated with new technologies has been remarked upon by several commentators (Vincent 1990).

Some account for these failures is placed on the doorstep of the 'engineering' approach to design that held sway during the 1970s and 1980s for which approaches like Checkland and Scholes' SSM were meant to be a corrective, as we have seen. Structured and formal design methodologies, in particular, deriving as they did from the engineering perspective, were particularly vulnerable to the criticisms just reviewed. Nonetheless, such methodologies constituted something of a revolution themselves when they first began to replace previous systems-design methods, and from the late 1960s dominated the design and implementation of information technologies in the commercial and industrial world. They are still very much in evidence. That they did so (and still find a role) is hardly surprising. The need for accurate, shareable and traceable information to be disseminated among large design teams, the orientation of design towards new rather than old ways of working and risk avoidance among IT professionals were just some of the reasons for the prevalence of formal and structured methods in the 1970s and 1980s.

Nonetheless, the relevance of the productivity paradox to our argument is not only to do with the history of the perspectives we have reviewed. It underlines the need to recognise that the matters of relevance are fundamentally empirical, practical ones. Thus, the success or otherwise of formal and structured methods in design, and the engineering approach that underscores them, is not and should not be judged in terms of theoretical features of those approaches. A more salient measure is to be found in their practical effectiveness.

One of the things that has arisen as a result of the technology paradox is that the issues surrounding the implementation of new technologies and associated changes in work processes is that even those who are completely unfamiliar with change-management practices are nonetheless aware that undertaking change is a serious affair. As a result, they seek to handle such change differently than hitherto. For example, there is now a common recognition that effective implementation of new technologies cannot and should not be measured or oriented to solely technical criteria, but must be oriented to organisational needs; something that BPR, SSM and, to a lesser extent, Participative Design are all intended to help achieve. And, disregarding any particular change management philosophy, this is shown in the shift from 'supply led' to 'demand led' IT strategies. As Peppard notes, IS/IT decisions are too important for management to delegate completely (or indeed abdicate) to the IT professionals in the organization.

This has been a result not so much of the impact of new approaches that have drawn attention to the need to take IT seriously (such as BPR), but are a practical reaction to the 'black hole' of technology into which large sums of money have historically been poured with varying results. The scale of this hole has been so great that management increasingly see technology and particularly IT strategy as a central concern. In many organisations decision-making about IT has been taken away from IT professionals and relocated in the hands of those responsible for core-business strategy.

The reasons for this shift are nicely expressed by Bart O'Brien (1992), who quotes from Frederick Brooks' (1975) seminal book *The Mythical Man Month* (in turn paraphrasing Shakespeare):

'I can write programmes that control air traffic, intercept ballistic missiles, reconcile bank accounts, control production lines.' To which the answer comes, 'So can I, and so can any man, but do they work when you write them?'

(*ibid.*: 15)

56 Part I

O'Brien updates this telling remark in the following terms:

> 'I can make strategies to transform your business, turn information into a management asset, incorporate IT into end products and services, and bring competitive advantage in the Information Age.' To which the response is, 'Why so can I, and so can any man; but will they work when you do make them?'
>
> (*ibid.*: 15)

The result of this kind of overconfidence is that IT strategies and implementations frequently disappoint. He remarks that too often:

> when the systems are finally operational at the price of tremendous effort, nothing very momentous seems to have been achieved at all.
>
> (*ibid.*: 16)

Assessing management of change and technology-design perspectives

From this view, the technology paradox is a reminder that what we are interested in are not the theoretical underpinnings of the approaches we have reviewed, or even the moral implications they may have. The latter may seem particularly appealing to those who would wish to compare approaches on the basis of the role of the user – something of particular salience to Participative Design. Our concern instead is to consider the approaches in terms of what they offer as practical resources for action. But this does not mean to exclude any consideration at all of the theoretical stance that these approaches take, so much as to address what any particular stance leads them to offer in terms of empirical descriptions of the organisational settings they are trying to effect.

Let us take BPR. A key insight of BPR is that technology is but one feature of a wider 'system' and that the design of the technology must orient to the system in the large. Underscoring this is the belief that the process or processes in question can be determined through the kinds of techniques BPR recommends. But it seems to us that there are aspects of working with technology which are complementary to processes and these need comprehending too. For example, when standard procedures are implemented through new technology, what one might call local knowledge and skills are typically persistent and indeed necessary to ensure the continual flow of work. Further, and this is particularly important given BPR's emphasis on new technologies as a vehicle for providing organisational gains, the deployment of local knowledge and the emergence of informal collaboration (such as asking for codes to enter on screens or information about how to complete routines), are often effective 'ways to cope' with the inadequacies of new computer-supported processes. That is, and to adapt a phrase of

Garfinkel's (1967), there are often 'bad organisational reasons for good organisational practices'.

Related to this is the importance of investigating how technology is 'made to work' by skilful interventions often called 'work-arounds' (Button and Harper 1996).[14] Often times the sheer invisibility of such work-arounds problematises conceptions of skill, especially if they are simply described as functions of overall processes. Work-arounds all too often slip from view in BPR since the perspective assumes that such phenomena are insubstantial, if not irrelevant to the level of description that is being provided. The absence of such accounts is all the more worrying since the existence of work-arounds can invert the usual way skill and technology are related, insofar as it is sometimes skill impacting on technology and not the other way round. This is not to ignore the concern with chronic problems in BPR nor the need for the observation of actual work as against understanding work simply as described in specifications. It will be recalled that BPR analysts recognise that such problems are often difficult to see. But for BPR it is reference to the system as a whole that enables their recognition and, further, their importance is measurable against a set of values.

What we are talking about here, however, are interactional properties much closer to the point of technology use. These are lost from sight to the BPR analysts by dint of their concern with higher-level measures. Such measures are in turn concerned with assessing whether tasks or skills should be done away with (i.e., do they add value). What we are arguing is that there may be a need to specify what interactional properties at point of use might be. All the more so, we might suggest, if these properties actually allow larger-scale phenomena such as the processes that concern BPR to occur. We are suggesting that, irrespective of whether one calls these interactional properties the display and use of local knowledge, skill at work-arounds or whatever, such skills and their deployment are hardly likely to be incidental to the concerns of process redesign. After all, even if one accepts that it is a sensible task to reduce discretion down to a lowest common denominator, it is likely to prove useful to know how it is constituted and how it relates to existing processes and technologies. What we are arguing here is not only a matter of detail, although it is that in part. It is also a question of analytic focus. We are suggesting that there are much more complicated properties to the relationship between processes and action, between technology and procedural requirements than may be apparent in the way these things are treated by BPR. Though BPR fully recognises the distance between what ought to be and what actually

---

14 One caveat here is that occasional problems may be equally significant, but in different ways. For instance, in safety-critical environments occasional problems are potentially disastrous precisely because operators may be unfamiliar with them. One argument for ethnography is that prolonged exposure to the domain usually prompts recognition of occasional but nonetheless important problems.

gets done, its top-down focus means that certain properties of 'situated work' disappear from view. This is not say that BPR fails to provide substantial insights into the matters of concern. It is to suggest that in certain situations there may be a need to supplement the view of BPR with another that looks at the kinds of issues that are beyond its vision.

This can be exemplified in a different way. The importance of the computer interface in making machinery 'usable' is by now well attested. What we are getting at here is that 'usability' itself can be a function of what may be called the 'mutually elaborated' character of work activities, where both the technology and the user (and indeed teams of collaborating users) make or 'accomplish' that usability through intermingling skills, know-how and the affordances of the technology into a functional whole. Sometimes even customers participate in these processes (Randall and Hughes 1994; King and Randall 1994). What we are getting at here is that though BPR orients to such matters as technology, process and the customer as primary foci of the value chain, nowhere is it recognised that what staff (or even customers) do in terms of local, collaborative, interactional processes, or how technology is used as part of a 'texture of relevance' (i.e., as one item among many that are part of the work setting), might be important.

It is our view that given BPR's strategy, taking these interactional properties seriously is very difficult. In essence, the BPR strategy is decompositional. It derives from its clearly stated objectives, which include providing a measurement system for organisations and a means to standardise processes. 'Problem' and 'solution', that is, exist in a hermetic relationship in which each can only be understood as aspects of 'healthy' and 'unhealthy' processes. Observation of the current state of play is conceived in terms of the analysis of task performance, the obstructions which may be associated with it, and evaluation and comparison of different task performances. In other words, when a BPR analyst is observing work, he or she is either looking for what is wrong with it, and defining it as process failure, or at examples of 'good' strategies which can be codified into the new processes. At root, although sources of discretion and variation – what we have called local knowledge – may be of some interest, the task of BPR is either to eliminate them or provide methods for their universal application. The solution to organisational 'problems' lies in understanding how, for instance, 'culture and politics', methods of 'task performance' and so forth can be conceived as variations which can be removed, wherever possible. In so doing, BPR offers considerable insight. But there is a compromise between the high-level valuations of BPR where its decompositional stance where it tick-lists components of an overall process or value chain, and the need to understand the often important but to our mind all-too-often neglected properties of interaction within any stage in these processes. Such properties may have to do with local knowledge, as we have put it, or the collaborative activities of participants and much more besides.

Participative Design is obviously a very different approach, all the more so since it would appear to have politically quite distinct underpinnings to BPR. But we see problems here too, primarily related to the role of the user as resource. It is, of course, blindingly obvious that requirements analysis, as computer scientists refer to it, cannot be considered a solely technical matter, but is fundamentally social as well. That is, it is always and inevitably a contested enterprise in which various stakeholders, with voices of varying 'loudness' according to the knowledge, power and influence they wield, will have often-contradictory views concerning what kinds of systems intervention might be appropriate. And yet, as all systems analysts know, the job of analysis and specification is to produce a consistent set of requirements. Consequently, methods have to be found for reducing and removing ambiguity and conflict. This has to be achieved in a context where the versions of what constitutes 'good' work and appropriate technology often vary across different occupational statuses, including for instance differences between managerial echelons, technical experts and 'shop floor' workers. Indeed, various stakeholders can present different assessments even among individuals with the same status and role in an organisation. Thus, in a study of Air Traffic Control (see, e.g., Bentley *et al*. 1992), it was noted that if twelve different air-traffic controllers were asked for an opinion, thirteen different answers were provided. Indeed, the study also showed that there was a considerable tension between managerial pictures of appropriate technologies for future work practices and those of controllers. Perhaps more importantly, it indicated that no group had particular confidence in the shape of the future of air traffic control (see Twidale *et al*. 1994). There was, in other words, a stakeholder problem.

This holds true generally, of course. One feature of this problem is that at least one group of stakeholders, management, is both considerably more powerful than others in the organisation, and likely to be defining strategy according to some theory of change. One consequence of this is that the managerial viewpoint will probably be extremely coherent and consensual. Management is likely to be increasingly engaged in the business of explicitly planning the future by programmatic means, including the use of approaches such as BPR and SSM.

Leaving aside the ethical issues contained in the stakeholder problem, the point is that the interests of diverse stakeholders are not as easy to settle as the Participative Design approach assumes – and indeed as even some of its practitioners recognise, as we have seen. Organisations are not constructed simply by the management and the workforce. The divide between stakeholders is often complex, as the example from ATC shows. The problem for Participative Design approaches is that the methodology provides only a technique for understanding hierarchical organisations, yet few can be so characterised. Moreover, the interest of stakeholders can also be construed in part as 'working' interests, and these are not necessarily either similar to or in conflict with, those of management.

Workers in the organisation, whether or not they have other 'interests' which have to do with the issues of control, pay, etc., also have an interest in simply 'going on with their work' in effective ways. One need not buy the 'job design' movement in order to make such an assertion.

To broaden understanding of complexity, as well as understanding of how the work gets done across the board, necessitates empirical descriptions of many diverse groups and practices, as well as mapping of the components of processes that link complex organisational structures. Such investigations may point toward changes that will effect some users more negatively than others. These changes may also require deep understanding of components of processes that any individual group of users have little sight of. The reader may well be led to think that a method that might provide this may well be a variant of BPR, but with some of the political assumptions of Participative Design thrown in. This is to oversimplify the concerns that we are wanting to raise about Participative Design. In any case, as we have seen, BPR has its own problems.

But that aside, what should be made clear when one tries to assess Participative Design is that it has made substantial contributions to the problem of organisational and technological design insofar as it has shifted some of the assumptions. The same may be said of SSM, too. Checkland, for instance, rightly insists on the 'hard' systems origins of the bulk of design work that has led to the technology paradox. In different ways, various writers in the Scandinavian tradition have made the same case. More importantly, both Participative Design and SSM have been founded on the recognition that information should be treated in terms of its human symbolic quality rather than simply as data. Both can be read as cautioning against the 'measurement' tendency in change management, since interpretation by definition is not directly measurable – a criticism that can be placed against BPR. In terms of technology, both SSM and Participative Design treat information systems as involving both data manipulation and meaning attribution. Though SSM has become increasingly used as a method for deriving information-system requirements, the evidence seems to suggest that the system that results is arguably unremarkable (see, e.g., Patching 1990; Stowell 1991, for case studies of SSM in use in this way). Some of the reasons for this may also apply to Participative Design. Perhaps most controversially, what underpins both is a presumption concerning consensus. Here, the problem of what 'weight' to attach to different viewpoints is not adequately dealt with, especially in terms of the radically different opinion. This bias towards consensus, then, ignores the prospect that the 'voice in the wilderness' might be making a powerful argument.

Moreover, the political, cultural and social realities of work in the organisation which SSM in particular seeks to understand presumably necessitates what is called in sociology 'thick' description (Geertz 1993). Such descriptions attempt to convey the complex interplay of objects, persons and beliefs in such a way as to convey a sense of place. They are also requisite if one wants to provide the kind of analysis of the interactional properties we mentioned in relation to BPR. These are unlikely to be provided by the methods generally advocated within a SSM framework alone. Techniques such as informal discussion, formal questioning, scenario writing and modelling are insufficient, it seems to us. We are not alone in this. BPR researchers are aware of the limits of these techniques, as we have seen. And indeed we have left SSM to the end of our discussions – or at least an assessment of it – precisely because, of the three approaches, SSM is the most naive when it comes to data capture. As we have seen, the problems in BPR have to do with how it necessarily focuses attention on comparison and measurement; and with Participant Design, the techniques offered are flawed by an over-simple conception of organisational life and of the design process more generally. In the case of SSM, though it emerged in the wake of perceived problems with formal and structural methods and pointed towards what would be better ways of proceeding, it does not offer any insight over and above BPR as regards how to uncover processes. Further, its concern with incorporating every factor into the design process means that it achieves the opposite of Participant Design by producing overly complex views of organisation. With Participant Design there is too little to choose from, with SSM too much.

4 Ethnography and change

INTRODUCTION

The purpose of this chapter is to provide some detail of the ethnographic approach to organisations. We will do so by reference to the analytic purchase that the method brings to the understanding of work. We have already used a number of phrases to hint at the kind of analytic view we have in mind, ranging from a concern with the world as 'encountered phenomenon', through to 'local interactional properties' and 'the lived experience'. All of these can be encapsulated in the phrase 'real time, real world work'. As we have seen in Chapter 2, our emphasis on this – leaving aside what it means for the moment – stands in rather stark contrast to many accounts of organisational life. These all too often have very little to say about the actual work which goes on within the setting under study – about what makes this work 'bank-work' say, or 'insurance-work' – and both the worker and the fashion in which work is accomplished tend to disappear into theoretical abstraction. A desire to be attentive to the work is one of the motivations for the use of our approach to research. In contrast to a common attitude which views specific social settings as sites of generic, abstract 'social processes', the approach we use, by contrast, is particularly focused upon the distinctiveness, the specificity, of the settings under study. It is our view that this can be a particularly useful aid in the management of change, as it can bring into view materials that the other approaches to change, such as those just reviewed, ignore. Of course, just how the approach we are about to outline does this is one thing, just how it might fit into a broader programme of organisational change is another. Our goal then is not only to outline our approach but to point toward – and this is all we can do in this chapter – what role this approach may play in supplementing and complementing the management of change approaches.

The chapter will be organised in the following way. First we say something about the general purposes and history of ethnography. Here we will begin to remark that ethnography has had an increasingly high profile in system-design research, since it provides what may be called naturalistic descriptions of work (we shall have more to say about such descriptions shortly). Its role also reflects its concern with how people work together and thus avoids the pitfall of approaches that treat individual workers as operating as isolated units (albeit often conceived of as part of an overall process or value chain, as we have seen). We then turn to what doing ethnography involves and how it requires the researchers to immerse themselves in the setting in question. We will note that this leads to more grounded understandings of the role of IT, and thus also of the various factors that impinging upon IT use as well as process change. This leads us to what we will call ethnomethodologically informed ethnography, which is appealing to us since it eschews theoretical elaboration and focuses instead on the rationalities of those observed. By this is meant those sets of skills, practices and know-how that members of organisations have to use in their daily work. It means also recognising – and reflecting this in descriptions – that members of organisations are concerned with everyday aspects of their work, with all its mundane properties: that they have to worry about things getting lost or mislaid, that they need to attend to work regulations despite knowing that doing so can sometimes inhibit effective working. The approach also involves recognising that much of what is important in terms of what is described by the research is of a taken-for-granted nature to those studied, being background information, often rarely spoken about since it is, in a sense, simply too obvious. It is these properties that make up 'real time, real world' experience.

We then make some further remarks on why we think the approach we outline is useful in the context of organisational change and technology design. We discuss various roles such an approach can have, though the remarks will be deliberately brief because much of these issues will be discussed at later points in the book. Our approach, though helpful, has its limits, of course, and we will note that these are at once methodological and practical: time constraints being as much an issue as regards the role and efficacy of the approach as the scope of the descriptions it generates. Notwithstanding this, we conclude the chapter with some comments on how effective ethnomethodologically informed ethnography can be for technology design, and hence also for all change programmes.

WHAT IS ETHNOGRAPHY?

Originally developed to supplement the 'strange tales of faraway places' of early social anthropology and adapted for sociology through the 'naturalistic stance' of the Chicago School and Symbolic Interactionism, ethnography has acquired some prominence (not to say notoriety) in recent years within the study of computer supported-co-operative work (CSCW). Here it has gained prominence as a fieldwork method which could contribute both to a general understanding of systems in use in a variety of contexts and to the design of distributed and shared systems (Hughes and King 1992). Efforts to incorporate ethnography into the system design process have had much to do with the (belated) realisation, mainly among system designers, that the success of design has much to do, though in complex ways, with the social context of system use. Understanding this context, many believed, could not be achieved through turning to formal or structured approaches, or even the correctives offered by Participative Design or SSM. These latter, though better in many respects still had problems, as we have just seen. Moreover, a number of well publicised disasters around the world suggested that methods better designed to bring out the socially organised character of work settings were required. It was also argued that such methods needed to be more attuned to gathering relevant data in 'real world' environments; that is, settings in which systems were likely to be used rather than in laboratories or other artificial and remote environments. Ethnography with its emphasis on the *in situ* observation of interactions within their natural settings seemed eminently suited to doing this.

With its emphasis on the 'real world' character of work settings ethnography is often contrasted with what are commonly regarded as unrealistic and unsatisfactory notions about both systems and the users of systems that tend to be proffered by more traditional methods, such as the formal and engineering approaches briefly alluded to in the last chapter. These approaches have come to be viewed as obscuring, misrepresenting or ignoring the 'real world' of work. To an extent this holds true of the management of change programmes we reviewed in the previous chapter too. More specifically, the analytic deconstruction of work activities into various components, such as elements in an information flow within SSM or stages within a value chain for BPR, removes the essential 'real world' features which make them practices within a socially organised setting. The heart of this complaint is that work is, typically, collaborative. Though the activities constituting work are done by individuals, they are performed within an organised environment composed of other individuals and it is this which gives shape to the activities as 'real world' activities. Thus, the focus of ethnography is on the social practices which enable the very processes which methods such as BPR and SSM identify but which they somehow decontextualise. It is through the social practices that ethnography seeks to identify and describe that work processes are established and are, accordingly, rooted in socially achieved sets of arrangements.

Such an approach also meshes with the increasing use of information technologies within working life, or as is sometimes put, 'the information age'. As computers increasingly, and seemingly inexorably, are adopted and diffused into the world of work and organisation, there is a growing awareness that the ubiquitous nature of networked and distributed computing poses new problems for design, requiring the development and deployment of methods which analyse the collaborative, social, character of work. Systems are used within populated environments which are, whatever 'technological' characteristics they may have, 'social' in character and thus the intent to design distributed and shared systems means that this social dimension has to be 'real world' circumstances of work and its organisation (Goguen 1993). Given this 'turn to the social' and the need to study the 'real world' character of work, drifting toward ethnography to provide insight into this social nature of work is almost a natural inclination.

What is involved in 'doing' ethnography?

As a mode of social research, ethnography is concerned to produce detailed descriptions of the activities of social actors within specific contexts (Hughes *et al.* 1992, 1993b). It is a method that generates naturalistic descriptions, taken from material drawn from the first-hand experience of a fieldworker in some setting. Such descriptions seek to present a portrait of life as seen and understood by those who live and work within the domain concerned. It is this objective which is the rationale behind the method's insistence on the development of an 'appreciative stance' through the direct involvement of the researcher in the setting under investigation. It is, as Fielding (1994) suggests:

> a stance which emphasised seeing things from the perspective of those studied before stepping back to make a more detached assessment ... mindful of the Native American adage that one should 'never criticise a man until you have walked a mile in his moccasins'.
>
> (Fielding 1994: 156)

The intention of ethnography is then to see activities as social actions embedded within a socially organised domain and accomplished in and through the day-to-day activities of participants. It is this which provides access to the everyday ways in which participants understand and conduct their working lives and it is the ability of ethnography to understand a social setting as it is perceived by its participants that underpins its appeal.

Although ethnographic methods can take a variety of forms its chief characteristic is the researcher's immersion in the milieux of study, and the detailed observation of circumstances, practices, conversations and activity that comprise the 'real world' character of work settings. In ethnographic research the understanding of any work setting is derived from the study of that setting itself rather than from, say, any highly structured model of work processes such as provided by BPR. Thus, it ties itself closely to the observed data.

Hence, while the emphasis in many studies of organisations (and in particular 'virtual organisations') is on the use of IT to facilitate and enhance various forms of distributed working, the virtue of ethnographic approaches comes from the 'grounded' recognition that computers are enmeshed into a system of working as instruments – incorporated in highly particular ways – used, misused, modified, circumvented, rejected – into the flow of work. One of the virtues of ethnography lies in revealing these myriad usages in the context of work settings; furthermore being:

> more capable than most methods of highlighting those 'human factors' which most closely pertain to system usage, factors which are not always just about good interface design but include training, ease of use in work, contexts full of contingencies which are not the remit of system design ... even though design may be concerned with developing a completely new system, understanding the context, the people, the skills they possess are all important matters for designers to reflect upon.
> (Button and King 1992: 6)

In summary, the advantages of ethnographic methods in studying work lie in the 'sensitising' it promotes of what we have called the real-time, real-world character of work.

In attempting not only to document or describe activities but also in accounting for them, ethnography seeks to answer what might be regarded as an essential question in organisational change as to what to automate and what to leave to human skill and experience. Ethnographic methods thereby assist in the shaping or reshaping of work design 'problems' as a consequence of greater knowledge of the social organisation of work – the recognition that 'problems' need to be placed (and resolved) within the context of the work setting. It also helps in identifying the subtle and often unremarked co-operative aspects of work – the small-scale constellations of assistance and deployment of local knowledge that enable the work to be accomplished (i.e., the focus is on the interdependence of work activities rather than viewing, e.g., sales, as a single discrete task), and, as part of this, the identification of process and data variability – how routines (and data) are adapted to cope with the variability of work, and more.

Ethnomethodologically informed ethnography

Ethnography is not in any sense a unitary method but is a gloss on various and different analytic frameworks; thus there are, for example, Marxist, feminist and postmodern ethnographies. While an ethnographic stance arguably entails some minimum orientation of viewing the social world from the standpoint of its participants, one approach to this, and one which has strongly influenced our own work, is the ethnomethodological one, in which organisational participants' methods for accomplishing their work in and through the use of local rationalities becomes the topic of enquiry. While there have been a number of attempts to document the characteristics of 'ethnomethodological ethnography' (Dingwall 1981)[15] or 'ethnomethodologically inspired ethnography' (Silverman 1985) in general terms, our primary concern is the 'analytic purchase' of ethnomethodologically informed ethnography and, in consequence, its utility for organisational design and development.

When used from an ethnomethodological stance, ethnographic work involves an unprejudiced look at the phenomena in question, and hence does not lead to that phenomena becoming obscured beneath layers of theoretical abstraction and speculation. It sets out:

> to treat practical activities, practical circumstances, and practical ... reasonings as topics of empirical study, and by paying to the most commonplace activities of daily life the attention usually accorded extraordinary events, seeks to learn about them as phenomena in their own right.
>
> (Garfinkel 1967: 1)

The aim then is to observe and describe the phenomena of 'everyday life' independently of the preconceptions of received organisational theories and methods, to be 'led by the phenomena' rather than by the concerns and requirements of a particular standpoint. This means, in effect, that one takes an 'unmotivated' approach to the activities, looking just to see what people are doing, rather than seeking to identify things which are (in organisational research terms) theoretically interesting in them. Thus, one dispenses with any preconception that there are numerous things which people are doing which are trivial and thus not worth attending to, in a theoretical sense; that is, do not matter with respect to the kinds of things that organisational researchers think are (or, more accurately, should be) important about a given activity – the mere fact that people are doing it justifies the attention being given to it by an ethnomethodologically motivated ethnographer. In this way the 'false starts', 'glitches', 'diversions', 'distractions', 'interruptions', 'digressions', which are aspects of all activities, are notable features of the phenomena and not, so to speak, 'noise' to be eliminated from the data in order to reveal 'essential' or 'relevant' aspects of the data. Relatedly, the phenomena which are to be investigated are to be studied in their character as 'phenomena of everyday life' as 'everyday' occurrences for those who are involved in the activities in question, and the investigator is, therefore, seeking to ascertain what the phenomena mean for them. It is not for the investigator to decide what things are, what matters, what is important, or

---

15 Dingwall, for example, outlines the following characteristics: accomplishing social order; specifying actors' models; suspending a moral stance; creating 'anthropological strangeness' and depicting stocks of knowledge.

trivial, but to ascertain how things are judged in that way by those who are doing them, to examine the familiarity with and understanding of these matters possessed by those who must live with them.

In studies of this kind, the concern is with the depiction of 'the working sensibility' of those under study. The interest is remote from the kinds of general reflections that someone in an occupation can produce, and much more engaged with their consciousness and attention when they are 'at work'. Hence the kinds of questions that are asked include inquiring into what kinds of things members of organisations take for granted or presuppose in going about their work, what kinds of things they routinely notice, as well as what kinds of things are they 'on the lookout' for and how do they 'tune themselves in' to the state of being 'at work'. Thus, attention is focused – in a way which is otherwise almost unprecedented in both organisational and particularly sociological studies – upon the study of doing the work. The emphasis is on work in the raw, work as it is done, and in the ways in which it is done in actual practice, as opposed to work in idealised form.

The ethnomethodologically guided orientation to ethnography begins from the point of view of the social actor acting within a socially organised environment; that is, working within a culturally recognised environment. There is a presumption that the world is 'known in common', and this is key to enabling the integration or concerting of everyday actions. The relevance of this to the conduct of ethnography is that the multifarious ways in which the world is assumed to be known in common are apt to be taken for granted, to be treated as things which are of such patent obviousness and familiarity that they need not be paid direct and explicit attention by those who deal with them. It is, thus, that the investigator is not merely seeking to capture the standpoint and experience of the participant in the setting in respect of the things which that participant might note, explicitly comment upon or pay significant attention to, but also to identify those things which the participant is attending to, is indeed depending upon – which are, in the jargon 'seen-but-unnoticed' in the organisation of conduct within the setting but which have presupposed, taken-for-granted status.

A second presumption is that the people observed are engaged in practical action. It is assumed that this is the orientation which pervades the world of everyday life: its denizens give priority to getting things done, and that their action is therefore organised with respect to the necessities of practicality, that they are engaged in doing whatever it takes to get the thing done. The purpose of observation is, therefore, to identify the specific activities in which participants engage to deliver some specific end, and the character of those activities is dictated by the specificity of the circumstances. The essence of practical action is the need to do whatever is to be done under just these circumstances, and therefore involves the adaptation of the course of action to the exigencies of its circumstances. Hence the concern with the interplay of standardisation and specificity; with the way in which those involved in social settings seek to achieve standardisation; to engender articulated and structured procedures for carrying out relevant types of social action which they must, at the same time, enforce and implement in exigent, unforeseen, circumstances which may be more or less tractable to compliance with those standardisations. This accounts for the concern with plans and procedures, and with the way in which the 'idealisations' of courses of action and their circumstances must be articulated with 'actualities'. This engenders the desire to gain (fieldwork) access to the ways in which work is done in practice, and motivates the noticing of the ways in which people achieve (or fail to achieve) conduct in accord with the standardisations that they seek to implement. This gives a reason for putting the exigency and variability of practice into a prominent position in fieldwork studies, one which would be lacking from many more 'orthodox' ethnographic approaches, because those contingencies and variabilities would not, for those approaches, be considered significant.

Relative merits of the approach

In advancing ethnomethodologically informed ethnography and contrasting it with other and different approaches as discussed in previous chapters, we are not talking in terms of rights and wrongs, suggesting that our approach is right and other approaches are wrong; instead our emphasis is on relevance, with why this approach is particularly relevant to informing ethnographic studies of work, technology and organisations. Thus, it is a simple fact that many organisational approaches would not be motivated to do ethnographic studies at all, and that others which were motivated to do so would not, for their own good reasons, consider the practicalities of activities worth noticing. Another point of differentiation is that many approaches are inclined to shift attention away from the activities which are the stuff, or business, of the setting under investigation. As we have seen, the bulk of organisational studies have very little to say about the work which goes on within the setting under study. As Williamson (1989) claims, most of the depictions of humanity in this literature are such as to make them unrecognisable as humans; that '*Homo sociologicus* neither laughs nor cries' (and 'he' does not do much that is recognisable as 'work' either). Thus, it is a common attitude to view specific social settings as sites of generic, abstract 'social processes' and their purpose in surveying actual social settings is to minimise the differences between them, to abstract from data about them in ways which exhibit the commonality of such processes, to make the case that these are generic. By contrast, the ethnomethodologically motivated approach has every reason to attend to the distinct character of the work in the setting, to give priority to the fact that these persons are, for example, 'authorising a bank loan', or 'completing a standing order' and for directing its attentions to the activities which specifically, distinctively comprise those particular types of activity, and, thus, to give detailed characterisations of, and to seek to understand the particular circumstantial conditions for, carrying out those activities in actual cases. The relevance of this to understanding work, technology and organisations is, then, that it engenders studies directed toward understanding how the work gets done, and thus to describing the detail and intricacies of working practice for their own sake.

Work activities are concerted activities, they involve different people – often very many people – fitting their activities together in quite complex patterns from within the activity itself. The expression, 'accountable' character of activities is relevant here, since it has precisely to do with this issue of concerting work, with the way in which people engaged in an activity have to organise their own actions in ways in which other participants can see what they are doing, and can adapt to it. Participants in work activities have, therefore, to make visible the identity of their actions, to enable other people to identify those actions, and to identify also their purposes and intentions, such that they can respond appropriately to them, and can integrate their own actions, reciprocally, in the complex pattern that they are jointly, collectively, engendering. The notion of the 'accountable' character of activities emphasises, then, the degree to which activities are organised to be identified, recognised or understood as the activities that they are, the way in which they are done so that other people can see what is being done and, thus, how they can respond appropriately to concert their actions, to take their part in the pattern of affairs that is developing.

The fact that work activities are concerted – indeed all social activities – has long been commonplace in sociology and to a lesser extent organisational studies, but a concern to understand just how such concerting can take place, how people manage to make their activities fit together whilst ensuring the 'accountable' nature of this work as part of doing those activities, is not something that was much considered until the development of ethnomethodology. The influence and importance of ethnomethodological concern with 'accountability' can be seen in the work of Weick, for example, and his focus on sense-making procedures discussed in Chapter 2. The ethnomethodological concern with the question of how concerted actions are concerted, and the associated emphasis upon the 'accountable' character of work, has combined to give studies a focus upon the ways in which the pattern of complex activities are 'made visible' to those carrying out those activities, to the ways in which people placed within some complex of action can figure out what is happening around them and how they can fit their own activities into that complex (both when, e.g., the pattern of activity is a localised one, within their visual field, where the participant can directly monitor those activities which are relevant to their decision as to what to do next and when, on the other hand, they are engaged in patterns of distributed activities, where they cannot immediately monitor the activities of other, collaborating, parties but need, nonetheless,

Ethnography and change 71

to know in some more-or-less specific sense what those others are doing, so as to shape their own activity into the relevant pattern). This emphasis upon the accountable character of activities explains another relevant aspect of this approach to fieldwork, for the focus on the concerting of activities from within the activities ensures an interest in working under distributed conditions and of the role of 'awareness' in those conditions. That is, it points towards the extent to which, and the ways in which, participants in work can attune themselves to the state of the work process, and integrate their own activities – immediately or remotely – with those of other participants in the work process.

CONCLUSION

In light of this it should be clear that there are a number of potential uses for such an approach within the organisational change and technology design processes. Whatever role it may have, crucial determinants will always include such things as how much time is available 'in the field'; the relationship to and temporal features of a change programme (i.e., has programme started or has it been underway some time?), and the availability and suitability of existing data. There is also the question of whether those involved in the management of change are willing to heed another approach. As we noted in the first chapter, the ethnographic view may be simply another voice in an already cacophonous setting. But these are as we say practical problems and each instance when ethnography might be used will involve dealing with a particular set of practical circumstances. There is no way these can be comprehensively predicted beforehand. Nonetheless, the kind of role it can play can be illustrated in part by our own experience and in part by the more general use of the approach, especially in CSCW.

As to our own: we have undertaken a number of projects and in each the relationship between our research and other activities within the banks in question have varied. Our initial forays into retail financial services took place in 1990. They were occasioned by a request by a large computer company for us to 'sanity test' a previously derived process model of the bank's operations (in this case it was in fact a Building Society, since converted). The model concerned was intended to cover the full range of the bank's operations and our contribution was to be, for reasons of time, an assessment of its applicability in a limited context. It was determined that we would examine the work of cashiers in branches and mortgage processing at head office, largely because some of the claims made around the model in question had to do with the speeding up of customer-facing work. Mortgage processing at head office exemplified work that was both customer facing and involved considerable back-office work. This initial study was undertaken with no specific presumptions concerning 'requirements' for new processes or technology, but was more in the way of an attempt to characterise 'real time, real world' working and identify whether there were features of this character that had relevance to the model. By relevance we mean offered correctives to certain aspects, deepened particular elements and helped ground the model in better understanding. In this regard, we made it clear from the outset that our own study had to be seen as complementary to the model; that is, less a sanity test than an interest in what the model did not and could not encompass.

We should stress that our stance was 'innocent' (see also Hughes *et al.* 1992). That is, we were not interested in providing data with, let us say, a specific design relevance, but in characterising the setting in its own terms – a necessary part of 'seeing things from the point of view of the participant'. Though this should be clear from the preceding chapters, it is worth restating that our concern was to understand 'how things are now' before change is undertaken precipitately. It is, and was in this case, others with different approaches and techniques who proposed to undertake and manage change. Another way of putting this was provided by one of the consultants in the computer company who created the model: his view was that we were providing 'organisational knowledge' that would help assess the adequacy of the model, as well as provide a 'line of sight' to issues and aspects of the bank's practices that the model could not offer. We were to return to the same organisation over a period of two years.

A second strand of research we undertook was similarly concerned with providing better understanding between two organisations, one being a bank and another a supplier of technology and 'business solutions'. Our task in this case was specified by both sides and that was to provide an insight to the culture, working patterns and problems of the bank during a period when it was undergoing radical change – and indeed the pace of such change was expected to increase in the future. The goal was to share ethnographic insights with the supplier and to use these as a basis for deepening relations between the two organisations. It was understood that the findings would be of a research nature, intended to act as reminders of features of bank practice to bank staff themselves, and understanding of the inner world of banks that the supplier would not ordinarily have access to. It was recognised also that a considerable added value for the ethnography would be to provide richer, more comprehensive understandings of bank processes than would be generated by the supplier's own analysis techniques. In broad terms these techniques involved creating a model of organisational processes based on document flows. Like the prior research, no direct engagement with particular change programmes was required, and indeed this was seen as inimical to the research. Rather the hope was the research would produce unbiased views or at least analyses not preoccupied with particular change goals. Of key importance was to detail some of the processes that supported the various customer channels, as well as to describe and explicate some of the everyday features of work within those channels. The research programme took 12 months, and involved ethnographic observation throughout the main elements of the bank, and in particular in four high street branches, one regional processing centre, a telephone bank, an Internet bank service and central clearing and printing functions. This work was completed in 1997.

Output from the research demonstrated the achievement of its goals. In addition, though, the findings drew attention to how similar back-office processes within the various channels were undertaken in highly dissimilar ways, despite the recognition within any one channel that standardisation achieved great benefits. Such differences were particularly evident between phonebanking and the other channels. It drew attention also, and this was of greater importance, to the interactional properties that led customers to prefer to use one channel over another for certain tasks and other channels for other tasks. These properties were treated as 'interactional affordances', and analysis of them was used to re-evaluate the hopes and aspirations placed on the bank's various customer channels (Harper 1998). It is important to recognise that the last was done alongside much more extensive – and it has to be said costly investigations – involving large numbers of senior bank personnel as well as outside business consultants.

A third research activity we undertook was concerned with the examination of 'multi-skilling' in 'virtual banks' and the complex skills issues that emerge when the 'virtual' meets the 'real'. The research was jointly funded by the bank in question and a UK research council. It used ethnographic materials taken from observation of the impact of major changes in the bank's internal processes. These were heavily dependent on IT systems and were intended to facilitate decision-making, co-ordination and the flow of work across customer channels, but were particularly focused on new centralised back-office functions for high-street banking including business lending. Allied to this were developments in work practices intended to foster flexibility of working and encourage a more 'sales-oriented' approach. The project focused on key organisational aspects of these sales-oriented working practices, the creation and use of 'virtual teams' for the flexible organisation of routine work supporting branches, and the notional creation, by 'expert programs', of 'virtual customers' to support decision-making and risk assessment. Fieldwork for the project was undertaken in an 'old fashioned branch', in three new back-office service centres and four new lending centres, one of which was dedicated to business lending. The research was undertaken between 1997 and 1998.

More specifically, the research provided an in-depth understanding of the interactions between the 'virtual' and the 'real', between organisational change, performance and skill by focussing on the ways in which strategic plans were instantiated in day-to-day working practices. It reported on the implementation of a 'virtual team' to support consumer and business lending and tracked the emergence of the 'virtual customer' as it impacted on the day-to-day work of the organisation and its customer relations.

Outputs from the research served to supplement the bank's own research activities and acted as a contrast to some of the views generated by business-change analysts commissioned by the bank itself.

Other research we have undertaken has had a more direct concern with technology design, and we shall come to this in a moment. The role of these three projects just discussed was clearly different in each case, and this reflects in part the fact that the concerns of each financial institution were at different points in the change cycle or were seeking examination of distinct and particular issues. Our own experience should not then be used as illustrative of all that ethnographic approaches can do so much as an indication of how flexible its role can be. Organisational change, as in so much else, is a matter of responding to contingencies of various kinds. These will have a bearing on the role of ethnography. In other words, while not necessarily buying into the picture of the change process as a series of discrete, clearly delineated and phased steps, it undoubtedly has different objectives at different stages and, accordingly, implications for how change decision-making needs to be informed by relevant information about the domain.

In any case, ethnography not only has a potential role in broad change programmes but can and indeed has been demonstrated to have a role in technology design. Just what this role might be is still subject to debate, as we shall shortly see, but it is not only our own research that needs reporting here. There is now a substantial amount of reported activity in this area:

> ethnographies provide both general frameworks and specific analyses of relations among work, technology and organization. Workplace ethnographies have identified new orientations for design: for example, the creation and use of shared artifacts and the structuring of communicative practices.
>
> (Suchman 1995: 61)

Despite the extent of the research in this area however, the value of ethnography in technology design is still a matter of controversy (cf. Anderson 1994b; Plowman *et al.* 1995). As we have remarked earlier, there are no panaceas for the problems of design. We can only expect ethnography to have a modest utility to design and the role of ethnography, as we have practised it, is primarily as an informational input into design, and, as such, only one source of such information. The input can be of critical value insofar as it can advise the designer of actual practices of work and may clarify the role that actual practices play in the management of work, matters which may not normally be captured by other methods. Inasmuch as a position on the role of ethnography in design has emerged, it is in its ability to make visible the everyday nature of work. This can be more clearly stated as the principal virtue of ethnography is its ability to make visible the 'real time, real world' aspects of a social setting, seeking to present a portrait of that setting as seen and understood by those who live and work within the domains concerned. The intention is to see activities as social actions embedded within a socially organised domain and accomplished in and through the day-to-day activities of its users and to convey this information to designers.

This is, in fact, a partisan conception of ethnography, and is by no means universally shared by those who usually claim ownership of the ethnographic approach – sociologists and anthropologists. It does, however, have the advantage of focusing upon the specific and detailed organisation of activities which are carrying out and, thereby, upon the very activities which designers are concerned to understand, analyse and reconstruct. It is the ability of ethnography to describe a social setting as it is perceived by those involved in the setting (the archetypal 'users') that underpins its appeal to designers. In particular, it offers the opportunity to reveal 'needs' or 'practices' of users which they may not be aware of – because they take them so much for granted that they do not think about them – or which they cannot articulate – because of the bureaucratic or power relationships within which they are placed. As part of the initial process of requirements capture, ethnography is valuable in identifying the exceptions, contradictions and contingencies of work activities which are real conditions of the work's conduct but which will not (usually) figure in official or formal representations of that work, including the techniques of SSM and Participative Design, discussed in the previous chapter.

The assumption underscoring the use of ethnography has been that it is for designers to draw design conclusions from the results of ethnography. There can be a case made for ethnography having a more far-reaching impact upon design, insofar as it provides a means to rethink the nature of the social world that is being designed for, or to rethink the designer's role within that world (Hirschheim and Klein 1989; Anderson 1994b) but our concern is not with anything so immensely far-reaching as rethinking the world of design; it is with the contribution that ethnographic studies can make to the formulation of specific designs. The kinds of changes to design which will result from ethnomethodologically informed ethnography are intended to have an incremental rather than a comprehensively transformative effect. In any case, there is no intrinsic design significance to the results of an ethnographic study, for such significance must be relative to the nature of the design exercise itself: to the purposes, conceptions, methods and plans of those making the design. The nature of the exercises of design and fieldwork are very different. Design is a decision-making exercise, concerned with solving practical problems, whilst the fieldworker's role does not involve decision-making but consists, rather, in the concern to adequately and accurately capture and portray the ways of social settings, and the activities which occur within them.

By way of irony, though we have focused on design in this section, such an agnostic view is appropriate when it comes to participating in wider organisational-change programmes where sponsors of such programmes may have strongly held views about what should or should not be changed. Though it is certain that ethnographers will develop their own deeply held opinions doing field work, it is important that the investigation of the realities of work not be informed by the views of the sponsors, or indeed any of the theoretically driven relevances of organisational literature. The sponsors' views should provide a background and a reason for the inquiries but should not distract from the task of understanding, describing and conveying to the right parties the real-time, real-world character of the work in question.

Some problems of ethnography

Ethnography is not, unfortunately, a method without problems; many of which have been well documented (Randall *et al.* 1992, 1995). These generally focus on the 'standard' concerns of 'getting in, staying in, getting out' as well as issues of access and 'gatekeeping', reliability, validity and generalisation and so on. While these are clearly issues of interest to ethnomethodologically informed ethnography, here we are primarily interested in a number of specific problems that have arisen in our own usage of ethnomethodologically informed ethnography in the study of work, organisations and technology.

Ethnography is not, and indeed does not claim to be, a methodological panacea. Historically, ethnography has generally been limited to small-scale, well defined and usually quite confined contexts, well suited to the observational techniques employed. However, problems arise with the method's application to large-scale, highly distributed organisations. There are very real problems in the design and development of large-scale systems as well as in the processes attendant upon achieving large-scale organisational change. These have to do with obtaining adequate knowledge of the relevant domain, communicating this to relevant parties and organising the process of change. In commercial contexts these problems are deeply infused with the familiar commercial constraints of budgets, time and resources.[16]

To date the main use of ethnography has not only been within research settings but also confined to relatively small-scale and relatively confined environments, such as control rooms and other micro-interactional contexts. In such settings there tends to be a clear focus of attention for the participants, who are typically few in number, and in which there is a relatively clearly visible differentiation of tasks at one work site. Scaling such inquiries up to the organisational level or to processes distributed in time and space is a much more daunting prospect in raising issues of depth and

---

16 This is not to say that research contexts do not have their constraints of budget, time and other resources, only that commercial development has different ones.

representativeness – if these issues are of concern. In a similar vein, traditional ethnography has been a 'prolonged activity' and whilst 'quick and dirty' approaches have been developed the time scales involved in ethnographic research are often unrealistic in a commercial setting where the pressure is typically for 'results yesterday'.

Moving out of the research setting into a more commercial one also raises different sets of ethical responsibilities as well as making access to sites more vulnerable to the contingencies of the commercial and industrial world. Ethnography insists that its inquiries be conducted in a non-disruptive and non-interventionist manner, principles which can be compromised given that much of the motivation for organisational change is to reorganise work and, as part of this, often seek to displace labour. Less dramatically, but important nonetheless, fieldworkers not only require access to relevant sites but also need acceptance on the part of those who work in them. Protecting the identity of people, respecting the fact that the fieldworker is like a guest within their lives, and so on, become much harder to sustain in applied work of this kind.

Of course, few of these issues are easily solved. However, it is important not to be too ambitious for any method, least of all in organisational change where new methods follow one another with monotonous regularity. Organisational change is, at best, a 'satisficing' activity, often dealing with 'wicked' problems and a matter of doing the best one can with the resources available. Nevertheless, if it is accepted that those who are in the position to plan and implement change should be informed about the social character of work, and that ethnography is an important means of gaining such knowledge, then serious attention needs to be given to the variety of ways in which ethnographic studies can be used in such a task. For us, the important issue at the present time is to sensitise those undertaking change to the sociality of work as systematically and as effectively as possible. This becomes particularly useful when change is linked to the design and implementation of technology, as we have seen.

Part II

5 Taking customers seriously

> The classical model of bank work involved customers and staff in face-to-face trust relations. Banking was thus far from an exclusively impersonal set of accounting calculations and ledger entries. It was, and to a declining extent still is, based on intensive and often long standing personal relations.
>
> (Smith and Wield 1988: 275)

INTRODUCTION

As outlined in Chapter 3, the change-management literature has radically re-defined our notions of the organisation. Leaving aside the many variations, at least two core features are present in just about all versions of change management, and they are the notion of the 'value chain' and that of the 'customer'. The concept of the value chain is important because it emphasises an aspect of the organisation that is often glossed or ignored, and that is the organisation as an economic unit. The organisation, in this view, consists of a series of exchanges, and at each stage the product or service recipient is the 'customer'. Given that 'adding value' is the whole point of the exchange, it is not entirely surprising that 'customers' become a major feature of this kind of analysis. Here, we want to examine the idea of the customer in more detail, and in particular, the rationalist underpinnings of 'customers' as one end of a predictable, rationally based pole in the exchange dyad. But our angle is rather particular on this: we are interested in the rationalities exhibited in the actions and purposes of customers, what we have earlier called 'local rationalities'. We are interested too in the same as regards bank staff. Our focus will be on these rationalities as displayed at point-of-contact activities, especially face-to-face ones. This will involve describing in some detail how customer-facing work in financial services has been and is being done. Our interest lies in the contingent and skilful nature of this work, all the more so given that it is being done in institutions undergoing large-scale organisational change. As we have seen, how that work is done is typically glossed in the literature. We refer especially to arguments concerning the move towards a 'selling' culture, 'team-based' working and away from branch-based work towards more 'proceduralised' processing centres. Here one will find very little indeed on what actually happens in these places, except for the most gross and generalising descriptions. Besides, our interest is all the more pertinent given that, in this sector, the reconfiguration of the institutions has often been predicated on a 'process' model of transactions generated from within banks (albeit with much assistance from process-change experts, of course) and, as a result, some at least of the traditional 'face-to-face' qualities of interacting with customers have and are being eroded.

We present observations taken over a number of years in the various bank settings we have observed, including observations of what one may call the everyday interactions at the cash desk and interviews within high-street branches. We draw attention to what bank staff themselves call the unpredictability of customer behaviour. We will see that in certain respects the 'problem' in customer-facing activities remains what it always has been: ensuring that customers have confidence in the bank despite the fact that this confidence is undermined by the unpredictable behaviour of the customers themselves. The way in which a sense of confidence is provided for customers is, however, changing in that the medium through which interaction is managed is less and less often the medium of face-to-face talk with which bank staff are so experienced. It is moving into more technologically mediated forms that bank staff have to learn and adapt to. We will suggest that the consequences of these changes rely on what the characteristics of face-to-face talk are in the first place, and how these characteristics have changed as a result of new organisational structures and the new technologies meant to serve them. We will pursue the question of precisely how customer-facing work is becoming increasingly mediated by technology in the next chapter.

'TELLING' AND 'SELLING' – CUSTOMER CONFIDENCE AND DEMEANOUR-WORK

As we noted in Chapter 1, much has been made in the literature of the move from a 'telling' to a 'selling' culture, whereby all retail financial services have recognised their profit sources and begun to pursue them vigorously. In so doing, they have attempted, at least in the institutions we have looked at, to transform their organisational culture. Financial products of many different kinds are now on offer, and bank clerks and cashiers are regarded as the front-line troops of the selling army.

The most interesting aspect of this literature (as against the actualities of the changes in practice) is the way it presumes that the transformation has been straightforwardly effected. Our evidence is that it was not. In one of the institutions we observed, for example, the initial presumption was that a universal 'selling' culture could be implemented in which all operatives were to be equally involved in the sale of financial products through, for instance, the 'spotting' of selling opportunities in their routine interactions with customers and the customer database. Conversations with staff, however, consistently produced observations on their part of the following kind:

> it's very difficult ... after all, you usually know these people ... some of them are even your friends ... and suddenly there you are trying to sell them something.

This, along with commonplaces such as, 'It's embarrassing ... I'm not used to this', led us to the view that the transition from one 'culture' to another was anything but unproblematic. That is, we had been assured in advance of our studies that we would find a 'selling culture' in place – from the point of view of management, it seemed that because there had been a change in policy, we could presume a change in the reality – but we actually found at that point very little to indicate this general cultural change. In one instance, we noted the existence of a 'spot box' (literally covered in spots) in a branch we were observing. In this box any 'spots' (or opportunities for selling as they were in truth), identified by cashiers were to be placed for follow-up by the sales team. Over 4 weeks of observation after the 'selling' policy was instituted, we failed to observe even a single 'spot' being placed in the box.[17] Such instances are, of course, often held to be evidence of the 'resistance' to change by organisational cultures. Such a view ignores the different orientations the individual cashier or clerk brings to the distinct task at hand.

For there is no question that in dealing with customers, the cashier or clerk brings a sense in which they 'represent' the institution as a skilful, customer-friendly operative. At the same time, these people are quite routinely expressing their dismay at policy changes within the institutions in question, and there is much talk of 'low morale'. Most if not all of such talk is of course undertaken in places away from view of the customer – in what Goffman years ago called backstage settings (Goffman 1959). The point is that what appears to be a contradictory impulse dissolves as soon as one looks at it as context-dependent. Customer-facing work is a context where operatives engage in what we suggest is 'learned demeanour work' which is evident in what on the surface appear to be small matters: learning the right 'pitch' for the voice, learning to respond to difficult enquiries and

---

17 Of course, institutional policy in one sense at least recognises this inertia, and typically various 'targets' are instituted in order to provide the necessary pressure. Again, however, observation 'on the ground', and in more than one institution, led to some interesting conclusions about the results of target setting. Not least was the effort put into 'claiming', individual against individual and department against department, the credit for a particular sale, and in much the same way the transformation of existing sales into 'new' opportunities in order to meet targets.

learning to maintain customer flow. All of these constitute skilful forms of working.

Whilst this places considerable demands on staff, it should not be forgotten that the major source of work satisfaction is precisely interaction with the customer:

> I like working with the public ... it's the thing I like about the job ... you work much harder, mind, and when you get an awkward one it can ruin your whole day ... but when they're nice, which about 90% are, well it's what I enjoy.

Comments of this type abound in our data. Through their interactions with customers, bank staff resolve uncertainty, suggest sensible courses of action, sometimes sell appropriate products, deal with an extraordinary range of problems and in so doing maintain customer confidence. Our concern is to try to account for how and why this transformation of relations with the customer appears so problematic for those involved in customer-facing work. We will argue that it had much to do with the way in which operatives construe their work with customers as being to do with 'maintaining customer confidence'.

The confident customer

Initial interest in notions such as 'customer confidence' came from our earliest studies in retail financial-services institutions. To some degree it reflected our awareness that customer service was becoming a central management concern. Hence, it was suggested to us by one middle manager that it was an important platform for the selling work that management wanted done, and that there were, increasingly, clear expectations concerning the demeanour of staff. As he said:

> Most people in financial services know that you can't differentiate by product any more, so you have to differentiate by service.

In this respect, and as noted by Hochschild (1983), demeanour work (Goffman 1971) has become a management issue. Rules about how cashiers, for example, express themselves have become implicitly and explicitly set by management. There is, for instance, the general expectation that all staff have to defer to customers in terms of courtesy, etc. Management strategies to gain the best share of the market include rhetoric such as positive attitude, customer handling, customer care, etc. Moreover, the accomplishment of this is regularly tested with the visit of the so-called 'mystery shopper'. It was the job of these individuals to walk into high-street branches and pose as a normal customer whilst in fact making a record of the performance of staff.

A particular concern was to assess the ability of staff to deal politely and effectively with 'problems'.

Thus workers are asked to undertake public-relations work, promote sales and to 'represent the company', even in situations where customers are 'awkward'. It was not at all uncommon at this time to hear staff 'backstage' ask such things as:

> Have you ever had to deal with Mr X? ... he's a complete nutter ... you wouldn't believe what he said to me ... how I kept the smile on my face, I don't know.

As Hochschild (1983) argues, display is what is sold, and a principle of 'emotive dissonance' analogous to the principle of 'cognitive dissonance' is at work.

Nevertheless, the ontological status of staff identity in relation to this work was not, and is not, of interest here. Whether or not 'customer service' can be construed as an 'ideology', there is little doubt that employees orient to some conception of it. Branch staff routinely speak of the need to maintain customer confidence or 'trust'. It comes from the seamless and apparently unproblematic way in which staff are manifestly able to do the work necessitated by customer demands. That is, in order to do the work necessary to produce an orderly flow of transactions, cashiers must be seen to be competent in so doing. In some circumstances, this requires the cashier to engage in a significant amount of demeanour work – work which is an inseparable part of the service provided (see also Randall and Hughes 1994). This work is manifest in the way staff routinely explain as they go along the steps they are taking, what enquiries they are making of the screen, to whom they are telephoning, and so on. Competence is evident in this sense in the way the flow of interaction is maintained without palpable gaps in routine and minute-by-minute interactions both at the cash desk and in interview situations. After all, bank cashiers are the first point of contact for the majority of customers, and a customer expects service that is personal, pleasant, friendly and open to their queries and requests. In practical terms, and from the point of view of the cashier, this means maintaining eye contact with the customer, making pleasant conversation, in some cases promoting sales, whilst at exactly the same time dealing with a screen display and navigating through a customer database. In all these prosaic ways cashiers are 'representing the institution' to the customer. Unsurprisingly then, demeanour work involves deploying some quite ordinary techniques, techniques which are familiar to us as members of the social world at large.

None of this, of course, is a discovery. Nevertheless, these ordinary pleasantries have to be conducted in circumstances where, in some contexts, these normally unproblematic interactions become problematic. In dealing with these, staff have to show an especial competence.

Consider managing a queue. The work involved here – for it is a kind of work – shows how in the specific features of one kind of face-to-face interaction the skills involved in maintaining customer confidence becomes visible, and particularly so in situations where there is a customer-occasioned deviation from what one might call the 'script'. At the time of our early studies, many institutions, including the bank we were observing, had not even begun to separate queues according to the kind of service demanded – the 'service desk' was much less prominent then than now. Hence, in any given queue, there were customers who simply wished to undertake some routine transaction such as a money withdrawal; customers with complex queries about mortgages, current or savings accounts; and customers who wanted information about all three. The experienced cashier knew not only that these queries could be presented by any next-customer-in-the-queue, but also that the customer in question could present their queries in any way. As one cashier said at the time:

> the most common words you hear in here on a Saturday morning are oh, by the way.

That is, although much of the work with customers consisted of straightforward transactions such as withdrawals of cash, the sequence of tasks cashiers had to perform were customer-driven in at least two senses. First, customers took priority above all other work because it was perceived wisdom that customers did not want to wait long either in a queue; and second, and more concretely, it was what 'this customer wants here and now' that determined what kind of transaction the cashier was required to perform. Of key importance was the fact that adept cashiers were concerned to complete transactions within a reasonable period of time, but what was reasonable was determined by the interaction with the customer rather than with the terminal. Maintaining customer confidence required cashiers to be attentive to queues whilst at the same time meeting the needs of each individual to their satisfaction when they got to the end of the queue. The art of maintaining customer confidence in this regard was as much about being seen to be dealing with the problem as it was about actually dealing with it. That is, when staff were engaged in the myriad interactions with customers and each other they were, in Goffman's terms, involved in 'the presentation of self' as a 'front stage activity' (Goffman 1959).

The work of the cashier involved the routine display of competencies that nevertheless went largely unnoticed as important elements of the transaction process. This may be because the relevant skills could be construed as 'social' rather than 'technical'. Staff would routinely explain to customers what enquiries they were making of the screen, to whom they were telephoning, and so on. Customer confidence was engendered above all by the perception that the problem was being sorted out by cashiers or officers who were demonstrating their knowledge of the problem and its solution to the customer. Failing that, trust could be seen to be warranted by staff who were able to identify the steps that would have to be taken in order that the problem could be resolved.

That simple expectation on the part of the customer – that the cashier was competent – however, had enormous consequences for the flow of work; that is, the minute-by-minute ordering of activities according to 'what must I do next?' principles. For cashiers, the customer was, in this context, constructed precisely as someone in a queue, and dealing with him or her necessitated intuitions on the part of cashiers about customer interests and behaviour. These, as we have suggested, had to do with on the one hand 'keeping the queue moving', since it is generally assumed that customers do not want to be kept waiting unnecessarily; and on the other 'dealing with each enquiry satisfactorily', in that it was equally assumed that each customer would be happy only if their confidence in the institution to deal with their queries, as and when they present them, was maintained.

Were it the case that customers abided by the procedures established by the bank in question this would have been, for the most part, unproblematic from a managerial or design point of view. The fact was, however, that in their queuing behaviour they did not. Cashiers had to deal with each customer without knowing in advance what their requirement would be, nor indeed whether the customer's requirements would be met in full at the end of any given transaction. Customers could and did structure their requirements in a variety of ways, including making a series of requests at the beginning of their encounter with cashiers, or alternatively waiting for the completion of the processes associated with an initial request before making a second. Thus, the nature of a request would not be predicted, but neither could the way in which the request(s) would be structured.

It would have been surprising, of course, if customers did show any sophisticated knowledge of bank procedures, and indeed they seldom did. From the customer's point of view, satisfaction was a result of a variety of factors, including cashiers' ability to keep the queue moving so as to minimise waiting time while at the same time deal with the customers' requests at the appropriate time both adequately and expeditiously. In the face of these often unpredictable demands the demeanour work of cashiers was critical. In interacting with customers, cashiers had to lead them through the processes necessary for the completion of the transaction, and engage in the work of 'being a cashier' which was part of the service customers expect. In other words, they had to visibly demonstrate and confirm the competence that maintained customer confidence through their talk and, above all, in their actions. We shall come back to this.

None of the above problematises the idea of procedures and plans for dealing with customers. There are many such procedures in relation to customer-facing activities, as indeed there are for most other activities performed within banks.[18] That is, and not very surprisingly, bank management devote considerable attention to codifying, providing rules for, and attempting to ensure conformity of procedures. In large part the intent of doing so is to ensure that customer-facing staff display competency (though this is not all the procedures are intended for). One problem here resides in the fact that – as Wittgenstein noted many decades ago (Wittgenstein 1958) – 'no rule dictates its own application'. What this means is simply that, whatever the force or extent of rules and procedures, occasions can and must arise where decisions have to be made about whether to apply this rule in this circumstance. Consequently, and notwithstanding the fact that some rules are more tightly enforced than others, cashiers have to reason through what rules were applicable at any moment in time.

This is why we suggested earlier on that our concern was with rationality. Dealing with queues in such a fashion as to ensure that any member of such a queue is dealt with when they got to the end in a way that satisfies the customer achieves the intent of the bank's rules. But this achievement requires cashiers to exercise their discretion. The fact that cashier work was viewed during our research (and continues to be to this date) as a low-discretion task in the general banking literature (and indeed within banks themselves) underlines the importance of recognising this. It is indicative also of how much more discretion must underscore activities in more complex and more comprehensively rule governed activities as undertaken in relation to, let us say, lending (as we shall see in the next chapter).

Knowledge in action

In any event, it is by now a commonplace observation (Suchman 1987) that work 'routines' are not slavishly adhered to but, typically, involve the considerable exercise of judgement and the deployment of a variety of 'skills'. Such discretion 'typically' concerns the circumstances under which a routine is to be strictly followed and conversely the circumstances under which modifications or 'short-cuts' may be employed through, for example, the utilisation of informal teamwork or, as we have termed it above, 'local knowledge'. In other words, what we are pointing to here is the 'occasioned determination' of practices in the course of work. In this context, the issues had to do with what it was that cashiers needed to know in order that they could genuinely be customer-facing; what knowledge and resources they deployed in order to do the work of exhibiting competence; and the degree to which the existing rules and procedures encompassed these 'informal' methods.

---

18 Indeed, the very point of introducing 'service desks' now common in most branches is to train customers into more predictable behaviour by enforcing a regime where certain kinds of problem will only be dealt with in certain locations.

One key feature of exercising the local rationalities we are concerned with is that it has to be done in the face of what staff themselves call 'routine troubles', and these primarily have to do with customer unpredictability. Competent working, and the concomitant maintenance of customer confidence, is a matter of interpreting the existing rules and procedures and deploying local and personalised knowledge in such a way as to get the job competently done despite this unpredictability.

This local knowledge can take a variety of forms, but includes personal and/or biographical knowledge of customers. Knowledge of customers is an invaluable resource in all branches, but above all in the small ones, for doing the demeanour work that gives customers confidence. Names, knowledge of family circumstances, enquiries after relatives, etc. are all used as a means to ensure the 'flow' of the transaction. Such an understanding of a customer's profile becomes extremely important in dealing with customers' inability to comprehend procedures, for example.

From the cashier's point of view, regardless of the nature of an enquiry, decisions must be made on a fairly immediate basis about how to deal with them. In our early studies (from which the previous discussion has been drawn), such enquiries could range through a number of concerns, as we have seen. Many enquiries, of course, occur as other transactions are taking place, and was a major source of unpredictability (and this held true regardless of whether interactions were 'scripted' or not).[19] Whatever their provenance, enquiries have to be handled in some way:

CUSTOMER (withdraws a sum of money and asks): Oh, by the way ... I wonder if you could tell me if two cheques have gone through? ... one's to Manweb and the other ... it's for £105 ... I can't remember what they're called.
CASHIER (searches enquiry screens and responds): Manweb ... May 18th ... yes that's been paid ... £105 ... 105 ... yes that's gone out as well ... it was payable to the House of Fraser.
CASHIER to ethnographer: We try to discourage it 'cos it takes so much time ... we used to just print it out but the customers just asked more questions, like what's this? ... when it's an interest update.

Although this example is ordinary in the extreme, it illustrates the point that customers cannot be relied on to produce their questions in a fashion that is consistent with the institution's order of things, or furnishes all the information relevant to the query. Nor can the nature of the questions be predicted beforehand. Decisions must be made on a fairly immediate basis about how to deal with those questions and in a context where those

---

19 The problem of customer unpredictability remains a vibrant one even on the telephone. Customer satisfaction is very much a matter of concious deviation from the script.

enquiries may range in character through the status of an account, standing-order or direct-debit payments, advice about new accounts and concerns about lost cheque books. These enquiries are time-consuming, and occur frequently.

One of the ways cashiers manage these problems is by reference to knowledge of the flow of trade on a daily and weekly basis. With this, cashiers can determine whether or not other routine administrative tasks can be performed at various times without the development of large queues:

> CASHIER: Monday and Friday are the busiest days ... it's always like this after the school term starts – the customers come in after they've dropped the kids off ... Lunchtime's the busiest in this branch, and it's always worse 'cos there's only ever two cashiers on.
>
> ANOTHER CASHIER: There's a big (supermarket) near here, and I think we get a lot of custom from people 'cos it's easy to park and it means they don't have to go into town.

Consequently, when staff absence or a need to clear a back-log of work, required the employment of part-timers unfamiliar with this particular branch office, we noted in our fieldwork the following kinds of problems ensued:

> For these staff, the first day or two in a branch are largely unproductive. A considerable amount of time is spent in orienting to local practice ... staff were not always familiar with the available technology ... and frequently had to ask others what the appropriate codes for various screens were ... sometimes they asked which drawer relevant forms were kept in.

This demonstrates that in important senses standardised operations can never fully encompass local contingency. Even the simplest of things can be a problem for staff in an unfamiliar location.

Visible competence

Being seen to do the work competently, especially in front of customers, substantially informs the practices of customer-facing staff. Key to this is providing accounts of what is going on that demonstrate knowledge. For example, many enquiries generate phone calls, usually either because the information is not available on the screen, or because it cannot be deciphered. The following example illustrates the point. A customer wants to know what is the accrued interest on a Capital Bond since 1989.

> CASHIER: I'm sorry, the screen doesn't go back that far ... but I can ring Head Office and get them to provide the information. Will that be OK?

CUSTOMER: Yes.
CASHIER (phones, explains, and then says to customer): Right, I'll get that put in writing later today, and sent out to you.

Such enquiries require both an effective knowledge of information resources such as the computer screens and some paper resources, but also require a skill in eliciting necessary information from the customer:

CASHIER 1 (to cashier 2): God ... this woman wants to close down her Account and open up four in her kids names, with £500 in each ... I've recommended an X account for them ... I'll need four application forms and one for closing it, won't I? What's the number for an X account? ... the two last digits.
CASHIER 2: points to wall.
CASHIER 1 (to customer): Have you given any notice?
CUSTOMER: No, does it matter?
CASHIER 1: Well, you know you'll lose 50 days interest?
CUSTOMER: It's only money, isn't it?
CASHIER 1 (fills in Withdrawal with Penalty section on Withdrawal Form and then says): Shall I transfer it for you?
CUSTOMER: Yeah.
CASHIER 1 (then fills in Withdrawal Form with 'All' written in relevant section and says): I'll give you the Application Forms for the X Account.
CASHIER 1 (then gives the customer four copies of the form): You've got 14 days to complete the transaction – just come in with the Application Forms and we'll open the accounts.

Such transactions could take a great deal of time, since the institution's procedures insist on the customer's presence throughout the opening of a new account. Thus, practical decisions had to be made about whether the request can be dealt with 'here and now', or whether it is best dealt with 'in part' – as in this case – so as to minimise its consequences for the queue. But in either event, the choice had to be explained to customers. In other words, the 'rational basis' of cashiers' behaviour had to be made available to customers. Our observations convinced us that this is a natural feature of how customer-facing work was done.

The satisfied customer and everyday tasks

Trying to keep the customer satisfied is a matter of juggling a quite complex and potentially conflicting series of demands. In the last case recounted, a further demonstration of the need to manage the interaction accordingly was provided when the customer did indeed return. One particular element of this multi-tasking relates to the use if systems whilst managing the

92 *Part II*

customer. Indeed, inputting information to the screen displays is probably the single most time-consuming aspect of the whole process of, for example, opening a new account. Within reason, cashiers sometimes leave this work until the customer leaves rather than expect them to wait for unnecessarily long periods. This was and still is, however, a technical breach of procedure, in that as the cashier involved in the above transaction explained:

> We're supposed to get the customer to sign and check the headers ... and they get impatient 'cos they're having to wait while you put it all in ... and the number of times you get communication failure and have to do it all over again ... that woman who wanted to open four accounts ... I just had time to get them open ... there was a queue right out the door ... there was no way I was going to get the Statics done.

The point here is that managing the customer is appreciably more than simply dealing with routine transactions. 'Oh, by the way' questions are surprisingly common, and suggest that a view that looks at customer–staff relations as purely transactional – as many views of such relations do as we have seen – though satisfactory as a way of representing the formal processes involved, does not encompass the problem of how it is that customers initiate, structure and juggle the order in which the relevant (transaction) work has to be done. Typically, dealing with unpredictabilities is done in and through the rational application of local knowledge on the part of the bank's staff. The rationality and knowledge we refer to can concern customers and their demands, technological constraints and affordances, as well as procedures.

Another example will be helpful here, again taken from our fieldnotes:

> The opening of a new account typically takes some 15 minutes to complete as a result of the need to input a considerable amount of data into the customer 'static'. Static details represent the major element of procedure for the cashier, and often entail difficulty. For example, cashiers sometimes have difficulty organising names, especially for joint accounts, so that they do not exceed the character space available, and the process as a whole is compounded when customers seek to open and possibly close several accounts – a not unusual event, especially when accounts are being opened for children/grandchildren. Having received the two application forms required by the institution from the customer, if a passbook is involved, the cashier must issue the new passbook, obtain the next Account Number from a sequenced file, and then type in the Account Details on the Static Investment-New Account screen. Depending on the account, different codes have to be input governing frequency of interest payment. A separate Static printout is also generated and filed, along with the completed application form. Within reason, cashiers will sometimes leave this work until the cus-

tomer has left rather than expect them to wait for unnecessarily long periods. This is, however, a technical breach of procedure.

Here we see clearly the contrast between the demands of 'keeping the queue moving' and meeting organisational requirements, when relatively unpredictable events occur. Whatever the standard problem of opening new accounts might be, and however it has subsequently been dealt with, for instance by separating out such procedures from the normal branch queue, the point remains the same.

Breaking the rules

On occasion, customers can ask for services in such a way that dealing with it wholly in accordance with the rules becomes problematic for cashiers. For instance, customers regularly demonstrate their ignorance of the bank rules, and yet still expect the service to be provided. Hence:

CUSTOMER wishes to withdraw two cheques but the CASHIER replies: Uh, I'm sorry, but there's only Mr Smith's signature on the passbook[20] ... it hasn't got yours ... have you got a signature with you?
CUSTOMER: No.
CASHIER: I'll have to find a signature ... CASHIER (searches through card index file of customer details [application forms, etc.]): I'm just trying to find your signature card ... we should have a card for you and I can't find it ... I'll just get you to sign your passbook for the next time.

Eventually the cashier gives the customer a passbook with a waxed paper strip attached which the customer signs. In this case, the cashier recognised the customer as 'the wife of' the signee, and knowing this (and knowing also that therefore that same customer had no right to money according to the rules of the institution), was able to provide a reasonable route to ensure that the customer's needs could be achieved, whilst achieving the intent of the rules if not the words.

For another example:

> A customer who wants to cash a cheque from another branch ... handed over to section head to ring for authorisation ... rang several times, branch continually engaged ... phone still engaged, trying to contact bank via switch message ... after 35 minutes no reply to switch

---

20 In this building society, there were a surprising number of old-fashioned passbooks being used. It appeared that, 'We have a lot of older customers. They like to sit and look at the passbook ... see how much money they've got ...'

94 *Part II*

and phone still engaged ... customer asked if he wanted to reduce the amount to £300 ... his cheque was then cashed.

In this example, the problem for the cashier is that he had no clear evidence of whether this customer is a legitimate client of the bank or not. Attempts to establish his *bona fides* fail, and in circumstances where a possibly legitimate client clearly needs money, a decision was made to offer him the facility to withdraw a lesser amount. Such strategies constitute what Bittner (1965) calls 'gambits of compliance'; that is, techniques that enable workers to 'get the work done' whilst the appearance of complying with the formal rules. In both cases, local knowledge of one sort or another was used to do this.

In important respects, whether rules encompass the behaviours or not is irrelevant. Our point is that what occasions the kinds of behaviour we have been talking about is to do with the perspectival construction of the customer. Put another way, a customer is no single thing, and what he or she is is produced out of the circumstances in which he or she arrives in contact with the institution. Hence, much of what we have discussed hitherto refers to 'keeping the queue moving' simply because the fact that many if not most customers still meet the organisation in queues means that they will have to be encountered and dealt with in particular ways. Dealing with customers in these instances is largely a matter of 'keeping the customer satisfied', in the face of unpredictable demands and queries, and the need to keep a queue moving. As we have shown, and regardless of the degree to which these are organisational matters in respect of the existence of rules designed to deal with these issues, local knowledge of one kind or another is a resource for staff to do the work the organisation expects them to do. We turn now to a similar case of face-to-face interaction, albeit one where the queue is not at issue. We do so to identify in what respect dealing with customers might be perspectively different, if at all, when interactions are relatively extended. The case in question is the customer interview.

MAKING SENSE OF THE CUSTOMER: INTERVIEWS AND LOCAL KNOWLEDGE

Customer-facing work, then, is rather more unpredictable than one might be led to believe. One should be careful, however, not to conclude that customers are therefore largely unmanageable, for they are demonstrably managed, and are managed in ways which indicate the sometimes hidden skills of ordinary staff. One such way, as we have seen, is through the use of particular knowledge of the circumstances of the customer, their business and their account and so on. This provides a short-cut to processing.

The following fieldwork extract indicates how some of this 'local knowledge' is deployed in a lending interview – a substantially more extended customer interaction than occurs at cashiers' desks. In this particular case, a lending officer in the bank is considering an approach to borrow money to purchase a 'hairdresser's'.

By way of background, it is worth noting that the interviewer does not go to the customer 'cold'. Prior to the interview he had perused the 'customer brief' transmitted from the lending centre (which contains advice on how the interview might proceed and the various requirements of the bank), some interview notes as well as the file containing a range of computer printouts (these detail the general working of the customer's account). In addition, he had compiled his own set of notes, including a list of questions concerning the relationship between the people proposing to borrow the money, a number of aspects of the proposition such as the borrower's contribution to the purchase, the serviceability of the debt, and an outline of issues connected to hairdressing as a business proposition.

Given these various resources one might suggest that the customer exists in more than one form. First the customer exists as a set of information, collected and collated from a number of resources including institutionally available notes and advice, and more 'personal' resources. Also, the customer exists as someone whose identity and character has to be dealt with 'here and now'. This twofold yet multifarious interest in customer identity is something that we shall come back to, especially in the next chapter.

LENDING OFFICER: What can I do for you?
CUSTOMER: Been hairdressing for 10 years ... we've seen premises ... we were enquiring about money.
LENDING OFFICER: Where is it?
CUSTOMER: It's on ( ) ... I used to be manageress of the hairdresser's on the corner of the road ... I've got 500 clients I can't expand anymore ... this is the only way I can expand the business.
LENDING OFFICER: What figures are we talking?
CUSTOMER: 68K ... the Building Society say it's worth 65 ... we think it'll come down.
LENDING OFFICER: First question – what have you got to put into it?
CUSTOMER: My own home ... that's all ... we haven't really got any ideas.
LENDING OFFICER: For a commercial proposition to get off the ground we're looking at a third ... the Banks have had their fingers burnt in the past ... (explains) ... its 20K ... or something like that.
CUSTOMER: There's no way round it?
LENDING OFFICER: No ... that's the first thing that any Bank will ask.
CUSTOMER: I have got 15 thousand on my property.
LENDING OFFICER: How much is your mortgage? ... most lenders will only give you 80%.
CUSTOMER: So we have to get 20K.

LENDING OFFICER: Not necessarily – speaking as a cautious banker ... we're interested in your commitment to the business ... if you're raising money on your property ... (but) you're looking for the Bank to raise it all ... I'm being honest with you ... you'll incur a lot of expenses ... (and) you can't get a domestic mortgage on it ... (also) I'm talking off the top of my head (but) it's a lot of money for a hairdresser's ... the business has got to service that.

CUSTOMER: The reason we went for the place ... I know the area ... (and) it was kitted out as a hairdresser's (describes) ... You think that's quite expensive?

LENDING OFFICER: You know more about hairdressing than me ... I understand it's tight on margins.

CUSTOMER: There's a lot of chimneys round there ... we haven't thought about it ... my husband's a barrister ... and he said it's a bit dear.

LENDING OFFICER: Did you produce some figures? (looks at forms).

CUSTOMER: This is what we take a week each individually.

LENDING OFFICER: Has anyone looked at it?

CUSTOMER: My brother's a surveyor and he looked round it.

LENDING OFFICER: He thinks it's worth it?

CUSTOMER: He did say 58 ... do you think if we got a more realistic figure ... we would stand a chance?

LENDING OFFICER: There's nothing wrong with purchasing property ... (but) I'd be thinking more on the lines of 30 ... The first question on my pad is the contribution ... if it was 30 and you were putting in 10 then I'd think of it.

CUSTOMER (talking about current mobile hairdressing job and why she wants to move into a shop): I start at 8:30 ... I'm just running around.

LENDING OFFICER: What do you turnover a week?

CUSTOMER: (I put) about 450 in the Bank and ... does 350 ... talking about how much is needed ... we'd have to do 850 a month which I couldn't see as a problem (chat about flat attached to premises and letting) ... we're talking about hairdressing in a shop compared with mobile.

LENDING OFFICER: You've got precious little overheads ...

CUSTOMER: Yes ... but eventually for piece of mind and a bit of a life I thought it was the right thing to look into.

LENDING OFFICER: That was the starting point ... getting a third ... I think there are a lot of properties (talk about shop) ... have you not thought of letting somewhere?

CUSTOMER 1: Where do you look?

LENDING OFFICER: Estate Agents ...

CUSTOMER (talk about leasing, terms of lease ...): Could lose a lot.

LENDING OFFICER: But conceivably you've lost less than if you were servicing 60K of debt.

CUSTOMER: OK ... so if we find something different and get a bit of a contribution its worth coming back?

LENDING OFFICER: It depends where you get it from ... can I ask you one question about your accounts ... (talk about changing name) another point ... are you paying in your takings into your private account ... it looks to me as if this is a business account ... you shouldn't do it ... could we make a separate appointment (to discuss this) ... Do you think I've been hard?
CUSTOMER: You've been hard ... I won't sleep tonight now.
LENDING OFFICER: I'm going to play Devil's Advocate ... It's (the proposition) a lot of debt to have around ... cheer up ... it could be for the best ... I'm not prepared to let you use a personal account for business purposes (goes to get diary to arrange another interview ... makes appointment ... gives customer forms on business accounts).

This interview was immediately followed by a discussion between the ethnographer and the lending officer:

LENDING OFFICER: You've got to be cruel to be kind ... there's no way I'm going to lend the 68K with no contribution from them ... the risk is all with the bank ... (after looking at the) initial contribution I didn't delve any further ... if they're not putting anything in it's not worth going into any other questions. The problem is ... I know her account is crap ... there's an enforcement order on ... it's a waste of time I spend an hour going through them ... (the proposition) wasn't really thought through ... it's back-of-a-fag-packet stuff.

So in this case, the lending officer had made a conditional decision to the effect that this customer does not constitute a 'good risk' prior to the meeting. This decision was based on knowledge of bank policy concerning risk, and also on knowledge of the customer culled from account details. Further to this, the final decision was arrived at on listening to the customer account for their plans, or in this case the lack of them. More importantly, the principle of 'keeping the customer satisfied' is also visible throughout the interview, as when the lending officer explains 'the banks have had their fingers burnt in the past', and when he explains that the decision is one that any careful banker might make, as in: 'No ... that's the first thing that any bank will ask'.

The 'skill' here, then, is a constellation of knowledge and techniques, including knowledge of the bank's policy on small businesses of this kind, of the balance of risk, of customers' handling of their accounts, and the deployment of techniques for, in effect, demonstrating that a decision is a reasonable one.

Despite an emphasis on procedure and the range of sophisticated computer support for risk grades and so on, the decision also involves what one might call this lending officer's instincts concerning this customer. In this

98 *Part II*

respect, lending officers often speak of 'gut feeling' or as one put it:

> In the end do you trust him to pay the money back?

and another:

> A lot of it is just gut feeling... the only other thing you've got is how the account has run historically and income and expenditure breakdowns ... and they can't tell you anything.

To reiterate the point made above, it is not as if decisions of this kind are made cavalierly, with disregard for bank policy and procedure. Rather, they must be seen to be made in accordance with policy. Nevertheless, the existence of detailed resources for decision-making do not in and of themselves determine whether a loan will be made, nor how the interview will be conducted. Lending clearly benefits from the kind of detailed local knowledge of the customer commonly found in the branches. Such local knowledge, as deployed in the above examples, developed in a branch with a few thousand customers. It is obviously a useful resource in everyday work. But its use points towards how similar knowledge might be replicated in distributed forms of banking, or as it is called virtual banking, where the numbers of customers is much greater and the extent of face-to-face work much less. We shall come to this in the next chapter.

Visible competence and interviewing

The above interview powerfully demonstrates the need to maintain customer 'confidence'. Confidence here refers to customer attitudes towards the bank – evidently not as far as the bank is concerned a matter of giving the customer what they want, but of demonstrating that decisions are competently arrived at. This interactional feature we find repeated consistently in a wide variety of queue management and interview situations.

Demonstrating competence is not at all the same thing as being competent, however. Local knowledge is differentially distributed and so, of course, is knowledge of institutional procedure and policy. These widely differing levels of competent working, nevertheless, remain largely invisible to the customer. That this is so is in the main due to some simple expediencies such as asking others, and these for the most part take place in the 'back office'.

In any event, to illustrate the importance of 'visible competence', we provide a second and lengthy vignette, based on a mortgage interview we observed:

CUSTOMER: I came in and got told I was £700 in arrears and then, no, it was only £220 and I want to know why ... we left our payments running at a higher level thinking we were paying the interest off, which we obviously weren't ... and I came in to find I was £220 in arrears and I said 'No, I couldn't be ...'.

INTERVIEWER: Are you on Annual Review?

CUSTOMER: No.

INTERVIEWER: You've not been on arrears since the beginning. What we've got to try to do is find out where it's gone wrong ... let's have a look ... (the interviewer interrogates the screen) What it is, your insurance has just gone in, which is not on your mortgage.

CUSTOMER: I thought it was.

INTERVIEWER: No, only if you're on Annual Review.

CUSTOMER: It doesn't account for the £700 I got told I was in arrears by first of all ... that figure there (points to screen).

INTERVIEWER: No, but this column doesn't mean much, only the last figure.

CUSTOMER: Why weren't we informed that the insurance was due for renewal?

INTERVIEWER: Well, the insurance company should have told you.

CUSTOMER: No.

INTERVIEWER: If you're not on Annual Review we'll have to work it out annually ... it's the 29th of September every year, it should be on your statement.

CUSTOMER: What about renewal?

INTERVIEWER: We don't send them out.

CUSTOMER: If we don't clear the debt by January we get charged interest on it? (yes) Shouldn't we be getting a letter?

INTERVIEWER: Your statement does tell you when your renewal is and when it's due ... (points to statement customer has furnished).

CUSTOMER: But is it March or September?

INTERVIEWER: Hmmm ... it doesn't tell you.

CUSTOMER: At one point I was told I was £900 in arrears ... where did they get that from?

INTERVIEWER: I can only apologise ... you shouldn't have been told that ... your arrears balance has been reducing as you've been paying over the odds.

CUSTOMER: But shouldn't there be another 8 months of £30 (overpayment)?

INTERVIEWER: Have you ever been on annual review?

CUSTOMER: I'm not trying to be awkward, like ... I just want to know.

INTERVIEWER: Well, your arrears must have been getting worse and worse 'cos you've never paid your insurance ... there's four lots altogether since 1988 ... this column here is what we charge and this column is what you actually pay ... (calculates insurance arrears) ... now that comes to 31200 ... what we've got to do now is find out what you've overpaid ... (points) ... that was the first overpayment you made – your £159.80 ... now what's this £274.46? ... (the interviewer spends some time trying to figure it out) ... ah ... I know what it is, you've paid your first insurance payment and your mortgage payment together ... there should be another £144 ... it might be on the next screen ... (enters codes) ... there it is ... we've charged it to you 'cos you haven't paid it ... the £144 is the additional premium for your contents 'cos you took out Buildings and Contents ... can you see that? ... do you agree with that?

CUSTOMER: Yes, yes ... I can see that ... where did that £510 come from?

INTERVIEWER: That's just your interest payment for the year ... there's another £120.31 so the interest rate must have gone up ... (checks next screen) ... no problem there ... (checks next screen) ... your payment there is £239.70 and you've only been paying £229.70 ... that's (calculator) ... £13.54 difference ... 1,2,3,4,5,6,7 ... that's 7 ... (calculator) ... another £94.78 ... (points) ... there must have been a cut there but you've still been paying ... not enough ... that's ... (calculator) ... 3 times ... 4 ... £104.32 ... (looks at screen) ... there your payments dropped and you've been paying over the top ... (calculator) ... £30.18 too much ... You've never ever been on Annual Review?

CUSTOMER: No.

INTERVIEWER (phones Mortgage Accounts to ask): Can you give me a hand on this one? ... Annual Review, he doesn't think he's ever been on it but I'm wondering whether in fact he has ... I've taken all that into account ... screen 09, is it? ... start of year ... I've added all the insurance premiums together ... they're coming to over a thousand ... it's got to be at least two of the insurances, but usually it tells you the day they've come off, doesn't it, on an 07? ... (points) ... that was for your bikes ... (on phone again) ... so where's the rest of his payments coming from? ... 'cos I'm still covered in arrears.

INTERVIEWER to CUSTOMER: She'll do a breakdown and send it out to you 'cos it's going to take some time.

CUSTOMER: I just can't understand it ... they keep sending us letters asking us if we want to reduce and at the same time they're letting the arrears build up.

INTERVIEWER: We need to look at it pretty thoroughly 'cos there's something wrong ... according to this you're not really in arrears, 'cos it's just this insurance payment, but I can't see where you've paid them ... they're not on here.

CUSTOMER: Am I looking at £800 arrears or £200? ... it doesn't fill me with a great deal of confidence.

INTERVIEWER: I imagine the computer will be right, but no, I do understand.

CUSTOMER: Do you need any more information from me?

INTERVIEWER: You can't recall making any payments over the counter? ... cash sums? ... (no) ... I'll have a word with my boss, 'cos she's very good at this sort of thing.

CUSTOMER: And when will I hear?

INTERVIEWER: Oh ... 1st thing next week?

CUSTOMER: Shouldn't I have been told ... don't you think I should have been told?

This interview lasted some 45 minutes in total, and we have substantially shortened the transcript. In any case, no transcript can give an adequate flavour of the emotional responses in this case. For the observer, the change from a 'concerned but reasonable customer' to someone who was 'demonstrably angry' was one of the most striking features of this interview, and in fact was the only occasion in this study where things developed in this fashion.

Our reason for examining it here is because it exhibits precisely customer reaction when the visible competence we have been speaking of is not adequately demonstrated. This is no reflection on the competence of the interviewer – the reasons for the deterioration in relations have to do with inadequate information on the customer-account screens, delays in the interaction caused by searching through various screens, and the absence of a solution after a telephone call. But what is interesting is that the interaction provides the resources (or we should say additional resources) for the customer to become rationally and accountably angry.

More specifically, the initial customer complaint had to do with the fact that he has been given two radically different versions of the arrears on his mortgage account. The interviewer makes an early assumption about why this might be, largely because it is in her experience the usual explanation, which has to do with annualised accounts. She decides that insurance payments are the likely explanation, and explains to the customer why this is so. But at this point the customer asks why it is that he has never been notified that insurance payments should have been made. The interviewer suggests it is a failure by the insurance company. But at this point the interview begins to deteriorate when the customer asks again why he has not been notified of annual insurance renewal. The interviewer tries to point out that this information is contained on his statement. But in fact the renewal date is not indicated. The customer's evident frustration with what he considers to be inadequate information then spills over into a further question, to do with a third debt amount that has at some time been given to him.

At this stage, a number of things happen. The interviewer apologises, the customer begins to ask some detailed questions concerning his account while emphasising that his enquiry is a legitimate one, and we see the interviewer begin again to construct a plausible explanation for the confusion. She is using, we should point out, some standard techniques with the customer, including sharing the screen with him so he can see all the relevant information, and taking him through each calculation step by step, soliciting agreement for her assessment at relevant points. But a further problem occurs when this detailed analysis fails to provide a figure that looks anything like the level of mortgage arrears the customer has been told he is facing. The assemblage of techniques on display, techniques which would normally constitute exactly the display of competence expected by both parties, are thrown into sharp relief by the fact that the interviewer cannot now provide a plausible competent account. It is at this point that the customer seeks help, knowing that some kind of orderly explanation is now vital. A point to mention here is that the telephone call made to another department is made on the assumption that there is expertise there that can provide the solution, expertise the interviewer does not have. As it happens, the situation worsens because they too, do not know.

Leaving aside the fact that the information in this case was not available, normally such appeals to others' expertise are made 'out of sight'. Thus customers will not be made aware of differential levels of expertise. That the interviewer does so in this case implicitly acknowledges that she cannot provide a solution herself and can be heard as a slightly desperate attempt to show a kind of organisational competence, individual competence having failed. No obvious answer is provided so she resorts to a further technique which is to tell the customer that it will take some time to examine the problem and he will be sent a letter explaining the situation shortly. The customer interjects a further complaint, and the interviewer can do no more than express puzzlement. Her last recourse is to suggest that 'back office' there is someone who will be able to provide a solution, and who can be relied on – again resorting to an appeal to organisational competence. The last few lines leave us with the impression that a very dissatisfied customer is about to leave the interview room.

This example shows then how being competent and showing competence are not at all the same thing. To an extent, it can be argued that two distinct failures arise in the incident: a failure on the one hand of visible competence, and on the other of organisational competence. Our point is that the latter is consequential in this case primarily because it happens in front of the customer, and as such no repair work is immediately possible. Such situations are relatively uncommon precisely because organisational competence is usually arrived at behind the scenes – in the 'back office'.

The relevance of this, of course, is that the directions of organisational-policy change is to increase the amount of back office work, and reduce the situations in which visible competence is necessary. Our example, however, is of interest because it presents one of those relatively rare occasions where one form of competence does not stand proxy for the other – where, if you will, compensatory work is unsuccessful. For the most part these two kinds of competence do stand in a complementary, or compensatory, relationship to one another. To better understand this, we now turn to examine back office.

Back office work

The examples show how, when individual displays of competence fail, claims to organisational competence can be made. That is, help can be sought from other members of the organisation. Of course, and to state what might appear obvious, help can only be sought if one knows where to look. Nevertheless, it bears mentioning that in real organisations individuals are seldom functionally equivalent and that every individual has their own particular job (albeit that sometimes groups have the same task). But along with this, everyone knows as a matter of routine what everyone else's job is. Hence, it is common knowledge who can be relied on to do what (as a function of the division of labour) and who has the relevant expertise.

Despite this, there is little mention of the importance of 'knowing who' to the smooth running of organisational affairs in the literature. In what follows, we expand our treatment of this issue because 'back office' sharing of expertise was and is a typical way of dealing with mundane problems.

We mentioned above that local knowledge is not equally distributed. As numerous researchers have noted, offices typically have one or more individuals who are regarded as 'fonts' of knowledge (Mackay, 1990). Whoever the font of knowledge might be, the salient issue is that resolving ordinary, routine problems is often a matter of teamwork. Given the varying degrees of expertise and experience to be found in any office, it is hardly surprising that one major resource constantly drawn upon is that of the knowledge of colleagues. Keeping in mind that the institutions in question make much of the customer-facing nature of the work, and that in face-to-face encounters we can see this emphasis has real consequences, we might ask how similar kinds of orientation are brought to 'back office' work.

To begin with, experienced members of organisational teams are typically a resource for the less experienced and for those undergoing training. Immediate policy – what to do – is decided on the basis of the mutual deployment of knowledge and solutions can quickly be found by the pooling of expertise. Here is a segment of talk between back office staff:

NEW MEMBER OF STAFF: If the advance is dead on 90%, would you times it by three or by 2.75?
OLD HAND: Does she need to have a multiple of three?
NEW STAFF: Yeah, it's dead on now.
OLD HAND: Put it in as 89 then and times it by three ... you're alright ... just ... doing it by 2.75 ... do it by 2.75.

Such examples are ubiquitous in our fieldwork, and raise an interesting question concerning more 'formal' organisational attempts to provide procedural and knowledge support. In all the banks we have looked at, a range of resources exist which were specifically designed to provide answers to routinely encountered problems. These variously include stand-alone computer systems, networked, screen-based help menus, as well as paper-based manuals and standing instructions. Yet the accomplishment of work tasks is frequently associated with informal teamwork, 'constellations of assistance' and the distributed use of 'local knowledge'. These often, if not always, were turned to instead of these resources.

Such 'local knowledge', as we have seen, can consist of knowledge of individual customers, the skills and experiences of colleagues, or particular processes and routines. What was striking about this knowledge was the way it was used to avoid lengthy perusal of, for example, 'action sheets' which describe what to do in any process, or screen-based navigation of electronic job manuals. The reason for this is simple, and lies in the economy of work. For example, in all the banks and building societies we observed, staff frequently maintain their own individually organised and paper-based files, often referred to as 'bibles'. Equally, most office spaces contain a wide selection of paper sheets, post-it notes, etc., all providing 'at a glance' information. The key to the existence of both may lie in what one clerk said to us:

> All this stuff could be on the screens ... the dodgy solicitors, the bad accounts, con men and thieves, interest rate changes ... you name it ... but we want it all organised so we can use it.

And again: here two cashiers use what they know about a customer to make a sensible decision about what to do with an account application:

CASHIER 1: What do I do about this account ... it's got nil written on ... you can't open an account without any money in it, can you?
CASHIER 2: It's Mr ... just put it to one side until he pays the £100 ... he's got over £30,000 in his other account ... don't actually open the account, just hold it ... he doesn't want to open the ... account unless he gets the Mortgage he's applied for.

This brief example of 'teamwork' illustrates that 'working together' in the simplest form – that of asking and answering a question – consists of deploying local knowledge in what may be described as economical ways: that is to say, efficiently and simply. It is quicker and easier to ask someone else when they are available. The organisational assumption that staff need large amounts of formal 'help' in the form of manuals, help screens, etc. does not appear warranted when we look at the expedients staff actually use to enable the 'flow of work' to be maintained.

CONCLUSION

Concepts such as team-based working, beloved of management gurus, refer to the policy of defining tasks to be accomplished by more than one person. That is, they constitute the proceduralisation of this distributed knowledge of local exigencies and of the rules, presumably on the basis that codification of this kind removes a level of uncertainty. The existence and utilisation of 'informal' teamwork practices and 'local knowledge' is in itself not a novel discovery and has been repeatedly found in a number of empirical studies in CSCW and elsewhere (Bowker and Star 1994; Bowker *et al.* 1997). Nevertheless, in our view, their importance needs to be recognised, particularly with regard to attempts to redesign the work process. Designing teams on the basis of presumptions concerning the nature of the knowledge and resources brought to the task under the prior regime is a far cry from investigating those resources. In the banks we have studied, while occasionally we saw semi-formal teams being created to deal with a particular 'problem' or task (usually a backlog of work), these often appeared to be inefficient, primarily because they often failed to incorporate the possessing of the kinds of local knowledge that would facilitate task completion.

These aspects of the work also suggest issues that computer-system designers might be attentive to. The fact that routine work in financial institutions is typically completed by more than one member of staff would suggest that – at very least – systems would have to support the judgements made about the state of play with lengthy processes such as mortgage processing. This would need to allow for 'bias discounting', and support the cues that staff regularly leave for each other on paper to indicate progress, work completed, and work that still needs to be done. In addition, there are occasions when the physical nature of paper, including the fact that it can be passed around, becomes an important resource for checking the accuracy of information with other individuals, or for appending matters for consideration.

This raises issues which have to do with the standard format of many documents in use in this domain and the functionalities of paper in the support of the teamwork activities that surround them, something that we shall come back to in Chapter 8 (see Hughes *et al.* 1993b; Sellen and Harper, forthcoming). Comments in margins, additional scraps of paper, and written requests for attention to particular problems, by way of example, are typical manifestations of routine work in the domain and arguably should not be ignored by the designer. The completion of work by a number of people requires an amount of mundane co-operation in many work environments, and in an electronic environment such details would have to be flagged and distributed.

The move towards standardised processes is interesting in part because it is as yet unclear what the relationship between knowledge work and process might be in these circumstances. For instance, occasions have arisen where more procedurally based working results in a more 'automatic' approach to dealing with matters arising. In one of the centralised centres we observed, complaints arose from the fact that customers were charged as a result of the delayed processing of standing orders which, at the time of the observations, had a 5-day backlog of work. The failure to cancel standing orders in time meant that accounts became overdrawn and incurred charges. Bank charges were automatically triggered on the computer when the agreed limit for accounts were exceeded. When the initial mistakes were rectified – typically after customer complaints – and the money paid back into the accounts, the charges levied were often overlooked, so initiating further complaints from the customers. As a manager commented:

> People aren't instructed to think through the effect of that change – they're only interested in putting it right.

This example serves to make the point that it is in the articulation of standardised procedures (or rules) and local knowledge and practice that work gets done successfully. Neither the procedure nor the knowledge guarantees the objective, but it does seem that in the appropriate articulation of the two, objectives are more likely to be met.

That is to say, though much has been made by the banks themselves of 'customer service' or 'care', equally many critiques have been applied to this new 'ideology', as we have seen in Chapters 1 and 2. Arguments of this kind normally take the form of assessments of the balance of power between producer and consumer, and seldom take customer/professional interaction as a starting point for analysis. In contrast, the details of these interactions have been very much our focus. We should perhaps stress that our purposes have not and are not 'conservative' in that we are not making an implicit defence of current practice. Rather, our purpose in this chapter has been to understand how, while some aspects of work activity can be shown to be constraining in that they are time consuming, repetitive, or unnecessarily complex, they can at the same time afford certain possibilities that good design of organisations and of technologies should not merely ignore. The key insight emanating from our focus on this particular aspect of social organisation is that 'system functionality', to borrow from computer-system design, cannot be considered to be a property of the system alone – meaning in this case the system as conceived by both the customer and bank staff and the technology supporting their interactions. Rather, it is better thought of as a property of the relation of the system to the use to which it is put, understood in and through the mutually accomplished purposes of participants, in this case both customers and bank staff.[21] That is to say, we have been concerned with the interactional properties of the behaviour of these individuals, and how these properties provide a bedrock for consumer–bank relations, including the use of attendant technologies.

---

21 For a parallel investigation in more complex technologically mediated environments, see Bentley *et al.* 1992.

6 The virtual customer

INTRODUCTION

Our ethnographic studies were initiated in 1990 and are continuing. They thus represent a historical record of routine work by bank staff in a period of time which has seen dramatic changes in the retail financial sector as new technology, redesigned processes, changing customer behaviour and new forms of regulation have radically transformed the work (see O'Reilly 1994; Knights 1997; Burton 1994). We have argued that the ethnographic studies of the type we advocate are unlike other studies conducted by social science at large in that for the most part we are uninterested in the 'critical' perspective generally deployed by such writers. Rather, our studies are oriented to the 'real time, real world' of how things are actually done. As argued in Chapter 4, ethnography in organisational contexts can be used to 'sanity check' the strategic considerations on innovation and the design of new technology by careful analysis of, amongst other things, technology in use. Put another way, ethnography can be viewed as a means to inform requirements for new systems and/or processes, by producing alternative accounts of the 'problem' to be solved, emphasising the meaningful and practical human activity involved in the orientation of participants to each other and to technology (Hughes *et al.* 1993; Randall *et al.* 1993). Such descriptions, then, provide a base-line understanding into which new processes or systems may have to fit.

This is all the more important in banking contexts where the customer is being increasingly understood in and through technology. This 'customer' is oriented to in various ways by banks – through advertising and the tailoring of financial products, for example – but our particular interest is with the technological orientation, with the representation, development and deployment of the 'customer in the machine' and how this impacts on and is brought off in everyday work. Our interest is in how technology within a bank, giving access to a customer's account or relationship history, or 'expert' programs with their typifications of customer behaviour, are regularly brought into play as an aspect of everyday work. We are concerned with how various technologies, and the representation of the customer 'in the machine' they provide, are routinely deployed as an integral aspect of cooperating with the customer; as a factor in the configuring and reconfiguring of customer behaviour; and as an element in the relationship management, and 'demeanour-work' that marks customer interaction.

COOPERATING WITH THE CUSTOMER

> I'm actually seeing very, very few of my own ... customers ... we never see them. We've never even heard of them. (Bank Manager)

There is a set of intriguing issues of cooperating with 'absent' customers, with cooperating with the 'customer in the machine' (sometimes characterised as 'virtual customers') that is consequent on both the massive organisational changes in banks and the changes in consumer behaviour that have occurred in recent years. Financial service providers have reorganised to try to protect and develop their customer base. Most have embarked on a transformation of their 'traditional' organisation to enable them to meet the increasing competition in the financial markets. In one bank in particular – from which most of the following materials are drawn in this chapter – a strategic plan was implemented in various ways; most obviously through a general and comprehensive restructuring involving the centralisation and standardisation of processes and the creation of specialist centres, such as Lending Centres, Service Centres, and Securities Centres, all servicing 'high street' branches. As the bank began this process of reorganisation there was a recognition of some of the tensions that would develop between a policy of centralisation and a desire to continue to appear as a local 'high street' bank, particularly as this might impact on its avowed policy of customer service. This tension manifested itself in a number of ways,[22] most notably in the conflict between 'relationship management' (in the sense of managing accounts according to what was 'known' about the customer as the product of a longstanding relationship); and in the tension between responding to the customer as an individual and what might be seen as 're-configuring the customer' to act in accord with organisational procedures.

To some extent (but not absolutely) this was resolved at the level of the account with those customer accounts deemed 'core' or 'mass market' being

---

22 Perhaps the most bizarre was that in the early days of the centralisation process staff in the centres answering the phone would pretend to be at the local branch. On one occasion this lead one member of staff, after answering the phone at a vacant desk, to cover the mouthpiece of the phone and shout 'Where am I?'

largely managed 'by the machine'. As one manager said:

> because of volume we are process driven ... we haven't got the time to make exceptions ... we know the Bank will stand by us ... because it's rule driven ... it works because we're dealing with sheer volume ... we're not being asked to get involved deeply with every customer who comes on the phone.

Moreover, these changes were bound up with technology. As the same manager put it:

> (lending is) ... a lot more process driven ... the machine will give you a recommendation. Assistant Managers can override the machine, Controllers can't ... if the machine says 'No' and that decision is overridden it's 90% likely to go down the pan ... loans 'down the pan' have reduced considerably since the introduction of machines.

However, even important business accounts were subjected both to various expert risk-grading packages and to a formal process of report; and similarly even customers in the mass market were liable to make complaints that demanded a personalised, managerial response.

The centralisation process within the bank was driven by a variety of factors, one of which was the attempt to ensure standardisation and consistency in decision-making and procedure not only through increasing reliance on the technology but also through an attempt to re-configure customers and staff. As another manager put it:

> whether you go into a branch ... or apply for a loan ... in Manchester or in Southampton ... you should be treated the same way.

This involved developing a set of expectations as to how accounts should be handled; a set of expectations that emphasised the application of standard procedure as opposed to the more personalised approaches of the past. So, for example, a standard, graded set of templated letters were developed to send to accounts that were 'out of order', accompanied by a 'script' to be used whenever customers complained:

> She wants to know why we bounced the same day she paid in ... Did we not write back and say same day was too late? ... Take the normal line with her and see how it goes.

Of course, this did not guarantee that customers would respond to what were effectively computer-generated letters informing customers of the state of their account in the same impersonal way. One customer responded to a computer-generated letter in the following manner:

Might I enquire as to what particular charm school gave you your wonderful way with sarcasm and barefaced cheek! You were bloody rude ... I demand, by return, an apology. Your failure to do this will result in my solicitor writing to your head office to take the matter further. May I remind you, the bank is in business to make money, not high handed moral judgements. You have overstepped the mark (with this letter) in a most appalling way and in your position cannot be excused.

The examples then suggest some tension in the 'customer care' process, but it should not be thought that 'skilful' demeanour-work is absent here. The latter is equally prevalent in mediated communications such as telephone work – indeed operatives often refer to this as 'smiling down the phone'. Such demeanour-work was also apparent in more innovative and experimental approaches to the provision of financial services such as videolinks (Hughes *et al.* 1995).

The move to selling was similarly accompanied by a focus on the provision of 'scripts' for various kinds of sales activity. Table 1 documents just a few of a wide range of suggested, scripted, responses to possible objections that might be raised by customers concerning advice that they consult the bank's personal-financial adviser. Whilst this might be seen as an attempt merely to ensure standardisation in the presentation of the bank to its customers another view might be that as the customer increasingly becomes merely a representation in the machine standardised scripts are not just a reflection of standardised processes but effectively become mandatory, i.e. they are essential to the processes.

Local knowledge and the 'customer in the machine'

The centralisation process, explicitly or not, effectively re-designed jobs to depend less and less on 'local knowledge', partly due to the increase in the number of accounts with which a worker was expected to deal, and partly due to the introduction of more procedural formalities in dealing with accounts. Although, and perhaps surprisingly, the use of local knowledge remained and continues to be a regularly observed feature of the work, as the process of centralisation continues even to this day – leading to some centres having over a million accounts – a pervading goal in our research was and continues to be to see whether, and how, such local knowledge is maintained. The managerial take on this is, not surprisingly, rather different, suggesting that such local knowledge is not invariably beneficial and has in the past resulted in inconsistent and 'bad' decisions. Furthermore, the suggestion is that any relevant local knowledge will in the future be available 'in the machine' through a standardised approach to maintaining their customer-relational database.

Table 1 Outbound telephone training – suggested responses

Objection	Consider whether you can 'ask it back'	Opening phrase	Explanation	Confirm satisfaction
'Not interested'	Consider whether you can 'ask it back'	That's alright, many of our customers have felt exactly the same way. However ... (Play down importance)	Having met with ... our PFA, they can see that there is real worth in having a financial review every 12 months or so	Surely that sounds reasonable, doesn't it?
'Can't afford it'	Consider whether you can 'ask it back'	I can appreciate why that would concern you; however (Handling) ... they do go through a full income and expenditure breakdown to ensure funds are available (Apparent agreement)	This is advice ... of the highest standard without any obligation on your part	That sounds reasonable, doesn't it?
'Too busy/no time'	Consider whether you can 'ask it back'	I can appreciate how busy you are; however ... (Play down importance)	Our adviser will visit you at a time convenient to yourself. A quick review will only take around 45 minutes	How does that sound?

In these circumstances what becomes important in such customer work is orientation to the customer record – in effect attentiveness to the 'virtual customer' represented in organisational records of various kinds – but predominantly 'in the machine' – and attentiveness to unravelling the history of the customer's account using the available technology. In these circumstances issues of representation and standardisation of the customer record become especially important for organisational actions. The importance of the electronic record is manifested in the everyday fact that practically every instance of customer contact – such as a phone call coming from the Telephone Liaison Office – begins with the provision of an account number so that details of account working or customer notes are available before the customer comes on line.

Demeanour-work and the 'customer in the machine'

As we saw in the previous chapter, when using technology cashiers must 'weave' interaction with the technology into the flow of interaction with customers and in such situations the technology ideally should be 'invisible'. The concept of 'customer care' has a force in these situations which may not be fully encompassed by the idea of the event-generated scripts described earlier, because it is precisely the difficulty of navigating through the screens and reading the information they contain whilst simultaneously trying to maintain customer confidence that generates many of the difficulties, as we saw in the vignettes of lending interviews.

There is, however, a reverse side to this in that the developing electronic representation of the customer may facilitate aspects of customer-facing and demeanour-work. In the next fieldwork extract a stroke victim, concerned about some aspects of the management of his money and account, has come into a branch for an interview with a lending officer.

CUSTOMER: It might be something or nothing ... (shows statement) ... how's me doodah? ... me account?
CASHIER (using machine – accesses account): Currently it's in credit ... (shows screen) is that more than you thought? (Chat about car insurance ... customer concerned about whether his car insurance premium had been paid).
CASHIER (using machine): Who's it with? ... no, that's not gone out yet (points to screen) so you'll have to take it out of your balance.
CUSTOMER: I paid some in.
CASHIER: Yes that balance includes ... did you pay it in after 3:30? ... would you like me to print you a mini-statement?
CUSTOMER: I'm not thick but this half of the head (pointing) isn't working.
CASHIER: Generally ... if you hadn't enough funds we'd return it ... I'll tell you what we'll do ... we'll see what's going out in the next few days and see if you can cover it ... let's see what has gone out ... (using machine brings up screen) ... your direct debit to British Gas ... has gone out ... and a cheque for £XX.

In this instance the technology was used to resolve customer concerns through a mechanism whereby the customer is effectively introduced to 'the customer in the machine', that is to say, to their electronic selves. In this way the technology can be used to make visible to customers the working and patterning of their virtual selves as embodied in their accounts.

Identifying 'difficult customers' in the machine

Technology and the careful and skilled perusal of the 'customer in the machine' can clearly enhance features of everyday work such as the 'managing out' of difficult, non-profitable customers. The systems provide a number of 'warning signs': 'frequent, urgent requests for increased facilities'; 'cheques issued in round amounts, in sequence to the same payee', 'post-dated', and more. These are important resources for proactive responses by staff:

> We have the opportunity to monitor the trend of performance ... The stage at which we can successfully manage-out risk situations is paradoxically whilst the customer's business still seems potentially viable.

This points to claims as to the predictive power of the technology and the usage of information. In a similar fashion, the bank's 'action sheets' outline a whole series of possible frauds: 'money laundering'; 'cross-firing' or 'kite-flying'; 'tizzy hunting' and the 'flip-over fraud' that staff need to be aware of as they peruse accounts on a daily basis. In this way the machines are being deployed normatively; used as part of a moral assessment of character through the assessment of the record 'in the machine'. The various warning signs for 'money laundering' – large cash transactions; sudden large activity over dormant or previously inactive accounts; large payments immediately followed by transfer out or request to draw the proceeds in cash – require an awareness of features of the electronic record as revealed in the following fieldwork extract where a manager is passing an account over to a member of staff responsible for signing off overdrafts and loans, a lending officer:

MANAGER: It was an account I picked up ages ago (as problematic) ... we've reported it ... every 3 or 4 months have a look at it ... there's some big entries going through at the moment ... two cheques going through for two and a half thousand pounds ... I'm sure it's money laundering ... there are big payments going abroad ... now the account had been dormant for 12 months ... and then it suddenly started.
LENDING OFFICER: I don't think it's money laundering ... I think they're trying to siphon off ... I think it's cross-firing.
MANAGER: Yeah he was ... but all that was a while ago and then it went

very quiet in the last 6 months but I've just ... this money that's going through ... they're doing something.
LENDING OFFICER: They're doing something.
MANAGER: But I don't know what exactly and why ... there's two cheques this last week for 5 grand ... so just keep your eye open ... I'm sure there's something happening there.
LENDING OFFICER: There's always been something fishy there.
MANAGER: To me it ... stinks ... something must be going on.

The manual of warning signs for 'cross-firing' demands a similar sensitivity to variations in the electronic record. Signs include increasing turnover out of all proportion to the type of account; a substantial uncleared position; credits containing cheques for large amounts: a number of cheques for round amounts; cheques which cannot be regarded as cleared within the normal clearing cycle (e.g., those drawn on branches of banks in outlying parts of the country or on non-clearing banks and so on). All of these and more are all indicators that can be potentially derived from the 'depiction' of the customer 'in the machine'.

However, a moment's consideration of this reveals an important facet of such nuanced uses of the technology. The numbers representing certain kinds of activity on a customer's account have no absolute significance in and as of themselves. Rather it is the situated arrival at some kind of meaning for those numbers, according to whatever relevances are currently being brought into play in a particular set of circumstances that provides any set of numbers with their significance. It is this matter of how numbers are actually used to render 'the customer in the machine' an effective, everyday resource that we shall now turn our attention to.

MORE THAN A NUMBER: RELATIONSHIP MANAGEMENT AND THE CUSTOMER IN THE MACHINE

We start out in this section by considering some of the everyday difficulties that can arise in interactions with the 'customer in the machine' – notably the tension between the customer as a 'real' person and the customer as merely an account number with an accompanying relational database of 'customer notes' – the 'customer in the machine' or 'virtual customer'. Out of this analysis we will explicate the way in which it is the very abstractness of this resource that allows it to become an effective means of supporting practical action. Furthermore, we shall attempt to demonstrate that staff in the bank share an awareness of the abstractness of the customer in the machine. Rather than orient to some absolute meaning for a particular machine-based representation or set of numbers, bank staff use such numbers with consummate skill to achieve their objectives in the face of everyday contingencies. It is precisely in this kind of light that 'the customer in the machine' can be seen as an effective contribution to working practice. It is when such representations are taken out of their contextual use and instead used to drive gross generalisations and presumptions about customer behaviour (e.g., see Winder 1988) that they become less tenable. By proposing some absolute and cross-situational significance for a certain set of numbers, such accounts overlook the very efficacy of their situated use.

In the early stages of the move toward centralised centres, organisational inertia and longstanding legacy issues magnified the problems in adjusting to new organisational forms and priorities. In the initial movement towards a selling organisation, for example, the dedicated mortgage adviser was unable to actively search the relational database to 'spot' potential customers (which was provided by the regional office) but instead was forced to develop and rely on a range of haphazard and time-consuming manual search techniques. Although the data and the potential customers were 'in the machine', obtaining access proved difficult.

In this fieldwork extract, below, a mortgage adviser is attempting to prepare for a 'first-time buyer initiative'. Since she would be away when the proposed sales initiative was due, the mortgage adviser was trying to get a local customer base established and consequently was discussing with an assistant manager just how she might go about building up such a base from the records:

MORTGAGE ADVISER: Can I chase back in your records of what's been opened recently? ... I want to see if they are in rented accommodation or with their parents ... also joint accounts with different names ... they're usually saving up to get married?
ASSISTANT MANAGER: responds by scanning through the computer printout by age (she has just thought of how to use the computer printout). She scans by whether they are homeowners, tenants, etc. Eventually the targeting involves the study of printouts on the basis of: personal loans; change of address; credit/overdraft limit; new applications. The scan involves spotting names and then calling up their account on a monitor and deciding whether in the light of these circumstances, they merit an approach. Eventually the manager says: Look's fine to me. Go ahead.
MORTGAGE ADVISER: A lot of it's just trial and error ... if it doesn't work try something else.

Managing change

The difficulties produced by the policy of functional specialisation and centralisation were clearly manifested in the work of the various managers who often had to effectively balance and resolve at a practical level the tensions involved in reconciling the centralisation of processes with the decentralisation of customer service. A further tension arose with the centralisation of administration and record keeping with the decentralisation of 'selling'. Managers were consequently obliged to reconcile organisational realignments with changes in consumer behaviour, the most notable of which was the relative disappearance of the customer from the banking hall with the increase, for example, in telephone banking and the use of ATMs. As one manager commented:

> Whereas in the past the branch manager could stand in the banking hall and recognise ten of his customers ... now he might not know any of them.

For the branch manager this created an interesting problem:

> If you take out the business customers, and you take out the runners ... if you take out that lot, then you take out the customers of other branches, I'm actually seeing very, very few of my own ... customers. So then we got to say 'where are the rest of them?' because I can produce a printout that says I've got 14,000 customers. And that was the answer to it: 'How well do you know your customer?' 'Not very well'. Some of them have credit balances of £20,000–£30,000. And we never see them. We've never even heard of them.

This branch manager can 'see' – 'in the machine' – that he has 14,000 names; 14,000 customers on a computer printout, but most of them he never sees or recognises in the course of an ordinary working day. Yet the computer tells him that they are his customers so they must be there. The problem then becomes how do you sell your products to someone you never see?

For one bank the answer to this problem is a strategy entitled 'Managing Local Markets' (known as MLM to bank staff), a sales approach focused within the particular bank's Customer Service Bureaux and Business Centres where face-to-face customer contact has been retained. Initially all staff underwent an exercise to develop some understanding of what they needed to know about customers involving going out and finding what lay 'beyond the walls' of the bank. Employees went out in the streets on walkabouts and drivearounds, collected newspaper cuttings, advertisements of house sales, etc. trying to assess the character of their particular area and gain some measure of the competition.

MLM is computer supported with customers being categorised into 5 basic categories – A+, A, B, C and D – with the A+'s being the 'super accounts' and the Ds being the ones that 'cost money to run'. These categories are based upon a thorough knowledge of the customer's dealings with the bank, the nature of their credit balances, the running of their account, credit cards, investments, mortgages, insurance, etc. In the early stages, it was found that there were large numbers in the B and C categories, so further classifications are now being applied. Customers are variously listed as being: 'Retireds'; FIYAs (Financially Independent Young Adults); YSs (Young Singles); and Mid-Markets, BOFs (Better Off Financially) and WOEs (Well Off Establisheds) who are all aged 31 to 50 with the classification being based on the amount of money that passes through their accounts.

The target products in MLM – insurance, pensions and so on – tend to be ones that are currently in focus throughout the bank, and a complimentary sales drive operates under the banner of 'Business as Usual' where they attempt to sell the same products to the people they do see regularly. To establish the ones they do not see they use the customer database to discover their normal mode of contact with the bank. Beyond this they will engage in other considerations such as what products customers already hold (there is little point in trying to sell one of your mortgages to someone who has already got one) in order to better target their potential customers. Where it was once the case that 'Products in Focus' would be the subject of blanket mailshots their aim is now to develop a 'Local Market Tactic' and to specifically target certain customers they do not see and send them a letter, perhaps following up with a telephone call.

In the actual context of the workplace it becomes quickly apparent that MLM has a number of important implications for the achievement of effective IT since computer derived models of market segments are being used to devise a whole set of organisational and marketing rationales which underlie an increasing number of management activities and decisions and the way these are achieved. Additionally there are efforts underway to arrive at ever-better depictions of customers within the machine of the 'virtual customer'. And there are at least two important aspects to this. One of these is the representational issue of the nature of such virtual customers and how they are arrived at and engaged with from day to day. The other is the question of how managers (and others) negotiate some sort of 'fit' between 'virtual customers' and the 'real' customers they see over the counter or talk to on the phone.

This tension between the customer as a person and the customer as an account number, the 'customer in the machine', is most clearly seen in the work of the business managers since their work involves a high degree of face-to-face interaction and 'relationship management'. Nevertheless, a whole range of technological support and 'expert' decision-making packages become a resource that they are expected to draw upon in daily interaction. Whilst the manager is clearly aware of, and makes reference to, this organisational backdrop, particularly in accounting for and justifying lending decisions, in practice such decisions frequently come to be based upon personal knowledge of the customer. The manager is effectively a locus through which the 'virtual' ideal and the need to practically achieve the 'real' work with 'real' customers gets negotiated. While he must engage with his customers and arrive at practical decisions, he must account also for those decisions in the terms (or the 'style') of the organisation within which he resides, as it is made manifest within the forms and procedures, the edicts and notions of 'best practice' that his environment provides. Increasingly, such managers must do so through their interpretation of the 'virtual' customer – the 'customer in the machine'.

'Virtual' customers are representations 'on file'. 'Types' of customer, manifest 'in the machine' in terms of utilisations of bank products, spending and income patterns along with protocols representing the 'rationalities' governing customer behaviour become the primary basis for 'customer facing' work. Breakdowns of the working of the customer's account over the year and the 'Customer Notes' which contain a record of every contact between the bank and the customer, are used to construct a 'picture' of the customer which then plays a part in the complex interaction between the customer and the various managers. This, increasingly computerised, record is valuable not simply or merely for the attribution of blame but through its procedural implicativeness in informing and guiding the actions of others, constituting an important component in the individual worker's 'sense of organisation' – enabling them to quickly obtain a grasp not only of 'what has happened' but also 'what to do next'. The following fieldwork extract shows a business manager orientating to the various forms of data:

> this ... is a limited company account and it works very well ... (looking at file/printouts and computer information) yes, used to quite a degree, ... a limit of 50K ... I did look at the 836 and the 838 printout again to see this utilisation of an account, see what it's doing (looking at printout) ... it works very well, no excess there ... is there at all, no excess days ... that's a very important part of information produced from the computer system ... number of days in credit is important so it's not in overdraft all the time ... shows that credit balances are seen ... we know that by those days (pointing at printout) but it does appear ... together with maximum facilities are fairly lightly used ... that's the company account.

Here, judgements concerning the running of a business account are made on accumulated evidence from transactions on file. Similar information might equally be used to identify 'troubles'.

In the following example, a business manager explains how the various computer screens, forms and notes present a particular lending history (in this case one of overborrowing) and thereby shape his decision-making:

> Basically, he's heavily borrowed ... (shows figures/folder) ... but he's got a private loan account of 38, a business loan account of 20 and business OD ... o umm ... of 29 there's a lot of borrowed money there ... on a business and clearly he's having difficulty in servicing it all ... had a couple of discussions with him (looking at file) at least a

couple, probably a few ... and the latest, the last thing agreed was ... so it was agreed that we would increase our limit which was 27,500 ... I think it goes back ... were things properly bottomed and properly dealt with at the outset ... (looking through file) ... totally overborrowed.

With the assistance of the various paper and computer records and aided by the knowledge that the account is 'under report', the business manager is able to come to a rapid understanding of 'what's going on'. This allows him to make a quick decision and to offer a reasonable justification, a rationalisation for his actions. More specifically, he concludes that since it is 'under report' the account is not to be allowed to 'drift up' over its maximum borrowing allowance.

Reconfiguring the borrower

This following extract from the fieldwork observations illustrates some more of the skilful subtleties involved in the use of the technology to construct an account of customer behaviour and history, and how the technology is deployed as an aspect of reconfiguring that behaviour. This case, observed in one of the new lending centres, unfolded over several hours and involves a businessman whose account cards have been retained by the bank's ATM but who claims that somebody at the lending centre – 'Mark' – had already verbally agreed an increase in his overdraft limit. In a very skilful fashion the manager and the phone team member who is dealing with a call mediate between the 'real' customer, angry because he cannot get access to any money, and the 'virtual customer' presented in terms of an account with a borrowing and relationship history on the computer screen. In this first extract, the customer has gone into the branch where his cards have 'been eaten', has related his story, and is now 'playing merry hell', over the phone:

PHONES TEAM MEMBER (to manager): I've got ... branch on the phone ... card retained (explains case) a high risk grade account ... we've got all the markers on ... he said Mark agreed ... he said to me are you calling me a liar ... I said No, I'm just trying to determine the facts ... he's now gone into the branch and is playing merry hell.

Manager goes with phones team member to her workstation to look at the account on screen – using screen to examine working of the account.

MANAGER: I think he's trying to pull a fast one ... As far as I'm concerned (it's) No.
PHONES TEAM MEMBER (talking to branch): I've talked to my manager ... it's against Bank policy.

Some hours later, having perused the customer's account history and notes, the manager is preparing to phone the customer about his complaint. Again he uses the accounting package and the relational database to look at the working of the account prior to and during the call. Here we have only the transcript of the manager's talk:

MANAGER: Hello Mr X ... my name's ... How can I help you? OK she's told me a lot of the info ... I understand we've sent a couple of letters (can see that this is the case from 'customer notes' on screen) ... now you've been into ... branch and it's (the card) been retained and you went into the branch (to complain).

You spoke to someone called Mark I understand ... Normally what happens if you ring up and we agree ... we mark an interview note to that effect.

I'm not doubting what you're saying but the only person called Mark was on holiday ... We haven't got a Mark on my floor.

You're saying it was definitely last week? ... There's no interview note to say it.

I know you spoke to Mark on 8th February (looking at customer notes) ... but you say you spoke to Mark since then ... and there's no notes on this at all.

In this potentially fraught customer interaction the manager uses the computer and specifically the accounting and database packages containing customer notes, account working and transactions through the account to carefully manage the situation, demonstrating a mastery of the details of the account's working. He then explains the way forward, again using the technology, weaving it into his telephone conversation.

It's a two way process ... If you tell us ahead of time ... Yeah that was a cheque you put in wasn't it (reboots machine) ... When you have a conversation with someone at the lending centre ... for us to bear with you (to let borrowers exceed their agreed borrowing terms) ... they have to mark a limit on the account ... Now we have to sort it out today ... I know maybe a few years ago the bank said we'll bear with you ... The way the system works now is you have to stay within an agreed limit ... We have to mark the limit ahead of time ... (otherwise the account will automatically appear as 'out of order').

I'm just getting some info on the screen ... (looking at account) ... What sort of work are you doing at the moment? ... What sort of turnover? ... OK ... That's not what's been going through the account recently has it? ... Seasonal ... (using machine – customer notes) ... I take your point ... I'm just looking at some of your customer notes.

What's your business card limit at the moment ... 'cos that was increased back in December wasn't it ... yeah ... Have you sent a business plan?

The things to do for today ... We can look at increasing your limit ... the re-issue of your business card ... and the getting of a (new) business card for you.

If we were looking to increase your limit what would you want it increased to? ... We're just not going to bear with you if the limit is 400 and the balance is showing 550 O/D (overdrawn) ... We're not going to be paying out.

Let's just (using machine to check balance) ... You stand at ... your balance on uncleareds is 791 OD against a limit of 400 ... until cheques cleared ... When did you pay cheques in? (yesterday) ... They're not going to clear until Thursday.

I know you requested £3000 ... which we wouldn't agree to ... I think if we agree a £1300 limit ... for a 12 month period ... It doesn't mean you have to use all that.

In this case, then, the manager is dealing, through the technology, with a customer he has never seen, negotiating a 'fit' between the customer as represented in the computer records and the customer as presented through the telephone and thereby attempting to reconfigure customer behaviour to a new regime. This regime consists of ensuring that there are sufficient funds in the account before withdrawing money or issuing cheques; to getting an agreement on new spending limits before exceeding existing limits; to supplying requisite financial information on request. It is a regime that is implicit within how the technology provides a representation of a customer's account, though the relevance of this representation, and the application of the regime, requires contingent negotiation in each particular case. This process is facilitated by frequent reference to the electronic customer record and is accompanied by a number of instances of what we earlier called 'demeanour-work' (Randall and Hughes 1994; Randall *et al.* 1998). The other interesting feature of this example – 'I think he's trying to pull a fast one ...' – is how it hints at the way some customers have adapted their own behaviour in response to what they perceive as features of 'virtual' banking organisation (the most extreme example being, of course, fraud which in a number of cases is actually facilitated by certain aspects of distributed working and the record-keeping enabled by the technology).

Taken together, the above examples show how the balance of 'visible' and 'organisational' competence has begun to shift. Face-to-face explanation and justification with customers is less common than previously, and decisions are more likely to be made on the basis of information on record. Orientation to the customer record – in effect attentiveness to the 'virtual customer' represented in organisational records of various kinds, and attentiveness to unravelling the history of the customer's account and complaint using the available technology is the preferred method of account management. In these circumstances issues of representation and standardisation of the customer record become especially important for organisational actions.

Yet, as we have already observed, the materials that drive the machine-based representations of the customer have no inherent meaning outside of their situated use. It is rather through the way the numbers in question provide for a working representation of what are, after all, necessarily contingent phenomena in such a way that those phenomena can be classified, and rendered open to flexible transformation and communication in a form that is common-sensically recognisable to anyone else engaged in similar activities as an appropriate representation (Lynch 1990). It is, if you like, a mathematization of the necessarily unique, contingent, and unpredictable in such a way that it becomes generalisable and predictable. It does this, of course, in the context of particular working practices.

This is the essential point to grasp about this use of information about this material. Just what sort of generalisation or prediction can be made out of the virtual customer is something that always has a negotiable and situated relevance. Ultimately it is the way that an account of 'this is what customers do or will do' can provide a means of accounting for 'what this particular customer has done or will do' that enables such representations to have some kind of practical applicability. Members in the bank draw upon what could be seen as a common stock of knowledge regarding what a set of information might or might not mean in a certain set of circumstances. This is not used as a rule for what that information will always mean, but rather as a visibly oriented to resource for arriving at just what the set of information means in this particular set of circumstances, as we saw in the example where a business manager was trying to arrive at an appropriate understanding of a customer file. And this, of course, attests to the awareness members have of regarding the abstractness of the machine-based representations. It is precisely in the way such representations provide for particular accounts of particular action in such a fashion that that course of action can be seen to be a recognisable and justifiable course of action for anyone else engaged in the same kind of activity that the efficacy of the 'customer in the machine' resides. In that case it is not so much a matter for support that ever-more complex, refined, and 'powerful' computer-based representations of customers be provided, for at the end of the day they will continue to serve primarily as a resource for accounting for particular action where their precise relevance is always a contingent affair. It is more the case, as with the mortgage adviser and to some extent still with MLM, that the data be readily available and open to hugely diverse and different kinds of situated enquiry if it is to provide for the wholly contingent kind of relevance that gets negotiated for any body of data in practical action.

CONCLUSION

'Real world' activity in the locus of customer services, whether or not it is computer mediated, requires appreciable sense-making work on the part of bank staff, achieved out of a constellation of awareness skills, demeanour work, knowledge of customers and their unpredictabilities, and awareness of the work of others. 'Re-configuring' customers can, in this sense, be seen as a skill with a developing importance, as new technology and standardised processes apparently reduce customer unpredictability and the importance of local knowledge, informal cooperation and so on. Nevertheless, despite the increasing importance of the 'customer in the machine', issues of skilfulness, local knowledge, or cooperation and coordination do not 'go away' when the mundane activities of the operative are machine mediated. Local knowledge remains a stubbornly persistent feature of decision-making. Whatever the classificatory regimes imposed by expert systems, the problem of determining exactly what each 'case' is a case of, especially in relatively unusual circumstances, remains one of 'occasioned determination' in the course of the work itself. And this, of course, is the point we were making with regard to how the information in the machine always has an achieved meaning according to its relevance and significance here and now.

'Cooperation' is a gloss for complex interactions; nevertheless, cooperating to do the job remains the job. The strategies being evolved to embody the 'customer in the machine' demonstrate the point. While demeanour and 'being seen to be competent' may in some sense be less important, the demonstration of competence remains significant through the production of 'results'. The suggestion in the bank discussed in the latter part of this chapter is that any relevant local knowledge will in the future be available 'in the machine' through a standardised approach to maintaining their customer database. Where face-to-face interactions can be maintained by the simple expedient of asking questions, relevant knowledge 'in the machine' relies on other staff having regularly, rigorously and routinely input information. It also makes important demands on the technology in an evolutionary sense. Thus and for instance, the reconfiguration of these technologies to incorporate this 'informal' knowledge implicates the operative in 'making the knowledge fit'. Database fields have standard sizes, and may well have standard notations. For staff, the job of work is to fit their knowledge to these standard formats in such a way that relevant knowledge of the customer is trustably incorporated. The point is that within the database this customer information has to be such that other people can 'work with customers', thus maintaining the levels of trust, etc. From the point of view of the customer, and regardless of a bank's structures, policies, technologies, etc., confidence in a bank as an institution is produced out of the customer's here-and-now experiences, whether this be knowledgeable staff referring to local knowledge of the customer's financial circumstances, a letter from the bank pertaining to oversight, bad management of the account, etc., or a response to a complaint. Where, in the context of face-to-face interaction, the successful handling of customers is a matter of 'being seen to be competent' by using knowledge of the customer, procedure and the work of others in the vicinity, the move to 'virtual' relationships implies a shift in the mechanics of 'work awareness'. 'Awareness of work' problems, then, remain and indeed become more difficult to resolve.

Our point is that whether or not technology intervenes in communication, decision-making or complaint, some underlying principles remain the same. The issues of 'trust' and 'competence' are fundamental to customer-facing work. Our early examples in the previous chapter show how, in the context of face-to-face interaction, staff have strategies for determining how and in what ways they can orient to customers in order to visibly maintain the trust and confidence needed. Using their knowledge of the customer, referring to each other, cooperating to make sense of problems, judging the course of the interaction and reacting to customer interjections, and doing demeanour work are all examples of just this orientation. The problem of customer confidence and trust in the system does not go away when customer-facing work becomes machine mediated.

In this chapter, then, we have looked in some detail at how cooperating with the representation of the customer in the machine is actually achieved in organisations that are moving towards more and more intensely technology-mediated work. It is a matter of some confusion (and possibly an echo of broader arguments about the impact of technology) that some commentators – including members of the banks studied – see the customer-configuring practices inherent in the hope for organisation-wide standardisation offered by technology as threatening the individuality of the consumer, whilst others embrace the possibilities of new technology (e.g., Internet banking) as a hope for further empowerment of individual consumers. In some ways the picture we have painted here is an altogether more mundane one for the single most noticeable thing about the role and introduction of new technology as an agent for change, at least in the context of our own studies, is the extent to which it becomes a tool through which to achieve 'business as usual'. The introduction of new technology in banks, both in the context of customer-facing work and in interactions with 'the customer in the machine', has not so much completely re-written the relationship between banks and their customers as necessitated the development of new routines, and new competencies that reflect the age-old problem of banking: that is, bank–customer relations. These competencies relate to both the continued maintenance of trust when engaging with customers face-to-face despite the implicativeness of changing technologies in those interactions, and the need to make decisions about such things as overdrafts whose rational basis consists of both what the system allows and those properties of acceptable reasons proffered in face-to-face communications. Given this, the questions for organisational change, including process re-engineering and new technology design, is not to abandon the past through making certain processes and tasks obsolete so much as to recognise that certain components of banking will remain the same. Currently, staff at the 'coal face' of banking have to make technology and the new processes they have to instantiate, 'fit' into these requirements; in the future those who plan and implement process and technology change need to ensure that what they provide helps the fitting through making the distance between the changes and the fundamental requirement of bank–customer relations as small as possible.

7 Taking technology seriously

> IT will turn ... services from highly labour intensive, paper shifting, minimal technology activities into fully-fledged tertiary mechanised industries, with massive leaps in labour productivity in a comparatively short period of time – hence the analogies which some writers draw with the Industrial Revolution.
>
> (Prandy *et al.* 1982: 17)

> It is curious that more attention has not been focused on the ways in which individuals actually accomplish their work in environments highly dependent on new office technologies.
>
> (Blomberg 1987: 196)

INTRODUCTION

One feature of contemporary interest in organisational change is the attempt to understand organisational behaviour by reference to major transformations in the social and economic environment in which organisations operate. There are various diagnoses of these transformations, as we saw in early chapters, but some common themes emerge both as issues for theoretical investigation and as practical strategies for change. There is the need for a greater reliance on knowledge creation and conversion; the decentralisation of organisational structures; and the creation of more flexible patterns of intra- and extra-organisational relationships. All of this, of course, turns on the use of technology. Financial institutions have long been in the forefront of the use of large-scale and distributed computer systems, and cash point machines – or the ATM, the American name for them – are but one public manifestation of this. More recently, however, banks have begun to explore, in conjunction with major changes in the motivation behind the services they provide, the increased use of information technology (or IT) to support decision-making, quality control and new customer channels. Though some of these systems are highly advanced and push the role of technology in new dimensions – for example, with video kiosks and such like – much of it is of a more mundane character: network systems of accounting, relational databases and email.

If in the previous chapters we have looked at how bank staff have had to take customers seriously, and then at how their point of view of the customer has shifted towards being increasingly mediated by technology, now in this chapter our concern will be with how bank staff need to take the technology seriously. By this we mean how it is they have to deal with the processes that the technology provides for them and which at the same time the technology insists on presenting in certain ways; how those processes are manifest in both the electronic display of information and in the vast swathes of computer readout that are ubiquitous in all banks; and how the technology is but one information resource for bank staff alongside their own paper-based notes and files as well as their collaboratively constructed systems of local knowledge and expertise. As with the previous chapters our concern will be, too, with what we view as the rational properties of behaviour with and around technology and how this is exhibited in the manifest ways bank staff have to reason through what they have to do with any particular set of materials in hand (including computational ones) at any particular point in time. In a phrase, what we are interested in is what taking the 'technology seriously' means in a context where the technology is often central and where the technology can sometimes (as we shall see) loom larger in the actions of bank staff than the customers that the technology is intended to support.

More specifically, we will cover a number of interrelated, empirical themes. First, we discuss the constellation of materials produced and made available by technology to support the process of managing 'accounts in trouble.' This task relates to accounts that are going overdrawn, on which cheques are being issued with insufficient funds and so forth, and which constitute the run-of-the-mill concern of any and all banks. The banks we report on are all major players in the market place so the volumes of such accounts is large, and consequently the kind of work devised to manage it is heavily systematised and undertaken through an elaborate though not overly complex division of labour. We will be particularly interested in how bank staff have to move between different computer-generated media for this – at one moment reading through printout; at another, juggling between applications on a screen. We will then report observations of some advanced technologies, including workflow applications. As regards the latter, we will report on the use of one such in a securities operation and examine how one of the curious properties of this system (and indeed we believe it is the same with workflow systems in all workplaces – see Sellen and Harper, 1996) is that the patterns of their use underline how working processes are much more complex than the process models used in workflow technologies allow. The notion of 'exception cases' which enables these systems to be more flexible in the face of contingency is a poor representation of the relationship between process structure and the orderly properties of organisationally motivated action. We then turn to the use of management information systems in the finely controlled environment of phone-banking and indicate how, even in these heavily Post-Fordist environments where the processes have been pared down to the lowest level, the interpretation of the management information system reporting on the doing of these processes relies heavily on the skill and local ingenuities of staff. This will allow us to reiterate the claim that the meaning of computer-mediated information as representations of persons and activities is replete with situated understandings of relevance and interpretation. These cannot be provided by even the most sophisticated suites of software applications. We then turn to the real bugbear of banking, legacy systems. For if it is the case that the future of banks will be one where new technologies will offer great opportunities it is also the case – and this perhaps is more important to banks themselves – that banks are burdened down with the technologies of the past. These do not enable the banks to reach forward to the hi-tech future but instead tie them down to processes and at times unfathomable tasks that reflect requirements embedded in systems, the purpose of which have long been forgotten. The ghost in this machine is not the virtual customer, but the applications programmer who has long since left the organisation.

TECHNOLOGY INSIDE BANKS

Like many other financial institutions in the UK, one of the banks we studied wanted to transform itself from 'traditional' structure and services towards what it perceived as a more competitive form. To meet this challenge, the bank saw a need to change the culture of the organisation from its traditional, predominantly 'administrative culture' to what was regarded as a modern 'service and selling culture'. This strategic plan was implemented in various ways primarily through a general and comprehensive restructuring involving the centralisation and standardisation of processes; but also through more experimental and radical modes of business. Both of these approaches involved considerable IT support for organisational developments. The most significant organisational development involved the centralisation of 'back office' processing and the creation of specialist centres, such as lending centres, service centres, and securities centres, all servicing 'high street' customer service branches. We have already reported some research into these and similar centres in the previous chapter.

These changes required considerable investment in developing and configuring what was called 'the retail banking platform': basically those sets of applications and associated terminals that supported high-street banking as we know it. In addition there was a series of more innovative IT initiatives, undertaken as pilot projects, exploring the possibilities of remote access through videolinks to specialist advice; the electronic transfer of documents between the bank's highly distributed sites, and so on. As is common in commercial circumstances these systems were effectively 'parachuted-in' to the particular locations.[23]

Accounts in trouble

Although a great deal of the technology in banks is 'task specific', throughout the bank we are reporting on here two 'workhorse' packages, an accounting package and a relational database, were commonly available. Consequently, their use was a regularly observed feature of routine, everyday work.[24] Instances of these two packages in everyday use come from the new lending centres created by what was called 'delivery strategy' to perform the lending-control functions previously carried out at branch level. Here the work was organised by the creation of a number of separate lending teams which serviced particular branches. This division of labour was also a division of responsibility, instantiated in the lending limits attached to each position. Observation of everyday work in the centres revealed a developing history of using the technology to inform decision-making and eventually – and to all intents and purposes – to make those decisions.

The 'routine' lending, monitoring and control work of the new 'lending teams' centred around dealing with the daily computer printout that detailed the accounts that were 'going out of order'. This entailed examining each identified account, first by calling it up on the accounting package to see both how the account had historically been managed and was currently being run. Next the relational database was used to peruse the customer's notes to see the history of the customer relationship, what action, if any, had been taken in the past, whether 'concern' letters had been sent, cheques bounced, and so on. Finally a decision would be made on what course of action to take.

By checking the working of the account and the history displayed in customer notes as well as viewing all the relevant post and letters, the lending team ensured that work on the 'out of order' printout took place with full knowledge of the circumstances of each account. The following extracts from the fieldnotes illustrates the use of printouts in teamwork; the

---

23 Bannon (1996) uses this term to refer to 'the literal "dropping" of technology onto an unsuspecting populace, and then watching what happens' (pp. 423–443). He also comments 'While such an approach can on occasion be fruitful and provide evidence for completely unexpected uses devised by the populace, in general, the lack of relation between user needs and the technology provided usually results in the total abandonment of the technology.' Whilst agreeing with this analysis, the point we would like to make is how common such an approach is in commercial life, and how such an approach is driven by necessity.
24 More 'specialist' software packages were made available according to the particularities of organisational location.

relationship between printouts and computer use; the extent of checking and the deployment of local and tacit knowledge.[25]

14 Looking at printout – accounts going out of order.
15 Logging in for details of account – using account no. from printout.
16 Uses yesterday's printout – compares with today's.
17 I know I spoke to him the other day and I want him to send me an income breakdown ... I know he's got a cheque guarantee card – he's cashing them in a local newsagent.
19 Decision making – looking at screen – when payments come in; extent of OD (overdraft) in the past – 'because we haven't written to them since last February ... I could bounce his cheque. I'll send an LC (letter of concern).'

Here the accounts package and the database are being deployed and combined with local knowledge – 'I spoke to him the other day' – in order to come to a decision about the account. By initiating different enquiries on the account the lending officer is able to see 'when payments come in' for example, whether a regular salary cheque is likely to be paid into the account within the next few days, and whether there are likely to be any regular payments out of the account in the form of direct debits or standing orders that will potentially worsen the financial position.

Similarly, an enquiry regarding the working of the account over the previous 6 months or year will provide a picture of the 'extent of OD in the past' and give the lending officer some clues as to whether the current circumstances are unusual or, for example, confirm a picture of growing 'hard debt'. Finally, examination of the relational database of 'customer notes' furnishes a synopsis of dealings with the customer and a justification for any proposed course of action.

In the following case the lending officer considers whether a customer's cheques should be returned unpaid:

> I could bounce his cheque but since (doing so) is usually either a reaction to unusual circumstances or the end-product of a long period of negotiation and graded warnings – but we haven't written to him since last February.

Given this, a different reaction was proposed, in the form of a return to the regular warning cycle of 'letters of concern'. Indeed this is what happened.

A further illustration of this kind of work comes in the following, very brief, extract where a lending manager is interrupted by his assistant:

25 By way of an aside, some of the extracts used in this chapter are organized around a numbering system for each stage within the observed behaviour. We have chosen to preserve this annotation for empirical accuracy.

Interruption – assistant shows him screen and discusses case – asks for a decision – talks about decision: 'whatever limit we give him he'll be up to it.'

Here the assistant is dealing with a customer who has asked for an increase in his overdraft limit and accesses screens detailing the working of the account over the previous 6 months and year. This includes figures giving the 'risk-grade' for the customer, highest and lowest levels of credit and debit on the account, number of days the account is in credit, commission, interest and so on. The screen readily reveals that whenever the customer has been given an increased limit on his overdraft within a relatively short period of time that limit has been reached, as the manager says. The decision then becomes one of whether the account can sustain a new overdraft limit or whether the account is effectively drifting into a position of 'hardcore' debt. This decision in turn is facilitated by accessing other screens such as 'linked accounts' (which will reveal whether the customer has other accounts that are in credit) and the 'customer notes' screen that will give some indications of the customer's business and dealings with the bank. The example indicates how the skill involved is related to the ability to bring to bear understanding of relevant though electronically separate relationships the bank may have with the customer, or more simply, other accounts a customer might have.

This next extract highlights the interconnections between the different software packages as they are used in the everyday work of dealing with accounts in trouble – in this case the decision to 'bounce' (return unpaid) customer cheques – and the implicativeness of these actions for other work, both for the manager and for other sections within the bank:

1 Doing 'out of order' accounts printout.
2 Calls up screen – enters account number.
3 Decides to bounce – customer had phoned and was sorting it out – branch phoned about outstanding tax bills – had changed decision.
4 Writes on printout – underlining – adds notes in margin for action by assistant 'He's supposed to be a good account – but I know he isn't – I know because I've spoken to him on the phone'.
5 To look at on Monday – to send cheques back as 'late returns' – highlights to see if items likely to be paid in/cleared on Monday.
6 Interruption – phone.
7 Working through printout using screen – customer interview notes.
8 Shouts across the room – to someone in debt recovery about the account.

Here the lending manager is dealing with an account in trouble and, having been informed by the local branch of an outstanding tax bill on the customer's account, reverses his previous decision to allow the customer to 'sort it out' and determines to 'bounce' instead. This decision will have been shaped by perusal of the historical workings of the account and the bank's dealings with the customer – in particular whether the escalating programme of 'letters of concern' to the customer has been followed through. Having made the decision to 'bounce' the manager then shows his awareness of the three (actually four) day clearance cycle for cheques so that cheques already in the system can physically be found and returned. He also needs to record his decision in the 'customer notes' and takes the opportunity to inform debt recovery – to whom the account is being transferred – about the circumstances of the transfer.

Decision-making applications and 'accounts in trouble'

As 'delivery strategy' was implemented throughout the bank, work became far more obviously 'rule-driven', based on the careful implementation of organisational plans and procedures supported and achieved in various ways through technology. This held true for accounts in trouble activities too. Thus there was, for example, a far greater reliance on various kinds of decision-making software, particularly in the form of credit ratings, to the extent that over-riding the machine was regarded as exceptional, if not mistaken. Similarly a large proportion of the routine work was effectively automated through the introduction of a new printout (the WE058) – a system that essentially involved 'computerising' existing manual processes.

More particularly, the WE058 printout contained details of the customer's account working and an indication of what level of concern was appropriate – in the form of an 'A', 'B', 'C', 'D' identification. 'A', for example, was where the account was overdrawn against 'uncleareds'; that is, the customer had funds paid into their account but they had not yet cleared (e.g., when cheques were still in the clearing system and could still be returned unpaid). 'B' was where the account was regarded as a 'good' account, with a reasonable income but the account had become overdrawn because its credit zone needed to be increased. 'C' accounts were where customers were up to their maximum possible overdraft limit given the level of their income and, in consequence, leeway was more limited tending to take the form of consolidation loans. 'D' accounts were:

> the crud – basically all we do with them is bounce, bounce, bounce.

'Actioning' possibilities for 'out of order' accounts consisted of four 'letters of concern' (two 'soft' and two 'hard') followed by returning cheques unpaid and recalling 'plastic' – cheque guarantee cards and so on. Each of these involved further work with the technology. An assistant would use the accounting package to instigate a balance enquiry to see the state of the account and to discover whether there were any savings that could be transferred. Then he or she would use the relational database to examine the customer notes to have a look at the history of the account, and to see if there has been any recent contact with the customer; for example, there could be a note saying that the customer had phoned to say they would be 'paying in' tomorrow. If a 'letter of concern' was to be sent the assistant would use the computer to produce a standard template for the letter concerned – 'LCH1', for example, produced the 'hard' letter one – and would enter the account balance and the manager's extension number.

Despite the implementation of the WE058 process, the emphasis on 'control' and 'checking' in the form of a managerial perusal of the range of screens and printouts remained an important, daily, routine task for those in the lending teams. For example, we often saw assistant managers looking at the WEO58s and checking that computer-generated actions had been done. They would also check 'over-rides' – where computer decisions had been over-ridden. Indeed our fieldwork notes are replete with such instances. Lending managers would verify that lending limits have been marked on, that the 'customer notes' recorded any decision that has been made; and so on. The managers also needed to ensure that where a computer decision, for example to 'bounce', had been over-ridden, the over-ride was done in the light of full knowledge of a customer's account. This would involve checking the customer notes to see whether the customer had recently contacted the bank or any agreements had been made. Other inspections would include the level of security of the customer (whether the bank held deeds or shares as security against a loan). Another routine everyday check would involve examining the historical working of the account – for example over the previous 6 months – to view and compare the historical debit and credit levels. Further checking procedure would be to look for 'linked accounts' – to see if there were funds in other accounts to cover the debit.

Examples of these kinds of everyday managerial, administrative and technological work that preceded decision-making are detailed in the following abbreviated field notes, documenting some of the routine work of a lending manager.

1 Looking at – printout 'accounts out of order' – for branches.
2 '+' marked against accounts means transferred accounts – looking at transfers.
3 Does an 836 (account working over past 6 months).
4 Does 'li' – linked accounts – notices customer has £21,000 in another account.
5 Does 'cn' – customer notes – sees 'power of attorney' ... 'I know this fellow ... it's an old lady ... that's her nephew' (points to screen). 'I'll do a transfer for them' writes on printout 'We'll do £100 across' fills out transfer form – highlights code number. 'We don't usually do transfers – but with all that money there ... if we'd taken charges you can bet your bottom dollar there would have been a complaint'.

Next example:

1. Using machine – looking at WE017 'diary notes'. 'These are "baddies" and we're considering plastic recovery'.
2. 836 and 'cn' customer notes. I've given them a bit longer to do it ... she's quite nice ... I might write to her, she's not a rogue, she's only marginally over the limit we agreed (points to customer note). I've spoken to her ... I may write to her and ask her to write to me'.
15. Typing letter – 'normally I wouldn't do that ... but from what I know of her she hasn't been getting post' (explains basis of decision-making process) 'what I know about this person'; 'naughty v non-naughty people'; 'intent v irresponsibility'; 'fate (letters not being received)'.

In the first activity in the extract the computer system has marked the account as one 'out of order' because the level of debit exceeds the limit marked on the account. The fact that the account is marked as a 'transferred account' alerts the manager to examine the account in more detail, in particular to see if this account is 'linked' to others (either held by the same person or, in this case, by a relative). In this instance the account is being administered by the nephew of the account holder and funds can be transferred to balance the account. Next, the manager is considering an account that has clearly been 'out of order' for some time because, 'these are "baddies" and we're considering plastic recovery'. Examination of the computer record of the account and customer notes shows that 'letters of concern' have already been sent to the account holder and the recovery of credit cards and cash cards is being considered. In this particular instance, however, the decision is clearly not simply a product of the technology but of the manager's 'sense' of the customer; that 'she's not a rogue' but has been unlucky as a consequence of not receiving letters from the bank.

Advanced technologies and practical actions

In recent years financial institutions have begun to explore the increased use of various new technologies including expert systems and workflow. These have been provided for informational databases, risk grading and decision-making. In this section, we want to pay some attention to this technology and highlight how these systems are utilised as part of everyday, routine work.

As part of the implementation of 'delivery strategy' a number of new 'expert' software programs were placed in the bank's specialised centres. The GAPP (grading and pricing policy) machine, for example, was a recent addition to the business centre). The software on this machine had come from the regional offices and it was used to calculate the 'risk-grade' of businesses. This in turn influenced lending decisions and the pricing policy that should be adopted on a customer's business account. 'GAPP' had been introduced both to support decision-making and to improve the speed of processing thereby giving staff more time to be 'proactive' – to develop customer relationships and sell bank products.

The following extract shows a business manager's assistant carrying out a 'GAPPing' exercise prior to a business manager's visit to a company. Each stage consists of a separate set of interaction protocols with screens (or pages) of the application:

1. Gets screen – 'customer new record' – fills in details from GAPP data input form (obtained from company's accounts).
2. Screen 'customise' – (name) – fills in details – date account obtained, etc.
3. Screen – 'business definition'. The assistant then asks: 'What does pharmacist go under?' – discusses this with other assistants – 'try that one' – clicks on various titles – the assistant then asks: 'what's other?' It is a list of non-standard occupations – assistant goes to other screens – eventually finds pharmacist under other.
4. Screen – 'audited management accounts'. The assistant calls out: 'Do you put a minus in here if it's in brackets?' 'Yes – it will print up them' – the assistant fills in details from form.
5. Screen – 'management details' – (series of questions – yes/no clicks) – management assessment; financial monitoring; trading environment; short-term problems.
6. Screen – 'facility summary' – 'new customer facility' – as each section of the screen is entered 'help/explanation' messages appear at the bottom of the screen.
7. Prints out – 'risk analysis summary' – gives risk-grade and ratings on facilities (what should be charged).

So although the system was intended to automate certain aspects of work, what it actually required was a rather long-winded process of data entry and searching through various sub-applications to find acceptable data-entry criteria (such as whether a pharmacist is an 'other' occupation). Bound up with this are issues to do with moving between various screens in the application as well as cross-searching between one and more applications. It is important to recognise that GAPP was simply an addition to the existing risk assessment and pricing 'devices' – in some senses merely automating what had previously been done (and continued to be done) manually.[26] The GAPPing procedure, although an integral and compulsory part of the lending process, often appeared as a mere additional check. This meant that GAPPing seemed less important as a decision-making device than as a

---

26 There were some additional features of the program which, because of its recent introduction and apparent novelty, appeared to be unused.

'security blanket' for decisions already made, and as a starting point for negotiation with the businesses concerned. As an assistant manager said:

> You cannot say straightaway ... just because the computer program says 1 per cent higher ... you can't just impose a 1 per cent rise ... You've got to use it as a tool ... You've got to sum up how much the overdraft is and whatever.

In this next instance of using the GAPP application, a business manager is considering a request for a £100K loan to a college for building work. This is a loan that he is quite keen to expedite because of the bank's perceived commitment to community and educational projects. However, there are a few problems, both with the accounts themselves (against which the loan will be assessed) and the precise legal position of the college (whether it 'owns' the buildings – affecting its ability to offer security for the loan).

1. Considering £100K loan to X college – for more buildings (Science Lab).
2. Looking at draft accounts – has been looking at accounts and liaising with the college for some time – some problem over ownership of land.
3. Developing some questions for answers from college – agreement in principle to loan with some conditions – fixed-price contract; staged payments; site visits.
4. Discussion of criteria for borrowing.

What seems significant here, and it is a practice we regularly observed, is the skilful teamwork between the business manager, his assistant and various other bank personnel. This ensures that paperwork and computerwork are appropriately interleaved and plans and procedures are interpreted in the light of 'local knowledge' and 'local logics' to accomplish the work in a fashion acceptable to both the bank and its customer. Consider the following extract. This describes the activities of the business account manager's assistant (who sits at the desk next to him) is also working on this account. Here she is preparing the essential paperwork, in this case assembling the data so that the accounts can be 'GAPPed' – run through the 'grading and pricing policy' software program which will give an indication of the likely level of risk and the appropriate levels of remuneration to negotiate:

1. Assistant – GAPPing accounts – instructions for GAPPing – talk about problems.
2. Phoning college – arranging papers – principal not available – another problem over the constitution of the college – whether they are legally allowed to borrow money, etc. – lending – problem of powers of college

Taking technology seriously 137

to borrow money. Three main worries – land; powers; ability to repay – re: £40K deficit.
3 Calculating depreciation. – using computer – BAF – to work out possible repayments.
4 Inquiries menu – repayment info menu – various options = O/D; loan – fixed term; loan – fixed repayment; actuarial structured loan (business development loan) – types in figures – £23K per annum.
5 Balance sheet carding – taking college accounts and putting onto balance sheet card – 'balance sheet carding for individuals and firms' – when finished will put on screen and then GAPP them.
6 Problem with GAPPing – advice from region applies to polytechnics and universities not colleges.
7 Still working on balance sheet – using screen – 'update financial accounts' – enters figures from balance sheet onto screen.
8 Interrupt – message – still entering data onto screen – looks at figures produced – looking at guidelines.
9 Interrupt – business manager – has found a different set of accounts – show a surplus – management figures – 'Which shall I enter?' 'I don't know'.
10 Back looking at instructions/guidelines.
11 Account has been GAPPed – came up with Risk Grade 6 – 'I just followed the instructions – I'll send it to region now and they can play around with it'.

Later, the assistant picks up the work again:

1 Working on college report in preparation for business manager's interview with principal. Discusses with business manager – rates for loan; had phone conversation with principal re: land; talk about alternative uses, etc. (alternative uses of buildings and land, etc. – effects valuation for security).
2 Filling out two loan forms – calculating rates for loans.
3 Business manager dictating letter to college – assistant still filling out forms. Asks manager to sign and then she'll key it into machine. – looking at form 'It's a matter of interpretation, isn't it?'

In this case, the software was used to confirm rather than determine decisions. This may have been a consequence of the inclusion in the program of 'non-financial' information which could significantly influence the risk-grade obtained. This information was dependent on the manager's store of local and anecdotal knowledge; for example, 'are there any signs of creative accountancy?'; 'are there any anecdotal signs of problems?' It may also stand as a reflection of managerial experience and scepticism about the information provided – an awareness of the variety of techniques that could be employed to disguise the 'true' nature of an account. It may also be, as

Feldman and March (1981) suggest, bound up with the fact that much of the information used in the bank had been gathered primarily for 'control' rather than decision-making; that is, it was gathered in a 'surveillance' rather than a 'decision-making' mode.[27] Be that as it may, the important point is that a system that purportedly automated processes actually shifted some work away from human hands but in so doing, extended and duplicated the overall system of work.

Another recent intrduced program was 'TecSec', a workflow system introduced into the bank's securities centre for the taking and maintaining of securities. Workflow management is the automation of procedures where documents, information or tasks are passed from one participant to another in a way that is governed by rules or procedures (Workflow Management Coalition 1994). The 'workflow' approach has diverse origins drawing, for example, on scientific management and systems analysis perspectives with their emphasis on flows of information around organisations, as well as the longstanding tradition of office automation (Abbott and Sarin 1994; Hammer and Sirbu 1980). Workflow is believed to be best accommodated by particular organisational forms such as those with extensive paperwork and standardised processes – such as financial services. Banks are also believed to have the organisational structures conducive to workflow technologies (Mintzberg 1979; Ramage 1994).

The rationale behind the creation of specialised securities centres lay in the requirement for technical accuracy in the taking, maintaining and releasing of securities. When carried out in the branches, securities had been a job entrusted to relatively high grade staff, and the comparative rarity of certain types of security meant that accurate completion was always problematic. By concentrating securities in a specialised centre servicing the branches of a region, and by developing appropriate software, it was argued that the process could be completed far more speedily and efficiently using lower-grade, lower-paid staff. One consequence was that work in the securities centre seemed far more intense than that encountered in the branches; an intensity related both to the complex nature of the work and the use of the new software – 'TecSec' – that effectively drove much of the work.

In greater detail, the process involved in taking, maintaining and releasing securities generally required the preparation of legal documentation and getting the forms 'executed'. While the branches completed the initial

---

27 Feldman and March (1981: 177) suggest that, 'When strategic misrepresentation is common, the value of information to a decision maker is compromised. ... Individuals develop rules for dealing with information under conditions of conflict. Decision makers discount much of the information that is generated.' Within the bank in general, and the business centre in particular, there was an awareness of how accounts could be managed to misrepresent a business's trading position; and there was similar scepticism about 'business forecasts' (especially when produced by the business itself). It was not, however, the situation that Feldman and March (1981: 177) describe, where 'Decision makers learn not to trust overly clever people, and smart people learn not to be overly clever.'

paperwork most of the work was done by the securities centre using the TecSec software. That is to say, once the branch had filled in the forms, they were then checked by the securities centre, whose staff then typed the information into the system. Thereafter the software essentially drove the process through the release of 'formalities' which directed the staff in the completion of the various procedures.

But it was not as simple as that. For workers in the securities centre 'doing the work' involved a complex series of interactions between themselves, other workers in the branches, the software and the 'paperware'. Examples from the fieldnotes illustrate the variety of these intersecting activities – making phone calls, data entry, gathering paperwork and so on – that typically constitute such 'work'. They also serve to illustrate the intensity, the persistent checking of procedures and the largely computer-driven nature of much, though not all, of the work in question.

The following segment of fieldnotes reports the activities of one member of staff in the centre. The assistant has already looked at what is called the 'outstanding worklist' and then having keyed in items (i.e., items on the workflow-task list), the application immediately releases certain procedures – 'formalities' – and requires answers to certain questions:

4   The questions are presented on screen with Y or N answer choices. If the assistant needs any other info, she will go into a second screen.
5   Security has to be revalued every 4 years – 'It's automatically picked up from the date I put in – we request a valuation from the branch – letter with facesheet and questions they fill in'.
6   Printing letter which tells the branch which per cent of the valuation they can take.
7   Prompt at bottom of screen – saying it's complete – so double-checks it.
8   Goes back into 'enquiries and prints'.
9   Selects 'blank forms and letters'.
10 Chooses letter to send off.
11 Back to main screen – 'current formalities' – more questions ... 'once you reach a certain point ... it will go to the assistant manager to check. And it will appear in checking file.'
12 Checking that paper matches the screen.
13 Goes off and gets form. Formality has prompted (the assistant) to go to land registry – to ensure no adverse entries on land and from entries already keyed in it prompts what to put on the form – appearing on screen – 'complete the application for a search (K16) using these details' – gives address to send form to.
14. Fills in form as per screen – uses stamp for address.
15. Goes back to screen – been given ref. no. – sends off to Plymouth to see if any adverse entries on the land ... 'because we can't answer a question it puts it in the diary' (can complete it only when form returned from Plymouth).

16 Going through screen questions on fire policy – when answers to questions screen comes up 'releasing formalities'.
17 Interruption – phone – writes details on pad; discusses on phone; goes off to consult colleague.
18 Back to screen – working through questions – 'releasing formalities'.
19 Going through 'work measurement' tally.
20 On screen – 'You have reached a checking stage: now pass file to checker … remember! Do you need to tally work measurement?'
21 Gets charge form and hands everything to assistant manager.

In the securities centre then, the work is driven by the computer software and, in a similar fashion to a production line, involves routinisation through the stepwise completion of circumscribed tasks. Indeed, the software is based upon and instantiates just this feature of the work as a series of clearly defined and specified steps. Yet this transcript points toward how, despite this routinisation, the practical accomplishment of the work depends upon dealing with various contingencies which invariably occasion the need to consult files or colleagues, refer to past actions and so on. That is, it demonstrates that staff need to draw upon a pool of knowledge and expertise that is informally available within the teams. Further, the appearance of 'routine' in the completion of what are complicated procedures is an achieved matter of being able to interweave the resources available within the work environment which includes not only the technology and the files but also the experience and knowledge of others.

A regularly observed feature of the day-to-day work of the teams was its dependence on various formal and informal team working and small constellations of assistance that were regularly drawn upon that address and resolve the various contingencies that arose during the day. Consequently, despite the apparently 'computer driven' nature of the work, successful job completion is heavily dependent on activities and knowledge independent of the software package, and the further up the job hierarchy the more obvious this becomes.

Another example of the importance of teamwork or 'informal constellations of assistance' comes from the lending centre. Here the development and maintenance of 'local knowledge' and 'local logics' (detailed knowledge of particular accounts or procedures) – what some might term 'organisational memory' – was facilitated by the 'open-desk' grouping of the team which encouraged the rapid exchange of information about particular cases. In this extract, for example, the assistant manager of the 'non-personal' team has been overviewing the 'out of order' printout – as he comes across a specific action he talks across the table to the particular lending officer involved:

ASSISTANT MANAGER (AM): I think you may have been a bit harsh on FF, check out the business account.

LENDING OFFICER (XX): Me being harsh, I can't imagine that ... I don't think there's much on the business account ... there's £700 over on the ...
AM: Is he? ... he's only gone £50 over on the other, that's all ... it's a little bit (harsh) ... I don't know whether you've written to him before?
XX: I think we've returned before.
AM: Oh we will have returned before ... whether at the £50 level ... (pause while AM confers with manager).
AM: It's more the old man that's ...
XX: Oh right ...
AM: It's a bad sign.
XX: I was generous!
AM: It's 3 months since we've written to him ... do an LC letter (letter of concern) ... LCH1 will do in this case.

Here the assistant manager's initial sense that the lending officer is adopting a 'strict' view of an overdraft, given the small sum involved, soon develops into a discussion – available to the rest of the team – into the conduct of the account and the nature of any previous action. In this instance the assistant manager has to balance the interest of the bank, the standard procedure for dealing with 'out-of-order accounts' and some notion of 'fairness' to the customer. Much of the observable activity is primarily concerned with developing a persuasive 'account' for that decision. This account also illustrates the way in which 'organisational memory' is constructed 'in the telling'; in a fashion similar to Berger and Luckmann's (1967) account of the social construction of marital memories.

A similar 'remembering' occurs in the following extract, where an interview brief for a branch, concerning a loan request by the owner of a take-away restaurant, is being prepared.

ZZ: I've seen this before ... we've lent to these people before ... let me check ... using machine doing search.
ZZ: No, it's not the same people, but it is the same restaurant ... they didn't make a go of it either ... it went to IDRD (insolvency and debt recovery). (The lending officer discusses the brief with the assistant manager, a discussion which soon involves other members of the lending team as they consider issues of insurance and security.)
ZZ: talking to assistant manager: Do you think this comment is fair enough? ... (reading from brief) ... on the issues for the proposition ... whilst we note comments on last report that business may be seasonal previous owners of the business did not make a success of the business, account at IDRD, and conduct of the account since opened gives great deal of cause for concern.
AM: Yeah ... certainly not give ... the OD (overdraft).
ZZ: I've put that on their (brief). I think they're going to have to consolidate it but on strict credit working and full security.

142 *Part II*

AM: I'm concerned at the lack of turnover through the account ... I don't think you've got a cat-in-hell's chance of turning it around.
ZZ: I don't.
AM: Get a charge on the lease ... even if it's of minimal value ... it will save him flogging it on and disappearing ... just put lease question mark ... tie him into the business if nothing else ... question terms of lease ... we've lost money on that business once – I've no intention of losing it again.
ZZ: I think we've already lost it quite honestly.
AM: Well, no more then shall we say.

Management Information Systems

The reorganisation of the bank was initiated through the redistribution and centralisation of functions. As the scale of the functional units increased issues of management control and information became paramount, particularly in the identification and calculation of labour costs. Management information served a variety of purposes and had previously been collected in a variety of ways, but as the move toward larger and more geographically dispersed units progressed various forms of electronic monitoring were introduced. Such management information systems (MIS) became increasingly important.

One example of this were the varied reports available via sophisticated monitoring software used in the various telephone 'call centres' called the 'monitoring kit'. Displays of this application were positioned on the manager's desk, and provided a real-time display of inbound, outbound, available and unavailable phones with times attached to each. It was used on a daily basis to monitor staffing, and to ensure, for example, sufficient staff were available to cope with peak periods of activity. Each 'operative' was represented on screen by a block – the colour of the block indicating their present status as inbound, outbound, unavailable, etc. – while on the manager's screen a series of calculations and indicators appear. These changed in accordance with the state of the service, for example: 'grade of service' (a calculation based on speed of response, waiting times, calls abandoned, etc.), 'queuing time' (in seconds), 'calls abandoned', 'total calls abandoned', 'calls recorded', 'average answering speed'. It was also possible to examine each indicator in more detail than was provided by the 'top view'. The equipment could show, for example, how long a caller was waiting before they abandoned – 5 s, 10 s and so on.[28]

The management information from this system was initially provided in the form of a number of computer-generated reports, which were sometimes

---

28 Similar systems were operated in all three of the phonebanks we observed and are more or less standard fare in these settings.

printed out. These included an 'agent report' which provided details of what individuals are doing throughout the day in terms of whether they are available or unavailable for calls, how many calls they took, average time of calls, etc. These reports were then used to create spreadsheets, again as part of a management information pack, which effectively summarises the information for those higher in the management hierarchy. This process is outlined in the simplified fieldwork extract below:

> Chris is talking about what MI (management information systems) is required and looking at a hand-written outline of the kinds of categories and calculations he thinks they should include. On one sheet of paper he has written a number of ideas: 'non-utilisation periods', 'R/E (reasonable expectancy) how many calls could we have taken?', 'what does the productivity gap equate to in man hours', 'speed/quality/control', 'industry comparisons' and so on. On another he has divided the sheet into columns as the precursor for producing a spreadsheet. Heading the columns are categories such as 'calls offered', 'staff required for 100 per cent calls handled', 'staff required for 90 per cent calls handled'. A series of comments are written down the side – these are later to form the basis of their discussion – 'figures as at certain date with customer base of X'; 'do subsequent charts/spreads for take-on of centres for rest of year multiplying calls offered by factor of X (customer base in future divided by customer base now)'; 'when new 'actuals are obtained from future information revise figures for comparisons and compare to model'; 'do we want to put in model numbers of staff to see divergence?' A final sheet has a complicated calculation by which they might obtain a measure of effectiveness.
>
> Whilst this is going on Les is looking at the BBS (balanced business scorecard) as it will be important that the measures reflect elements of the BBS both for the section and him personally and at a basic set of management information spreadsheets that they produced last week for the managers' meeting which forms the basis for this current MI pack.
>
> Chris uses the computer to get an Excel spreadsheet on screen – 'AOBT accuracy' (advice of borrowing terms) – they then chat about the layout of the spreadsheet. The talk centres on how much information they need to display and how to present it; the emphasis is on 'totals', totalling columns because '... all he'll (the centre manager) be interested in is that (pointing at total)'. They then work together setting up the various 'macros' (calculations) for the various parts of the spreadsheet, talking about its use for making predictions with the suggestion that 'that would be good for "Hours by Design" (a new initiative on hourly working within the bank). They then turn to the MI figures they produced last week – 'these are great ... but I think we need the

graphs and a comments box ... he (the manager) doesn't need all that (the detailed figures)'. They then use the computer to access the spreadsheets they produced last week.

The important point about this extract is the recognition of the 'work' and decision-making involved in the accomplishment of management information. Despite the use of relatively sophisticated monitoring software, the bald figures produced needed considerable interpretation before they could have any value as 'management information'. So, for example, one manager (in a different centre but using the same call-monitoring software) pointed to some of the figures and commented:

his per cent time was low because he kept wandering round the office ... I came in with a ball of string and tied him to his chair ... his times are better now; her time on the phone was low because she came in and then went out to work with another team.

or commenting on the figures for grade of service:

We try to keep it above 90 per cent ... last Monday it fell to 72 per cent ... three staff were on holiday and three were sick ... we couldn't answer the phones any quicker ... last week I promised them cakes if they got the GOS up to 94 per cent.

Above all, the main point to make about the decision-making process and the usage of information (whether on paper or computer) is concerned with appreciating the careful consideration that needs to be given to what the figures mean in terms of the actual events and circumstances which they index. That is, it is not a question, as Harper (1989) points out in his ethnography of accounting, of 'just any old numbers' but that making sense of the information, and any decision-making based on that information is dependent on certain 'nuanced' understandings, understandings which are frequently a product of local knowledge of the personnel and the particular circumstances of their work.

The careful construction of management information revealed in the extract becomes a resource for both rationalising future work and increasingly to predict or anticipate volumes of work and staffing. The description is not simply a description of a certain body of work done over a certain period of time. It is a description that necessarily informs their understanding of just what the work they are doing might amount to. Subsumed within it are representations of what a normal amount of work to be received and got through might consist of, revealed in both periodic totals and averages. Inevitably the production of an 'adequate' description of the work requires some sort of previous knowledge of just what 'adequacy', in the terms of the organisation, might amount to. The totals, percentages and so on that together make up the 'management information' amount to more than merely a 'truthful depiction of the work we did'. The pragmatic value of such number work resides in the way it comes to inform work allocations through understandings of what is and is not practically achievable, and to provide for rationalisations of particular instances of failure or success.

All of the above reveals the extent to which management information is not something that unproblematically resides within the computers, to be accessed at the simple push of a button. In fact management information is a 'representation' of the work of individuals, teams, and whole sections that has to be worked up and achieved in a rich interweaving of computer-based materials and paper documentation. Management information was one way in which managers sought to practically achieve a displayed orientation to the much vaunted principle of standardisation; to provide 'adequate' accounts of the work that their staff do in particular circumstances of accountability; and to arrive at practical decisions as to how to mete out the ongoing influx of work. Finally the practice of mathematising and rendering real-work phenomena open to further transformation and manipulation in 'standard' and 'generalisable' terms made management information a resource for the discussion of other issues to do with performance and staffing.

BANKING ON THE OLD TECHNOLOGY: 'LEGACY' SYSTEMS IN USE

> The scenario is all too common: An application has served the business needs of a company for 10 or 15 years. During that time it has been corrected, adapted, and enhanced many times. People approached this work with the best intentions, but good software engineering practices were always shunted to the side (the press of other matters). Now the application is unstable. It still works, but every time a change is attempted, unexpected and serious side effects occur.
>
> (Pressman 1997: 790)

> Banks are dinosaurs ... we can bypass them.
>
> (Bill Gates, *Newsweek*: 1994)

Information technology has often been the subject of quite unreasonable 'hype' and quite unrealistic expectations. Various commentators have suggested we may have to wave goodbye to the bank as we know it, and its accompanying scenarios of 'off-planet' banking remain, of course, inspired journalistic fictions and even relatively developed technologies such as video-conferencing, video-booths and Internet banking are currently still largely experimental or small scale. Instead, since financial institutions were among the first wave of business organisations to computerise many of their operations, a great deal of their basic functioning is now dependent on what are increasingly ageing systems. 'Taking the technology seriously' requires then not only that we understand the broader context into which the technology fits and (as just described in relation to accounts in trouble, for example). It also necessitates addressing the impact of 'legacy' issues on everyday working and organisational life.

Old systems and ordinary work

In one of the banks we studied, the main 'workhorse' systems in use in the accounting/bookkeeping package dated from the 1960s and 'had bits bolted onto it'; while the more modern relational database dated from the 1980s. Observation and conversations with users indicated a number of problems with these systems. Both were seen as 'dated', 'slow', prone to unpredictable breakdown, and not 'user friendly' and 'went down' or 'went slow' on a regular basis. Occasionally this was for considerable periods of time and resulted in great frustration. Work was still done but not without a little ingenuity. The accounting package was regarded as a particular problem. Whatever the nature of the difficulty, they were all captured under the term 'legacy'.

This is perhaps best illustrated by the 'problem of the phantom branch' related by one manager in a comment that resonates with the concerns of Pressman:

> if you go and speak to our systems people they would say there are parts of the software that they still don't know how it works because the original inventors of the package have long left the bank ... now and again they still change parts of it and it has effects that nobody foresaw ... there's a branch ... which has been closed a long time but we have to keep it open because when they tried to close it in the bank's books, the computer records ... it threw all sorts of things out ... and they haven't found a way yet of closing this branch out in the bank's books ... the computer still thinks this branch is open on a daily basis.

Whilst this may appear an exceptional, if not ridiculous, example – indeed we heard similar in at least two other banks we studied suggesting that the story was apocryphal – essentially similar circumstances would arise on a regular (if not predictable) basis.

This is detailed in the following extract from the fieldnotes where a manager provides a familiar explanation for the failings of the direct-debit system on a newly installed retail-banking platform. In so doing he also indicates some of the organisational concerns and skills and training issues that arise as a consequence of technological legacies:

1. Regular Payments screen – comparing screen to confirmation of customer's instructions.
2. Reg Payts Direct Debit Type 1 screen – hesitates.
3. MANAGER: We have a situation here. Screen has originator as GE Capital bank – letter says Dixons – correspondence to customer quotes Dixons and reference number – however, only information bank (goes to Regular Payments screen and points to entry) refers to GE Capital bank.
4. Problems with direct-debit system – set up by two experts some years ago – no longer contracted to work for the bank – system now isn't user-friendly – to put matters right would involve large resource and expense so they make do with what they've got.

Next example:

1. Pointing to customer instruction – studies screen – focuses on Co-Op bank card number on customer form – compares with screen.
2. The originator's name just comes up as 'Visa' – Co-Op bank's Visa department – however, 'Visa' is under umbrella of various banks ...

   MANAGER: We get situations where we get authorities (...) I mean this is erm.
   ASSISTANT: Oh yes it's come up as Visa.
   MANAGER: Yeah (...) I mean this is the Co-Op bank.
   ASSISTANT: Yeah the customer thinks he's paying the direct debit to the Co-Op bank.
   MANAGER: In a situation like this (...) if the customer comes on the phone and says 'I want to cancel my direct debit to the Co-Op' and they went through the screen (...) the first screen would be (pointing to screen). Well, there's no mention of Co-Op there so they'll go on to the next screen (...). There's no mention of Co-Op bank (...) so they'll go on to the next screen (...). There's no mention of Co-Op bank (points to screen). There's TSB bank (...). 'Are you sure you don't mean TSB? (...). No? (...). Well we go on to the next screen. Well we've got a Visa (...). Now that might trigger something off the customer (...) erm (...) but it depends how it's handled by the TLO (telephone liaison officer) (...). Now if it isn't resolved then ... the TLO will then make a service recovery sheet. ... So then we get passed the sheet to look into when really from the outset (...) if that information had been recorded on here (points to screen) it just wouldn't have been a problem.

Another example of the way in which organisational factors impinge on what seems a straightforward technical or software issue became apparent in the concern over 'customer notes' and 'letter templates' on the relational database. It is also informative regarding the way in which legacy issues emerge over time as a feature of organisational restructuring. The relational database was purchased in the 1980s prior to the massive restructuring of the bank and the change in focus from the administration of accounts to a new emphasis on sales and customer service. In these changed circumstances the field sizes allocated to customer notes (four lines) and templated letters suddenly became inadequate for the amount of information the new emphasis demanded while central control over the search facilities of the database tended to make local customer initiatives difficult to sustain.

CONCLUSION

These kind of problems are not, of course, unfamiliar to any organisation that has been at the forefront of computerisation and whose systems are rapidly nearing the end of their effective life. 'Legacy' as an issue is easily identified with ageing and creaking mainframes. This is not necessarily an indication of the unwillingness of those responsible for the development of systems to make appropriate changes but is an indication of just how difficult it is to modify systems upon which the work depends, not to mention the problems of technical complexity especially when these systems are in constant use. In significant respects, problems such as these are as much organisational as technological. This is because they direct attention to the need to reorganise work and implement new technologies in a more integrated way. Moreover, legacy concerns are not merely technological in focus but also organisational in the sense of being intimately wrapped up in the everyday accomplishment of work. Consequently, straightforward process approaches, despite their attraction to system modellers, are unlikely to take into account the various interactional subtleties involved in the actual doing of the work. Understanding how 'processes' may be made efficient and effective would seem to require a nuanced view of various factors, including working practice, communication and control problems, and indeed any number of complex articulations of structure, process, technology, and 'situated' knowledge. The fieldwork observations further suggest that in a number of instances the deployment of local knowledge and instigation of informal teamworking, such as asking for codes to enter screens, how to complete routines, etc., was effectively constituted as 'ways to cope' with the inadequacies of the computer systems. This brings to mind a phrase made famous by Garfinkel (1967), which when adapted says 'that there are bad organisational reasons for good organisational practices'. According to this view, any attempt to resolve legacy issues will depend for its success not only on finding the right answers but also upon deciding the right questions to be asked in the first place.

The general point is that organisational change, whilst constituting an attempt to move away from past practices and activities, will necessarily have to involve dealing with the past in some way. Recognising that technology is not the only legacy issue is important since it suggests that it is no longer enough merely to examine what one might think of as the technological *status quo* and project a new set of arrangements, as some more simplistic approaches to process modelling might imply. The examples of the intersection of local knowledge, interactional processes and technology use provided in this chapter indicate that there are many matters that need to be addressed when investigating the 'processes' of banks, especially with a view to their simplification and integration. Some examples particularly showed how not only was there extensive work involved in moving between applications, but also in undertaking processes in such a fashion as to reflect the posited order of those processes embedded in those applications. If workflow applications, for instance, represent best efforts to automate relatively straightforward and compartmentalised processes – which it seems fair to think – it is all the more difficult to recognise and track the integration of processes as actually happens in the 'real world' work of staff in the newly formed centralised offices of banks. The fact that the completion of 'due process'; that is, the performance of all stages in a formal procedure requires such extensive manipulation of resources, sequences of action and local know-how, leads us to suggest at the outset of this chapter that bank staff all too often lose sight of the customer and start to focus instead on the technology itself. It seems to us that what we have shown in this chapter is that a failure to deepen understanding of the work currently undertaken in the new regional and centralised centres will increase this distraction. Then it will not be the ghost of the departed programmer that haunts bank staff, but the ghost of the customers departing to go to other, less technologically distracted service providers that lingers.

8 Conclusion

INTRODUCTION

We would not be the first to point out that organisational analysis can take two very different forms. On the one hand there is 'prescriptive' analysis which has to do with problems of organizational efficiency, effectiveness and adaptability, and on the other analysis which is concerned with wider theoretical problems; what contemporary sociologists have come to call 'critical' sociology. This recognition that regardless of the object of study, the method of analysis and the kinds of conclusion reached depend fundamentally on research purpose is an instructive one. Indeed, from our point of view, organisational theory has in fact taken many different directions: directions so disparate that at times it is difficult to conceive of the various perspectives as being 'about' the same thing at all. Even so, and without wanting to recapitulate what we argued in Chapters 1 and 2, certain themes are discernible.

These include, first of all, a concern with developing new definitions of what organisations might be. Unfortunately there is little consensus about this, and so the debates and theoretical elaborations seem interminable. Second, there are those studies which are more concerned with particular groups within an organisation than with the organisation itself. These kinds of studies, associated with writers such as Strauss *et al.* (1985), Roy (1960) and Goffman (1971) (the latter whom we discussed in Chapter 5), have not been regarded as being 'about' organisations at all, largely because the people being investigated are not part of 'management'. Hence, Mills and Murgatroyd (1991) can assert quite reasonably:

> The work of Erving Goffman ... Alvin Gouldner ... and John Goldthorpe and his colleagues ... for example, were not considered by organisational theorists to be central to the discipline of Organisational theory.
>
> (Mills and Murgatroyd 1991: 5)

A third concerns itself with the discourses surrounding the organisation in question, and in particular whether 'critical' discourses or 'prescriptive' discourses are the appropriate theoretical stance. This latter is of considerable interest to us, since the focus of many of the studies we have been involved in has been the issue of technology and how we are to understand the relevance of technology to organisational work. We see the issue not as being a struggle between those who wish to critique conceptions of the organisation and those who wish to provide tools for the design of efficient, effective or adaptive organisations, but as being to do with what kinds of description confer most on our understanding, and for what purposes.

A fourth theme concerns the debate between those who think of organisations as structures, on the one hand, and those who take an 'action' perspective on the other. In recent times there have been various attempts, often based on general sociological theorising such as Giddens' structuration thesis, to resolve this distinction. This terrain has been contested not only by sociologists of different kinds, but also by psychologists for example. It has resulted in the revisiting of some classic debates in sociological theory as well as the philosophy of social science. They include debates concerning the nature of 'motivational' accounts and their relevance to 'job design'; the status of functionalist accounts as manifest in arguments concerning organisational structure and its relationship to the 'environment'; and much else beside. They include too 'postmodern' theories and broadly 'deconstructionist' accounts of organisational theorising, in which the object under scrutiny is less the organisation but writings about organisations. Many of these – though not all obviously – we discussed in Chapters 1 and 2.

A post-disciplinary approach to empirical research

Our own research in the retail financial services sector have to be placed in the context of these sorts of debates and concerns. After all, banks are organisations. But as should be clear, our take on the relationship between our research and the bulk of academic inquiries into organisations is quite particular. Our studies stand not as a test of the accuracy of organisational theory, but of the peculiar relationship theory has with empirical material. In the previous chapters we have reported just some of the considerable research each of us has spent in the field, in one case over a period of 5 years. In this respect we can claim to know a great deal about empirical aspects of work in banks. Yet as trained sociologists, we have been in the somewhat paradoxical position of seeing our research work being treated as manifestly relevant by a community of 'design practitioners', to wit those working in the field of CSCW, but as of much lesser interest to sociology at large. The latter ambivalence to our activities is a reflection of what we have explained as its inward-looking and essentially theoretical nature.

As it happens, the community of CSCW, despite the fact that it is largely concerned with the design of technologies for organisational use, seldom references organisational theory (see Eason and Olphert 1995). At the same time, design based on ethnographic study is becoming so commonplace that one can almost speak of a 'fashion'. We wonder, perhaps less than idly, whether this contrast between detailed empirical study and organisational theorising in different research arenas is a product of a lack of 'crossover' of the different intellectual purposes of the 'critical' as against the 'prescriptive' or 'design' discourse; and whether theorising work about organisations has in fact ever produced a body of useful work. For our interest lies not only in the retail financial sector, but in the nature and purposes of organisational analysis at large. Banks, building societies, financial retail organisations of whatever kind, though the locus of most of our work, are of interest primarily because they exemplify the way in which social science (and we use this term inclusively) has become a terrain contested on the one hand by those 'prescriptive' stances mentioned above, and on the other by an essentially 'critical' stance which the sociologically minded disciplines implicated in organisational analysis increasingly tend to take.

The term 'critical' here refers to studies which for the most part are oriented to a number of matters, which include uncovering the ideologies, discourses and assumptions upon which policy towards institutional management is predicated, particularly where they are 'objectivising'. Critical studies also wish to scrutinise these tendencies so as to provide a distinctive analysis which can be used contrastively (or put another way, the critical discourse is 'revelatory' of structures we might otherwise be unaware of). Needless to say this is a simplified version of what goes on and we are not here attempting to dispose cavalierly of a large and disparate literature (but see Thompson and McHugh 1990; Clegg 1990; Grint 1991 and Morgan 1990). Nevertheless, we would hold to the general view that these critical presumptions represent the typical discourse of modern, or postmodern, organisational literature. Based substantially on the view that prescription is wrapped in a scientific, and thus 'objective' language, critical studies are oriented to uncovering and exposing the hidden assumptions contained therein.

These 'critical' discourses are not something we have much truck with, for reasons which are not the topic of this book, but which can briefly be held to include the fact that firstly what is deemed 'hidden' is hidden only to social theorists. (That the relations between manager and manager, manager and worker, and so on, are political seems so obvious as to be unarguable, and we do not take issue with it, save to remark that organisational members do not need social scientists to point out the existence of power, and that their 'exposure' makes not the slightest difference to the purposes of those who seek to manage or control change.) Rather more importantly, we argue that the critique of 'objectivism' relies on a philosophical appeal. That is, the critique of objectivism gains its force by imposing impossible standards of objectivity in the first place. Our interest in this point derives from an ethnomethodological stance, and ultimately from Wittgenstein. That is, being rigorous and empirical as a matter of policy has nothing whatsoever to do with epistemological and ontological problems. Social theorists, who wish to make it so, cannot hold practical enquiry hostage to a 'failure' which is explicitly not the concern of practical enquiry. To put it another way, we are explicitly interested in what we might term the 'design' discourse, and which looks as if it is akin to prescription. It is not. For we are interested in the kind of social science which engages with the question of how to provide grounds for decision-making about change rather than specifying the changes to take place, or arguing why changes of a certain kind have taken place. The grounds here are rigorously collected observational data which are plausible renderings of the activities of those who work within organisations. They are data collected in the course of doing what we explained in Chapter 4 is ethnomethodologically informed ethnography.

In so doing, of course, we are open to a standard rejoinder from critical sociology in particular, which is something along the lines that we are taking a pseudo-objectivist position in order to do work which is supportive of management purposes. Critical argument is presumptively about the deployment and exercise of power relations, and how they are exercised and resisted, and we suspect would be inclined to critique our research on that basis. It is not our purpose to argue that studies of the kind we are engaged in might not be taken up and used by management, and used in ways that are persuasively 'powerful'. Nevertheless, we are deeply unhappy with the convenient and somewhat glib notion that studies which claim an empirical rigour (and not necessarily objectivity in any philosophical sense) are based on any such 'assumptions'. The problem is, in our view, precisely that such critique conflates practical matters with a position in the philosophy of science (something that Perrow (1970) is much concerned with as we remarked in Chapter 2). This is not to say that the status of this 'objectivist' literature is a comfortable one. Our concern about the large part of this literature is precisely that it lacks the empirical rigour we seek. That is to say, we have aimed to provide plausible accounts of the business of 'doing work' in banks. We have made no 'assumptions' about the forces which are acting upon them, nor about their moral and political consequences. We have simply wished to describe this work, in a context where massive changes are indeed taking place, as thoroughly and carefully as we are able. But in doing this we have also been undertaking a second task, and that is to present the role and contribution of the ethnographies we have been engaged in.

To remind ourselves of the goals we set in the early part of this book: our starting point has been that the status of observation within the analytic framework we have adopted and the procedural differences between it and the more theoretical stances of social science are quite great. There is an evident tension between social science and managerial work, a tension which critical sociology tends to treat without conscious irony as being constituted in rigid boundary categorisations, paradigmatic distinctions or epistemic breaks. That it may in practice be a manageable tension, one which is handled on a largely pragmatic basis seems to escape the analysis even while it is being done in pursuit of, for instance, research funding. The following remark, then, is unusual in proposing some synthesis of purpose:

> Managerial perspectives tend to seek normative and prescriptive solutions, whilst social science approaches are more interested in analytical methods and theoretical implications. However, each perspective can be mutually informative. Social science can inform managers why there are no 'quick fix' solutions, whilst managerial concerns can, and are, focusing research agendas on pertinent contemporary issues.
>
> (O'Reilly 1994: 7)

We are broadly sympathetic to the tone of this argument, if not its detail. We do not share the interest in theoretical implications, and we are also tempted to observe that managers already know there are no quick-fix solutions. Their problem is that the business of management is finding solutions of any kind, and being seen to do so. Nevertheless, the implication – that what appears to be radical disjuncture from within social science can be simply a matter of seeing other points of view – seems to us to be a broadly sensible 'way of looking' at organisational matters. In our view, this uneasy relationship comes precisely from theoretical sociology's interest in modelling 'structures' and 'behaviours' in organisations and its lack of interest in rigorous empirical detail.[29]

Such perspectives typically contrast paradigmatically, we have suggested, the 'assumptions' contained in various stances in order to explicitly render alternatives. One such example is the debate about 'rationalism' in the organisational literature, and the way this pans out in prescriptively oriented work. Hence:

> this brief overview of the IS/IT strategy and planning literature indicates much of it shares an unproblematic rational approach to management, organisation, and change, involving a set of rather mechanistic assumptions about how organisations function and managerial and non-managerial labour behaves. Organisations are seen to be no more than the planned outcome of rational decisions made by senior management.
>
> (Bloomfield et al. 1997: 14)

---

29 Again, we are not suggesting that no empirical work has ever been done in the study of organisations, for that would be manifestly untrue. Our interest here is specifically in the nature of 'rigour' and the empirical warrant for theorising.

Here, the question is seen by whom and for what purpose this research has been undertaken. Whether or not strategic management is 'successful', and whether or not the design and implementation of IT can be construed narratively as 'success' or 'failure' (Fincham 1998), for those people engaged in the work of making change work, such distinctions are irrelevant. Irrelevant in the very specific sense that 'getting on' with the job of planning must necessarily involve some rationalistic assumptions, for the job of doing 'planning' would make no sense whatsoever without them. The issue of whether these 'plans' are adequate (and in what sense) to the effecting of change is an empirical and conceptual one, and not much affected in practice by the accusation of 'rationalism', or for that matter its apparent converse, 'radical subjectivism'. Our research is very much about exactly the issue of how organisational practices do change and yet remain the same; how plans, policies, procedures and rules are encountered and managed on a day-to-day basis. We have aspired, in short, to describe the massively real experience of working in organisations, dealing with 'problems', encountering situations, and going about the minute-by-minute work of doing a job.

To achieve this we have organised our presentation in the following way. We commenced our descriptions with what is more or less the cornerstone of what bank staff have to do: and that is to take the customer seriously. By this we meant to treat the customer as an able, knowing and concerned individual whose various relationships with the bank, entailing as they often do a myriad of chequeing accounts, savings deposits and investments, necessitate complex interactions whose orderly properties are best thought of as an achievement. That is to say, dealing with customers, especially in face-to-face settings, is not a process of simply dealing with each component of the bank–customer relationship in turn; it involves a subtle and skilful juggling of those concerns – often in non-sequential order – whilst preserving at the same time a sense of due propriety and competence. Bank staff know that the way they interact with customers may be fraught with unpredictability (i.e., they may not know what the customer will ask next) but they do know that whatever is asked next they have to deal with it in such a fashion that the customer comes to believe that they are dealing with a bank whose staff are able, competent and proficient, and this is to leave aside questions to do with politeness and decorum. In other words, bank–customer relations in face-to-face settings particularly are far from the straightforward low-skill activities as are sometimes portrayed in the management-change literature or indeed in those research monographs that have reported on the gradual deskilling and transformation of this form of white-collar work. This is not to say that these other approaches have failed to recognise that there has indeed been considerable change in the patterns of these relationships and that the provision of certain sorts of skills has indeed altered; it is to argue that an ethnomethodologically informed approach to the examination of these activities draws attention to the kinds of locally displayed interactional skills and competences that most if not all other approaches to observation ignore. These properties are important to understand if one is in the business of scoping out what may be the form of customer–bank relationships in the future.

Dealing with the customer and treating him or her seriously is itself a serious matter; and when banks attempt to re-invent themselves with new channels, the need to preserve that serious intent remains. Detailed descriptions of how these activities are 'successfully' undertaken (and sometimes not so successfully as we saw in Chapter 5) is an important resource that needs to be revisited whenever banks propose to invest in new channels or to amend the processes attendant on the old. When they do so, of course, the customer does not disappear from view except in the literal sense that with new channels there may be much less face-to-face activity. This was the concern of Chapter 6. Here we reported on how the nature of the customer and those myriad forms of relationships just mentioned are instantiated in practical requests and communications between staff and customer we noted are becoming increasingly mediated by technology. Here it is not simply that the technology acts like a mechanism of communication – a telephone if you like in the form of a mainframe – it is rather that the nature of the customer as a sentient being comes to be understood in and through the materials that staff are provided with both by the immediate interactions with customers (say via the phone), and the informational resources the technology provides. Here too we drew attention to the fact that these resources are supplemented by paper-based sources and that consequently bank staff have to manage a constellation of media in their activities. It is in these ways that we suggested that customers are becoming virtual.

Of importance here was not that the relationship between banks and customers is becoming simpler (the ostensive goal or at least the hidden agenda in much of the move to centralisation and regionalised processing); far from it. Indeed we suggested that though the emergence of the virtual customer is bound up with much more comprehensive standardised procedures and relatedly more comprehensive divisions of labour, the customer as a phenomena is ever more complex. If in the past local knowledge about a customer's family and background was readily available through the talk and commonly shared understandings of staff behind the counter, now the same can only be consolidated through elaborate procedures of juxtaposition, comparison, cross-referencing and talk. In making the processes simpler, more centralised and technologically supported, banks are then making the particularities of dealing with customers more diverse in terms of the resources necessary to support those tasks. Thus the move to centralisation should not be thought of as one equating to simplification, though it certainly equates to cost reduction; rather it necessitates much more close examination and understanding of the specific features of how knowledge of the customer is created in any instance. The implication is not only that the skills used in the so-called 'paper work mills' at the end of the twentieth century are greater than had been envisaged, and that arguments about de-skilling seem to miss the point, it is that the incumbency on management to understand what bank procedures are in detail is now greater than ever. If before, the locally displayed competencies and rationalities comprised the resources through which banks provided good service, the move to centralisation has necessitated and will continue to necessitate much more fine-grained understanding of what is entailed. The purpose here is not to allow greater Fordism or Post-Fordism, but to recognise that the collage of activities becomes increasingly difficult to understand. Our approach offers one way in which such understanding can be built.

In the following chapter (Chapter 7) we focus less on the customer than on the machinery used to support customer-oriented processes. Here we considered a number of technologies and drew attention to how at times technology seems to have greater importance than the customer. One feature of this is the fact that banks are not so much in a position to leap into the future with new technology as they are already so constrained by the massive investment they made in technology in the past. This technology is far more obdurate and resistant to change than bank staff. So whereas this technology was originally implemented with a view to transforming organisational processes, culture and skills, years after implementation that same technology is preventing changes with the same goals. Indeed it is only with ever-increasing ingenuity and patience on the part of bank staff that the technology that was intended to do away with their work gets used at all. The implementation of workflow applications are but one instance of this and our remarks about the curious properties of such applications within banks are echoed in numerous other settings and research. Technology automates some components of action but the link between those and other components necessitates more work than before. The problems are not ones that can be easily done away with and despite the claims of BPR analysts who may suggest abolishing whole sets of processes or indeed technology vendors who may propose to simply electronify paper-based processes and automate, the fact is that banks are finding that technology complicates processes. Not in the sense that at any particular point the processes have become more complex but that, as a whole, the matters of concern both in terms of ongoing and routine management of plans and processes involve many more factors to deal with than ever before. This accounts for why senior managers in banks and indeed other organisations heavily dependent upon technology talk about the burden of their problems. The bold investments of the past are tying their hands in the present and hence handicapping their move into the future.

158 *Part II*

Placing a post-disciplinary approach to ethnography within a spectrum of techniques

Throughout the empirical chapters certain themes and issues raised themselves which constituted specific aspects of the more general issues just raised. These we think are important because they drew attention to the kinds of analytical foci that may be applicable to help deliver materials that can aid those trying to think through and implement change in organisations. We have argued that our approach, so-called post-disciplinary insofar as it is motivated less by an interest in improving sociological or organisational theory and more with effectively contributing to practical action in organisations, is to be thought of as supplementing other ways of conceiving of the management of change problems. These more orthodox approaches, as we called them, though offering powerful insights in various ways, suffer from limitations as regards what kinds of descriptive and empirical resources they provide.

To recapitulate our discussion from Chapter 3, we argued that methodologically there is a presumption within Business Process Re-engineering, Participative Design and Soft Systems Methodologies that knowledge of work is easily elicited. We suggested otherwise and argued that particularly 'local' knowledge, and important elements of 'skilful' working, were not made tractable or empirically observable by these methods. Second, we argued, especially in relation to Participative Design, that the complexity of organisations is not easily encompassed by user involvement alone. Users cannot hope to be representative, particularly in situations where both horizontal and vertical flows of communication and commitment may be crucial, as is increasingly likely to be the case in re-engineered environments. Third, obtaining consensus amongst users or groupings within an organisation as regards what any particular set of work practices achieves does not equate to solving the problem of generating good solutions to process change and technology design. This does not imply any assumptions about there being any one perfect solution, but does point toward the fact that consensus does not guarantee good design. Fourth, the kinds of descriptions and representations generated by these approaches are not sufficiently thick to convey the complexity of the political, cultural and social realities that constitute both the experience of work and the matters relevant at any particular point of organisationally situated action. All three approaches provide glosses on what work involves.

CONCLUSION

This cursory reminder of our concerns about the methodological recommendations of these approaches may suggest some similarity between these and the conduct of organisational ethnography. We explained in Chapter 4 that we do not, in fact, accept that the practices of asking questions, process walkthroughs and related techniques are similar to organisational ethnography in any but the most superficial ways. To restate a point we and others have made elsewhere (see Hughes *et al.* 1994; Button and King 1992; Anderson 1994a; Pycock *et al.* 1994), ethnography is not in any sense a unitary method, if indeed the word method is applicable at all to its varied practices, but is a label for various and different analytic foci.

By way of conclusion, we want to overview what have been some of the analytic foci of our own research as reported in this book, with a view to showing what these have allowed us to point towards in terms of specific matters related to design in organisations. In particular, and as the preceding summary should indicate, what we have demonstrated are certain issues that point towards the relationship between skills, know-how (local, tacit), customer–bank relations and the technological transformations of these. We have been especially concerned with pressing home the demand to 'take technology seriously'. Whilst conventional analyses of technology, when they examine technology at all, have focused on relatively simple issues of 'productivity' or technology and skill we have wanted to move beyond this to consider issues of organisational knowledge, the 'affordances' of technology and the related role of technology in coordinating collaborative and/or group work.

The analytic foci of a post-disciplinary approach

This leads us on to the relationship between technology and 'skill'. This continues to be the subject of profound academic and professional interest. For example, a range of 'labour process' studies, stemming from Braverman's (1974) work, have sought to analyse and relate changes in skill requirements to wider organisational and societal changes. This was originally with regard to the large-scale trend toward replacing craft skills with technology in manufacturing, but increasingly the argument has been extended to professional and service organisations (Edwards 1979). From within this perspective the rather bald question about skill becomes: Have technological developments made banking a skilled, a deskilled or a reskilled job? However, such a simplistic association of deskilling, degradation and routinisation of work with increases in technology argued for by such 'labour process' theorists has not been supported by, *inter alia*, studies of banking, including our own. Rajan (1988), for example, argues that IT has not brought about universal deskilling but has resulted instead in the work of middle managers and clerks becoming more skilled. Similarly, Bertrand and Noyelle (1987) suggest the emergence of a new set of competencies in banking and the development of new skills – 'reskilling' or 'compensatory skilling' (Penn 1990) – associated with changing market conditions while Austrin (1988) states:

to argue the teller's job or the bank manager's job has been deskilled by technology is simply absurd.

(Austrin 1988: 15)

And indeed, the preceding chapters demonstrate the accuracy of this comment quite clearly.

Looking at the changing skill requirements in banking, the general suggestion made by writers such as Penn and Rajan is that the emphasis on technology is misplaced and that procedural and technical skills are increasingly being replaced by interpersonal competencies – customer assistance, problem solving – with an associated need for knowledge of new and complex products. What emerges from our studies of bank work is the inadequacy of any simplistic, uni-dimensional and context free account of 'skill'. The message from our fieldwork, though rather complex, certainly suggests that 'skill' is a concept that needs to be 'unpacked'. While clearly work can be analysed in terms of skill and skill requirements, such an approach tends to ignore the interweaving of skills in work; the variety of approaches and skills used for task completion as well as the context in which skills are exercised. It is evident, however, that simplistic notions of skill requirements 'decomposes' workers and jobs into sets of skills that are deemed essential for the work but ignores both how most jobs are multi-skilled as well as the way in which skills mesh together. Workers in financial services routinely perform complex collaborative tasks deploying a range of skills and technologies and the ability to manage such complexity and collaboration is essential for many forms of everyday work.

Continuing to explore this relationship between technology and skill, another relevant sociological approach is informed by debates on skill as a form of knowledge. Whilst a classic 'labour process' perspective might suggest that human skill is replaced by being incorporated 'in the machine' a rather different approach sees knowledge as often partly informal, tacit and the product of the acquisition of the culture in which a particular work activity is accomplished (Collins 1987). What this highlights are the subtle but essential competencies involved in making sense of, and thereby being able to make it available to others, what is 'going on'. This is connected both to the idea of 'local knowledge' that we have already documented, and to more general CSCW notions of 'awareness' and could be described as the competencies required for 'mutual intelligibility' on the part of the members of a work team. This involves the ways in which, to put it generally, 'X's problem' can be seen as 'something Y knows about'. Thus, and for example, using the workflow system discussed in Chapter 7 was not simply a mastery of the specific skills incorporated in it – knowing the difference and the implications of land being 'registered' and 'unregistered'; knowing what 'voting rights' amount to, for instance. It is also knowing and being able to rely upon the fact that others in the team know the relevance of such knowledge for the work being done. As has been shown in other contexts

(Harper and Hughes 1993), this kind of competence is essential to a whole range of informalities involved in performing work activities, including 'knowing where others are in their work', 'getting round the inadequacies of the system' and more.

A final problem with such a 'skills' based approach to work and workers – particularly when the emphasis is on the replacement of human skill by technology – is the assumption that particular skills are important because they are seen as vital for the performance of a particular task. This suggests that there is effectively only one way of completing any particular task and for which consequently a particular, often technical skill is deemed essential. Research presented in this book has revealed, however, a whole range of personalised approaches to work among any group of employees – the way they prioritise work, how they go about diagnosing and solving a range of procedural problems, and so on. Workers in banks are not exceptional in doing this.

Furthermore, observation suggests that 'skill' is commonly regarded as important for very specific reasons at very specific times and is therefore inconsistently defined; that is, it is defined differently in different stages of the work process or by different groups in the working hierarchy. Skill requirements are constructed through a social process and in a particular social context and, in many ways, it is this process and this context that it is important to describe and understand. Work context influences and shapes both the opportunity and the motivation workers have to exercise skills that may be regarded as important. It is, perhaps, for this very reason that the creation of a 'selling' culture within banks has proved difficult. Turning 'tellers into sellers' requires rather more than new technology, executive mission statements, 'visions' or slogans – it requires an organisational context in which technological and selling skills become relevant to the work. Finally, in this context it is interesting, if nothing more, to note how, within each work site, the skills necessary to be let us say a 'good' lending officer or cashier would readily be identified. For example, 'good' lending officers are expected to have commonsense, an awareness of a bank's rules, communication skills, an ability to talk with customers – specifically (or more precisely) the ability to say 'No'. As one assistant manager summarised:

> they have to know what they are talking about ... to apply common sense to every decision along with the bank's rules ... (to) get the bank's viewpoint across ... (they) have to be able to get (the bank's) viewpoint across politely and concisely ... (I) don't like to hear raised voices or struggling to say 'No' ... I've got to sit here ... knowing that they can be left and relied upon to do that job.

In contrast the 'bad' lending officer is seen as indecisive, unable to make lending decisions themselves but always referring them upwards requiring the 'comfort factor' of higher sanction.

Without making too much of these members' notions of skill what is interesting is the absence of any reference to use of the technology in these comments. While a range of 'technical' competencies or knowledge, such as knowing the technical procedures for both paperwork and computer work that need to be followed, is fundamental to everyday practise in banks, this kind of technical competence – particularly that associated with using the computer – is often taken for granted. What this suggests is that approaching an appreciation of technology through a relatively narrow conception of skill is likely to produce limited answers. It is not that the skills involved, for example, in being able to use the different systems are unimportant – they are clearly essential – but so too are a range of skills or, better, competencies involved in everyday working within a team or working with customers and so on and, consequently, our interest needs to be directed to the utilisation of technology within these specific contexts.

A rather different, and more fruitful, approach to 'taking technology seriously' is suggested by Anderson and Sharrock (1993) in their heuristic adaptation and deployment of Gibson's (1979) notions of affordance and information pick-up and their suggestion that:

> we can treat ... phenomena such as technological artifacts as affording knowledge and as having been designed with this possibility in mind.
> (Anderson and Sharrock 1993: 144)

It should be clear from the empirical chapters that our own interest has been how the different information systems within banks, the accounts packages, the relational database and the securities workflow systems for example, are constructed so as to afford organisational knowledge in this sense. Though we have not used the term extensively ourselves, the thrust of our analysis has been the same. That is to say, we have wanted to highlight, as a matter for careful analysis, the organisational relationships into which systems are introduced. These organisational relationships – between functional units such as lending centres, customer service branches and service centres, or between different organisational roles and responsibilities within a single unit such as the securities centres – are effectively embedded in the system once it is in everyday use. Such everyday, skilful usage of the technology affords organisational knowledge insofar as:

> knowledge is not to be considered apart from the situations and courses of action within which it is deployed. Knowledge and action are conjoined ... The connection between knowledge and action is defined in constitutive terms. Patterns of knowledge and patterns of action define each other. Hence knowledge is seen as social through and through.
> (Anderson and Sharrock, 1993: 145)

So, for example we showed that the 'TecSec' securities system (discussed in the last chapter) afforded knowledge of an organisational division of labour in that at various stages in the work process workers are advised that they have reached checking or monitoring stages, or that their part of the process has now been completed and the (electronic) file needs to be passed on to others in the hierarchy. Similarly, we saw that those using the accounts package or the relational database of 'customer notes' are made aware of the purpose and activities of other sections of the organisation. We saw that the various electronic entries may document how an account has been passed to insolvency and debt recovery, or that an account merits suspicion as being involved in 'money laundering' and so on.

Organisational knowledge is then afforded through the integration of information systems into the distributed coordination that is a feature of modern financial service organisations. Distributed coordination refers to the various ways in which the coordination of people and tasks is accomplished as a routine feature of 'real world, real time' work. Both the activities and the people who perform them are interconnected, and in the case of banks in general they have to be treated not as isolated activities and persons but as part of some organisation of activities and persons. Much of this coordination work consists of distributing relevant information – for example, by inputting information into particular, relevant screens or by printing out electronic data – to relevant parties and keeping this flow of information going as a routine state of affairs. Coordination can also be a feature of specifically designed or evolved artefacts. As Yates (1989) describes, memos, files, standard forms, etc. evolved to solve problems of 'distributed coordination', as organisations became larger and the problems of management and control correspondingly increased. These 'standard forms' and formats are readily apparent in banks both in terms of paperwork and computer screens. These act as just such coordinating artefacts, initiating and coordinating various actions between the branches and the different specialist centres. A specific technological example would be the GAPP (Grading and Pricing Program) software package, routinely used as part of the annual review discussed in Chapter 7. The 'customer notes' one finds on various of the relational databases throughout all banks would be another example. Such artefacts facilitate the coordination of tasks by embedding descriptions of the task, along with other relevant information, within the format of a document as 'instructions', as 'items required' and so on, making available to those who know how to use the artefact its implications for the work of others. These artefacts serve as sets of instructions for a set of institutionally identified persons – the 'business manager's assistant', the 'records clerk' and so on – to perform particular tasks and, in addition, serve as a check on whether or not these tasks have been performed.

It is in these ways then that the social organisational properties of work are manifest. It is these properties that we have wanted to investigate in this book and to have demonstrated, thereby, how certain approaches to sociological inquiry can supplement and aid the pragmatic concerns and thinking of those involved in organisational change. To be sure, we have not provided answers to the dilemmas that these individuals face; what we hope to have done is shown how our approach can provide them with better information about what they are wanting to effect. This is what we believe good organisational research ought to be about whatever its disciplinary provenance. And this is what we hope to have empirically demonstrated. We hope that the others – sociologists, ethnographers of various sorts, as well as those from the disciplines more traditionally associated with change, will want to pursue the same empirical endeavours. Doing so will not be easy, of course, since there are so many factors effecting the kind of enquiries we espouse. But we do believe it is worth undertaking. After all, change is all about us, as we noted at the outset. Our post-disciplinary approach is one way of contributing to that change.

References

Abbott, K. and Sarin, S. (1994) 'Experiences with workflow management: Issues for the next generation', in R. Furuta and C. Neuwirth (eds) *Proceedings of CSCW '94*, New York: ACM Press.

Ackroyd, S. and Hughes, J. A. (1992) *Data Collection in Context*, London: Longmans.

Ackroyd, S., Harper, R., Hughes, J. A., Shapiro, D. and Soothill, K. (1992) *New Technology and Practical Police Work*, Milton Keynes, UK: Open University Press.

Amin, R. (1985) *New Technology and Employment in Insurance, Banking and Building Societies: Recent Experience and Future Impact*, Institute of Manpower Studies Series, Aldershot: Gower.

Anderson, R. J. (1994a) 'Beating the bounds: Who's the community? What's the practice?' *Human-Computer Interaction* (Special Issue on Context in Design), 9(1), 42–6.

Anderson, R. J. (1994b) 'Representations and requirements: The value of ethnography in system design', *Human-Computer Interaction*, 9(1), 151–82.

Anderson, R. J., Hughes, J. A. and Sharrock, W. W. (1989) *Working for Profit: The Social Organisation of Calculation in an Entrepreneurial Firm*, Aldershot: Avebury.

Anderson, R. J. and Sharrock W. W. (1993) 'Can organisations afford knowledge', *Computer Supported Cooperative Work (CSCW)*, 1(3), 143–61.

Argyris, C. (1957) *Personality and Organization*, New York: Harper and Row.

Atkinson, J. (1986) *Changing Work Patterns: How Companies Achieve Flexibility to Meet New Needs*, London: National Economic Development Office.

Austrin, T. (1988) 'Models of service and internal labour markets in banking', departmental paper, Department of Sociology, University of Canterbury, Christchurch, New Zealand (quoted in D. Burton (1992) 'Banks go to market', Ph.D. dissertation, Lancaster University).

Bagguley, P., Mark-Lawson, J., Shapiro, D., Urry, J., Walby, S. and Warde, A. (1990) *Restructuring: Place, Class and Gender*, London: Sage.

Bannon, L. (1996) 'Use, design and evaluation: Steps towards integration', in D. Shapiro, M. Tauber and R. Traunmuller (eds) *The Design of Computer Supported Cooperative Work and Groupware Systems*, Amsterdam: Elsevier.

Bannon, L. and Schmidt, K. (1991) 'CSCW: Four characters in search of a context', in J. Bowers and S. Benford (eds) *Studies in Computer Supported Cooperative Work: Theory, Practice and Design*, Amsterdam: North Holland, pp. 3–16

References

Bansler, J. P. and Bødker, K. (1993) 'A reappraisal of structured analysis: design in an organizational context', *ACM Transactions on Information Systems*, 11(2), 165–93.

Bardram, J. E. (1997) 'Plans as situated actions: An activity theory approach to workflow systems', in J. A. Hughes, W. Prinz, T. Rodden and K. Schmidt (eds) *Proceedings of ECSCW '97*, Dordrecht: Kluwer.

Barua, A., Ravindran, S. and Whinston, A. B. (1994) 'Organizational mechanisms for facilitating information sharing between cross-functional teams', http://cism.bus.utexas.edu/suri/in.html.

Bell, D. (1974) *The Coming of Post-industrial Society: A Venture in Social Forecasting*, London: Heinemann Educational.

Bentley, R., Hughes, J., Randall, D., Rodden, T., Sawyer, P., Shapiro, D. and Sommerville, I. (1992) 'Ethnographically informed system design for air traffic control', in J. Turner and R. Kraut (eds) *Proceedings of CSCSW '92*, Oct. 31–Nov. 4, Toronto, Canada: ACM Press, pp. 123–9.

Benyon, D. (1992a) 'The role of task analysis and system design', *Interacting with Computers*, 4(1), 102–23.

Benyon, D. (1992b) 'Task analysis and system design: The discipline of data', *Interacting with Computers*, 4(2), 246–59.

Berg, M. (1998) 'The politics of technology: On bringing social theory into technology design', *Science, Technology and Human Values* (Special issue on Humans, Animals and Machines), 23.

Berger, P. and Luckmann, T. (1967) *The Social Construction of Reality: A Treatise in the Sociology of Knowledge*, Allen Lane.

Bertrand, O. and Noyelle, T. (1988) 'Employment and skills in financial services: A comparison of banks and insurance companies in five OECD countries', *The Service Industries Journal*, 8(1), 7–18.

Bilderbeeck, R. and Buitelaar, W. (1992) 'Bank computerization and organizational innovations: The long winding road to the bank of the future', *New Technology, Work and Employment*, 7(1), 54–60.

Bittner, E. (1965) 'The concept of organisations', *Social Research*, 23, 239–55.

Blau, P. and Scott, W. (1963) *Formal Organisations: A Comparative Approach*, London: Routledge and Kegan Paul.

Blau, P., Falbe, C. H., McKinley, W. and Tracy, P. K. (1976) *Administrative Science Quarterly*, 21, 20–40.

Blau, P. and Schoenherr, A. (1971) *The Structure of Organisations*, New York: Basic Books.

Blomberg, J. L. (1987) 'Social interaction and office communication: Effects on user evaluation of new technologies', in R. E. Kraut (ed.) *Technology and the Transformation of White-collar Work*, New Jersey: Lawrence Erlbaum Associates, Inc.

Bloomfield, B. P., Coombs, R., Knights, D. and Littler, D. (1997) *Information Technology and Organizations: Strategies, Networks, and Integration*, Oxford: Oxford University Press.

Bloomfield, B. P., and Vurdubakis, T. (1997) 'Paper traces: Inscribing organizations and information technology', in R. Coombs, D. Knights and D. Littler (eds) *Information Technology and Organizations: Strategies, Networks, and Integration*, Oxford University Press.

Blythin, S., Hughes, J. A. and Rouncefield, M. (1997) ' "Never mind all that ethno' stuff: What does it mean and what do we do now?": Ethnography in a Commercial Context', *Interactions*, May–June 4(3), 38–47.

Boden, D. (1994) *The Business of Talk: Organisations in Action*, Cambridge: Polity Press.

Bowers, J. (undated) 'Understanding organisations performatively', COMIC Working Paper, Lancaster: Department of Sociology.

Bowker, G. and Star, S. L. (1994) 'Knowledge and infrastructure in international information management', in L. Bud-Frierman (ed.) *Information Acumen: The Understanding and Use of Knowledge in Modern Business*, London and New York: Routledge, pp. 194–209.

Bowker, G. C., Star, S. L., Turner, W. and Gasser, L. (1997) *Social Science, Technical Systems and Cooperative Work: Beyond the Great Divide*, Mahwah, New Jersey and London: Lawrence Erlbaum Associates.

Braverman, H. (1974) *Labour and Monopoly Capital: the Degradation of Work in the Twentieth Century*, New York: Monthly Review Press.

Brooks, F. (1975) *The Mythical Man Month*, New York: Addison-Wesley.

Burns, T. and Stalker, G. M. (1961) *The Management of Innovation*, London: Tavistock.

Burns, T. (1967) 'The comparative study of organisations', in V. Vroom (ed.) *Methods of Organizational Research*, Pittsburgh: University of Pittsburgh Press, pp. 118–70.

Burrell, G. and Morgan, G. (1979) *Sociological Paradigms and Organisational Analysis*, Aldershot: Gower.

Burton, D. (1994) *Financial Services and the Consumer*, London: Routledge.

Buttny, R. (1993) *Social Accountability in Communication*, London: Sage.

Button, G. (1991) 'Introduction: ethnomethodology and the foundational respecification of the human sciences', in G. Button (ed.) *Ethnomethodology and the Human Sciences*, London: Routledge.

Button, G. (ed.) (1993) *Technology in Working Order: Studies of Work, Interaction and Technology*, London: Routledge.

Button, G., Coulter, J., Lee, J. and Sharrock, W. (1997) *Computers, Minds and Conduct,* Cambridge: Polity Press.

Button, G. and Harper, R. (1996) 'The relevance of "work practice" ', *CSCW: An International Journal*, 4, 263–80.

Button, G. and King, V. (1992) 'Hanging around is not the point', workshop paper, CSCW '92, Toronto: ACM Press.

Button, G. and Sharrock, W. (1994) 'Occasioned practices in the work of software engineers', in M. Jirotka and J. Goguen (eds) *Requirements Engineering Social and Technical Issues*, London: Academic Press.

Canals, J. (1997) *Universal Banking*, Clarendon Press, Oxford and New York.

Carchedi, G. (1977) *On the Economic Identification of the Middle Classes*, London: Routledge and Kegan Paul.

Casey, C. (1995) *Work, Self and Society after Industrialism*, London: Routledge.

Castells, M. (1996) *The Rise of the Network Society*, Oxford: Blackwell.

Chanlat, J-F. (1994) 'Towards an anthropology of organizations', in J. Hassard and M. Parker (eds), *Towards a New Theory of Organizations*, London: Routledge, p. 156.

References

Checkland, P. (1981) *Systems Thinking, Systems Practice*, London: John Wiley and Son.

Checkland, P. and Scholes, J. (1989) *Soft Systems Methodology in Action*, New York: Wiley.

Clegg, S. R. (1990) *Modern Organizations: Organization Studies in the Post-Modern World,* London: Sage.

Clegg, S. and Dunkerley, D. (1980) *Critical Issues in Organizations*, London: Routledge and Kegan Paul.

Clegg, S. R., Hardy, C. and Nord, W. R. (eds) (1996) *Handbook of Organization Studies*, London: Sage.

Clegg, S. R. (1994) 'Power and institutions in organization theory', in J. Hassard and M. Parker (eds) *Towards a New Theory of Organizations*, London and New York: Routledge.

Cockburn, C. (1983) *Brothers: Male Dominance and Technological Change*, London: Pluto Press.

Collins, H. M. (1987) 'Expert systems and the science of knowledge', in W. Bjiker, T. Hughes and T. Pinch (eds) *New Developments in the Social Studies of Technology*, Boston: MIT Press.

Cowling, A. and Newman, K. (1995) 'Banking on people: TQM, service quality and human resources', *Personnel Review*.

Comic Deliverable D2.1 (undated) 'Informing CSCW system requirements', COMIC Working Paper, Lancaster: Department of Sociology.

Coriat, B. (1980) 'The restructuring of the assembly line: A new economy of time and control', *Capital and Class*, 11: 34–43.

Cressey, P. and Scott, P. (1994) 'Employment, technology and industrial relations in the UK clearing banks: Is the honeymoon over?, *New Technology, Work and Employment*, 7(2), 83–96.

Curtis, B., Krasner, H. and Iscoe, N. (1988) 'A field study of the software design process for large systems', *Communications of the ACM,* 31: 1268–89.

Czarniawska Joerges, B. (1992) *Exploring Complex Organizations: A Cultural Perspective*, Newbury Park, CA: Sage.

David Skyrme Associates (1995) 'The virtual corporation', http://www.skyrme.com/insights/2virtorg.html.

Davenport, T. H. (1993) *Process Innovation: Reengineering Work Through Information Technology,* Boston: Harvard Business School Press.

Davidow, W. H. and Malone, M. S. (1992) *The Virtual Corporation: Structuring and Revitalizing the Corporation for the 21st Century,* New York: New York Press.

Diaper, D. (ed.) (1989) *Task Analysis in Human Computer Interaction*, New York: Ellis Harwood.

Dingwall, R. (1981) 'The ethnomethodological movement', in G. Payne, R. Dingwall, J. Payne and M. Carter (eds) *Sociology and Social Research,* London: Croom Helm, pp. 124–38.

Donaldson, L. (1994) 'The liberal revolution and organization theory', in J. Hassard and M. Parker (eds) *Towards a New Theory of Organizations,* London: Routledge.

Ducatel, K. (1992) 'Computer networks in Britain: Communication technologies or technologies of control?', in K. Robins (ed.) *Understanding Information: Business, Technology and Geography*, London: Belhaven Press.

Eason, K. and Olphert, W. (1995) 'Early evaluation of the organizational implications of CSCW systems', in P. Thomas (ed.) *CSCW Requirements and Evaluation*, London: Springer, pp. 57–74.

Edwards, R. (1979) *Contested Terrain: the Transformation of the Workplace in the Twentieth Century*, London: Heinemann.

Emery, F. E. and Trist, E. L. (1965) 'The causal texture of organizational environments,' *Human Relations*, 18(1), 21–32.

Emery, F. E. and Trist, E. L. (1972) *Towards a Social Ecology*, Harmondsworth: Penguin.

Emery, F. E. and Trist, E. L. (1973) *Towards a Social Ecology—Contextual Applications of the Future in the Present*, New York: Plenum Press.

Etzioni, A. (1961) *A Comparative Analysis of Complex Organizations*, New York: Free Press.

Fayol, H. (1949) *General and Industrial Management*, London: Pitman.

Feldman, M. S. and March J. G. (1981) 'Information in organisations as signal and symbol', *Administrative Science Quarterly*, 26: 171–86.

Fielding, N. (1994) 'Ethnography', in M. Gilbert (ed.), *Research in Social Life*, London: Sage.

Fincham, R. (1998) 'Inside banks', paper given at *NCR Workshop on Retail Financial Services*, Lancaster University: Computer Science Dept.

Fitzgerald, G., Tolone, W. J. and Kaplan, S. (1995) 'Locales and distributed social worlds', in H. Marmolin, Y. Sungblad and K. Schmidt (eds) *Proceedings of ECSCW '95*, Dordrecht: Kluwer.

Foucault, M. (1977) *Discipline and Punish: The Birth of the Prison*, Harmondsworth: Penguin.

Garfinkel, H. (1967) *Studies in Ethnomethodology*, Cambridge: Polity Press.

Geertz, C. (1993) *Local Knowledge*, London: Fontana.

Gergen, J. (1992) 'Organisation theory in the postmodern era', in M. Reed and M. Hughes (eds) *Rethinking Organisation*, London: Sage.

Gibson, J. J. (1979) *The Ecological Approach to Visual Perception*, New York: Houghton Mifflin.

Glaser, B. and Strauss, A (1967) *The Discovery of Grounded Theory*, Chicago: Aldine.

Goffman, E. (1959) *The Presentation of Self in Everyday Life*, Harmondsworth: Penguin Books.

Goffman, E. (1971) *Relations in Public*, New York: Harper and Row.

Goguen, J. (1993) 'Social issues in requirements engineering', paper given at *Proceedings of RE 93: International Symposium on Requirements Engineering*, Jan. 4–6, San Diego: IEEE.

Greenbaum, J. and Kyng, M. (eds) (1991) *Design at Work—Cooperative Design of Computer Systems*, Hillsdale: Lawrence Erlbaum.

Grint (1991) *The Sociology of Work*, Cambridge: Polity Press.

Grudin, J. (1990) 'The computer reaches out: The historical continuity of interface design', paper given at *Proceedings of ACM CHI '90 Conference on Human Factors in Computing Systems, Evolution and Practice in User Interface Engineering*, ACM Press, pp. 261–8.

Grudin, J. (1991) 'CSCW: The convergence of two development contexts', paper given at *Proceedings of CHI '91*, New Orleans: ACM Press.

Hackman, J. R. and Oldman, G. R. (1980) *Work Redesign*, Reading, Mass.: Addison-Wesley.

Hammer, M. and Champy, J. (1993) *Re-engineering the Corporation: A Manifesto for Business Revolution*, Boston: Nicholas Brealey Publishing.

Handy, C. (1993) *Understanding Organizations*, 4th edn, Harmondsworth: Penguin.

Harper, R. (1989) 'An ethnography of accountancy', unpublished Ph.D. thesis, Manchester: University of Manchester.

Harper, R. H. R. (1997) *Inside the IMF: An Ethnography of Documents, Technology and Organisational Action*, London and San Diego: Academic Press.

Harper, R. (1998) 'Controlling customers: A brief history of the impact of new channels on customer behaviour', paper given at *NCR Workshop on Research in High Technology Financial Services and Other Organizations*, Lancaster University, Bailrigg, Lancaster, 13 May.

Harper, R. R. and Hughes, J. A. (1992) 'What an f-ing system! Send 'em all to the same place and then expect us to stop 'em hitting: Making technology work in air traffic control', in G. Button (ed.) *Technology and Working Order: Studies of Work, Interaction and Technology*, London: Routledge, pp. 127–44.

Harper, R., Hughes, J. A. and Shapiro, D. (1991) 'Harmonious working and CSCW: Computer technology and air traffic control', in J. Bowers and S. Benford (eds) *Studies in Computer Supported Cooperative Work: Theory, Practice and Design*, Amsterdam: North-Holland, pp. 225–34.

Harrington, H. J. (1991) *Business Process Improvement: The Breakthrough Strategy for Total Quality, Productivity and Competitiveness*, New York: McGraw-Hill.

Hassard, J. and Parker, M. (1994) *Towards a New Theory of Organizations*, London: Routledge.

Heath, C., Jirotka, M., Luff, P. and Hindmarsh, J. (1993) 'Unpacking collaboration: The interactional organisation of trading in a city dealing room', in G. de Michelis, C. Simone and K. Schmidt (eds) *Proceedings of ECSCW '93*, Amsterdam: Kluwer Academic Publishers, pp. 155–71.

Heath, C. and Luff, P. (1992) 'Collaboration and control: Crisis management and multimedia technology in London Underground line control rooms', *Computer Supported Cooperative Work*, 1(1–2), 69–94.

Hertzberg, F. (1966) *Work and the Nature of Man*, Cleveland: World Publishing Company.

Hertzberg, F. (1968) 'One more time, how do you motivate employees?', in S. J. Carroll, F. T. Paine and J. B. Miner (eds.) *The Management Process*, New York: Macmillan.

Hirschheim, R. and Klein, H. K. (1989) 'Four paradigms of information-systems development', *Communications of the ACM*, 32(10), 1199–1216.

Hochschild, A. (1983) *The Managed Heart: Commercialisation of Human Feeling*, Berkeley: University of California Press.

Hughes, J. and King, V. (1992) 'Sociology for large-scale system design', paper given at *CRICT Conference of Software and Systems Practice: Social Science Perspectives*, Uxbridge: Brunel University.

Hughes, J. A., Kristoffersen, S., O'Brien, J. and Rouncefield, M. (1995) 'The organisational politics of meetings and their technology – two case studies of video supported communication', in K. Kautz and J. Pries-Heje (eds) (1996) *Diffusion and Adoption of Information Technology*, Leangkollen, Oslo, Norway: Chapman and Hall, pp. 52–64.

Hughes, J. A., Randall, D. and Shapiro, D. (1993a) 'From ethnographic record to system design: Some experiences from the field', *CSCW: An International Journal*, 1(3), pp. 123–41.

Hughes, J., King, V., Mariani, J., Rodden, T. and Twidale, M. (1993b) 'Paperwork and its lessons for database systems', paper given at *Proceedings of the 12th Schaerding International Workshop on Design of Computer Supported Cooperative Work and Groupware Systems*, June 1–3.

Hughes, J. A., King, V., Randall, D. and Sharrock, W. (1993c) 'Ethnography for system design: A guide', COMIC Working Paper, Lancaster: Department of Sociology.

Hughes, J. A., King, V., Rodden, T. and Andersen, H. (1994) 'Moving out from the control room: Ethnography in system design', paper given at *Proceedings of CSCW '94*, Chapel Hill, North Carolina: ACM Press.

Hughes, J. A., Randall, D. and Shapiro, D. (1992) 'Faltering from ethnography to design', paper given at *Proceedings of CSCW '92*, Toronto, Canada: ACM Press, pp. 115–22.

Hughes, J., Rodden, T., O'Brien, J., Rouncefield, M. and Blythin, S. (1997) 'Designing with ethnography: A presentation framework for design', *Proceedings of Designing Interactive Systems '97*, ACM Press.

Hutchins, E. (1995) *Cognition in the Wild*, Cambridge, MA: MIT Press.

Jacobson, I., Ericcson, M. and Jacobson, A. (1995) *The Object Advantage: Business Process Re-engineering with Object Technology*, Wokingham, UK: Addison-Wesley.

Karpik, L. (1968) 'Expectations and satisfaction in work, *Human Relations*, 21(4).

Katz, D. and Kahn, R. (1966) *The Social Psychology of Organizations*, New York: John Wiley.

Keat, R. (1991) 'Starship Britain or universal enterprise?', in R. Keat and N. Abercrombie (eds) *Enterprise Culture*, London: Routledge.

Kensing, F., Simonsen, J. and Bodker, K. (1997) 'Designing for cooperation at a radio station', in J. A. Hughes, W. Prinz, T. Rodden and K. Schmidt (eds) *Proceedings of ECSCW '97*, Dordrecht: Kluwer.

King, V. and Randall, D. (1994) 'Trying to keep the customer satisfied', *Proceedings of the 5th IFIP Conference on Women, Work, and Computerisation*, July 2–5, Manchester, England.

Kling, R. (1980) 'Social analyses of computing: Theoretical perspectives in recent empirical research', *Computing Surveys*, 12(1), 61–110.

Kling, R. and Dunlop, C. (1992) 'Key controversies about computerisation and white collar work life', in R. Baeker, W. Buxton and J. Grudin (eds) *Computer-Human Interaction*, San Mateo, CA: Morgan Kaufman.

Knights, D. (1997) 'Governmentality and financial services: Welfare crises and the financially self-disciplined subject', in G. Morgan and D. Knights (eds) *Regulation and Deregulation in European Financial Services*, Basingstoke: Macmillan.

Knights, D., Murray, F. and Willmott, H. (1997) 'Networking as knowledge work: A study of strategic inter-organizational development in the financial services industry', in R. Coombs, B. P. Bloomfield *et al.* (eds) *Information Technology and Organizations*, pp. 137–59.

Knights, D. and Tinker, T. (eds) (1997) *Financial Institutions and Social Transformations*, Basingstoke: Macmillan Press.

Knights, D. and Sturdy, A. (1997) 'Marketing the soul: From the ideology of consumption to consumer subjectivity', in D. Knights and T. Tinker (eds) *Financial Institutions and Social Transformations*, Basingstoke: Macmillan Press.

Knights, D. and Willmott, H. C. (1987) 'Organisational culture as management strategy: A critique and illustration from the financial services industry', in *International Studies of Management and Organisation*, M. E. Sharpe Inc., vol. XVII, no. 3, pp. 40–63.

Knights, D. and Willmott, H. (eds) (1988) *New Technology and the Labour Process*, London: Macmillan.

Knights, D., Wilmott, H. and Collinson, D. (eds.) (1985) *Job Redesign: Critical Perspectives on the Labour Process*, Aldershot: Gower.

Kunda, G. (1992) *Engineering Culture: Control and Commitment in a High-Tech Corporation*, Philadelphia: Temple University Press.

Kuuti, K. and Arvonen, T. (1992) 'Identifying potential CSCW applications through activity theory concepts: A case example', *Proceedings of CSCW '92*, Toronto, Canada: ACM Press.

Landauer, T. (1995) *The Trouble with Computers: Usefulness, Usability and Productivity*, Boston, MA: MIT Press.

Lash, S. and Urry, J. (1987) *The End of Organised Capitalism*, Madison, Wisconsin: University of Wisconsin Press.

Lash, S. and Urry, J. (1994) *Economies of Signs and Space*, London: Sage.

Lawler, E. (1973) 'Satisfaction and behaviour', in B. Straw (ed.) *Psychological Foundations of Organizational Behaviour*, Santa Monica: Goodyear.

Lawrence, P. R. and Lorsch, J. W. (1967) *Organization and Environment: Managing Differentiation and Integration*, Cambridge, Mass.: Harvard University Press.

Lewis, A. and Pescetto, G. (1996) *EU and US Banking in the 1990s*, San Diego: Academic Press.

Llewellyn, D. T. (1996) *Banking in the 21st Century: The Transformation of an Industry*, Loughborough: Loughborough University Banking Centre.

Lockwood, D. (1958) *The Blackcoated Worker: A Study in Class Consciousness*, London: Allen and Unwin.

Loebbecke, C. (1966) 'Building the "Virtual Organization" at Gerling', *Proceedings of the 4th European Conference on Information Systems*, vol. 2, pp. 1245–57, Lisbon.

Lynch, M. (1990) 'The externalized retina: Selection and mathematization in the visual documentation of objects in the life sciences', in M. Lynch and S. Woolgar (eds) *Representation in Scientific Practice*, Cambridge, Mass.: The MIT Press, pp. 153–86.

Lynch, M. (1991) 'Method: measurement—ordinary and scientific measurement as ethnomethodological phenomena', in G. Button (ed.) *Ethnomethodology and the Human Sciences*, Cambridge: Cambridge University Press.

Mackay, W. (1990) 'Users and customizable software: A co-adaptive phenomenon', unpublished doctoral dissertation, Boston: Sloan School of Management, MIT Press.

McGregor, D. (1966) *Leadership and Motivation*, Cambridge, Mass.: MIT Press.

Manning, P. K. (1997) 'Organizations as sense making contexts', *Theory, Culture and Society*, 14(2), London: Sage, pp. 139–50.

Maslow, A. (1943) 'A theory of human motivation', *Psychological Review*, 50, 370–96.

Miles, L. D. (1972) *Techniques of Value Analysis and Engineering*, 2nd edn, New York: McGraw-Hill.
Miller, E. J. and Rice, A. K. (1967) *Systems of Organization: The Control of Task and Sentient Boundaries*, London: Tavistock.
Miller, P. (1987) *Power and Domination*, London: Routledge and Kegan Paul.
Miller, P. and Rose, N. (1988) 'The Tavistock programme: The government of subjectivity and social life, *Sociology*, 22(2), 179–92.
Mills, A. J. and Murgatroyd, S. J. (1991) *Organizational Rules: A Framework for Understanding Organizational Action*, Milton Keynes: Open University Press.
Mintzberg, H. (1973) *The Nature of Managerial Work*. New York: Harper and Row.
Morgan, G. (1990) *Organizations in Society*, Basingstoke: Macmillan.
Morgan, G. (1997) 'The global context of financial services: National systems and the international political economy', in G. Morgan and K. Knights (eds) *Regulation and Deregulation in European Financial Services*, pp. 14–41.
Morgan, G. and Knights, D. (eds) (1997) *Regulation and Deregulation in European Financial Services*, Basingstoke: Macmillan Press.
Morse, N. (1953) *Satisfaction in the White Collar Job*, Chicago: University of Michigan.
Mount, M. K., Barrick, M. R. and Strauss, J. P. (1994) 'Validity of observer ratings of the big five personality factors', *Journal of Applied Psychology*, 79, 272–80.
Mumford, E. (1983) *Designing Human Systems*, Manchester: Manchester Business School.
Mumford, E. and Henshall, D. (1979) *A Participative Approach to Computer Systems Design*, London: Associated Business Press.
Murray, F. and Willmott, H. (1997) 'Putting information technology in its place: Towards flexible integration in the network age?', in B. P. Bloomfield *et al.* (eds) *Information Technology and Organizations*, pp. 160–80.
Murray, F. (1989) 'The organizational politics of information technology: Studies from the UK financial services industry', *Technology Analysis and Strategic Management*, 1(3), 285–98.
Nonaka, I. and Takeuchi, H. (1995) *The Knowledge-creating Company: How Japanese Companies Create the Dynamics of Innovation*, New York: Oxford University Press.
Nord, W. R. (ed.) (1995) *Handbook of Organization Studies*, London: Sage.
Nord, W. and Fox, S. (1995) 'The individual in organizational studies: The great disappearing act?', in S. R. Clegg, C. Hardy and W. R. Nord (eds) *Handbook of Organization Studies*, London: Sage.
O'Brien, B. (1992) *Demands and Decisions*, Englewood Cliffs, NJ: Prentice-Hall.
O'Reilly, J. (1994) *Banking on Flexibility*, Aldershot: Avebury.
Orr, J. E. (1996) *Talking about Machines: An Ethnography of a Modern Job*, Ithaca, N.Y.: ILR Press.
Parsons, T. (1960) *Structure and Process in Modern Societies*, Chicago: The Free Press.
Patching, D. (1990) *Practical Soft Systems Analysis*, Guildford: Pitman.
Penn, R. (1990) *Class, Power and Technology: Skilled Workers in Britain and America*, Cambridge: Polity Press.
Pentland, B. (1992) 'Organising moves in software support hot lines', *Administrative Science Quarterly*, no. 7, 527–48.

Peppard, J. (ed.) (1995) *IT Strategy for Business*, Guildford: Pitman.
Perrow, C. (1970) *Organizational Analysis: A Sociological View*, London: Tavistock.
Piore, M. J. and Sabel, C. F. (1984) *The Second Industrial Divide*, New York: Basic Books.
Plowman, L., Rogers, Y. and Ramage, M. (1995) 'What are workplace studies for?', *Proceedings of the Fourth European Conference on Computer Supported Cooperative Work (ECSCW 95)*, Stockholm, Sweden: Kluwer Academic Publishers, pp. 309–24.
Polley, D. and van Dyne, L. (1994) 'The limits and liabilities of self-managing work teams', *Advances in Interdisciplinary Studies of Work Teams* 1, 1–38.
Porter, L. W. and Lawler, E. E. (1968) *Managerial Attitudes and Performance*, Dorsey.
Potts C. (1993) 'Software engineering research revisited', *IEEE Software* 10(5), September, 19–28.
Prandy, K., Stewart, A. and Blackburn, R. M. (1982) *White-collar Work*, London: Macmillan.
Pressman, R. S. (1997) *Software Engineering: A Practitioner's Approach*, London: McGraw-Hill.
Procter, R. and Williams. R. (1996) 'Beyond design: Social learning and computer supported cooperative work – some lessons from innovation studies', in D. Shapiro, M. Tauber and R. Traunmiller (eds) *The Design of CSCW and Groupware Systems*, Amsterdam: Elsevier, pp 445–63.
Pugh, D. S. and Hickson, D. J. (1976) *Organizational Structure in its Context: The Aston Programme*, Gower.
Pugh, D. S. and Hinings, C. R. (eds) (1976) *Organizational Structures – Extensions and Replications: The Aston Programme II*, Gower.
Pugh, D. S. and Payne, R. L. (eds) (1977) *Organizational Behaviour in its Context: The Aston Programme III*, Gower.
Pycock, J., Calvey, D., Sharrock, W., King, V. and Hughes, J. (undated) 'Present in the plan: Process models and ethnography', COMIC Working Paper, Lancaster: Department of Sociology.
Quintas. P. (ed.) (1993) *Social Dimensions of Systems Engineering: People, Processes, Policies and Software Development*, New York: Ellis Horwood.
Rafaeli, A. and Sutton, R. I. (1989) 'The expression of emotion in organizational life', *Research in Organizational Behaviour*, 11, 1–42.
Rafaeli, A. and Sutton, R. I. (1990) 'Busy stores and demanding customers: How do they affect the display of positive emotion?', *Academy of Management Journal*, 33, 623–37.
Rafaeli, A. and Sutton, R. I. (1991) 'Emotional contrast strategies as a means of social influence: Lessons from criminal interrogators and bill collectors', *Academy of Management Journal*, 34, 749–75.
Rajan, A. (1987a) *Services – The Second Industrial Revolution?*, London: Butterworth.
Rajan, A. (1987b) *Employment in Multinational Banking: Recent Trends and Future Prospects*, Sussex: Institute of Manpower Studies Working Paper No. 50.
Ramage, M. (1994) 'Engineering a smooth flow? A study of workflow software and its connections with business process reengineering', MSC thesis, School of Cognitive and Computer Sciences, University of Sussex, Brighton.

Randall, D. and Hughes, J. A. (1994) 'Sociology, CSCW and working with customers', in P. Thomas (ed.) *Social and Interaction Dimensions of System Design*, Cambridge: Cambridge University Press.

Randall, D., Hughes, J. A. and Shapiro, D. (1992) 'Using ethnography to inform systems design', *Journal of Intelligent Systems* 4(1–2), pp. 9–28.

Randall, D., Rouncefield, M. and Hughes, J. (1995) 'Chalk and cheese: BPR and ethnomethodologically informed ethnography on CSCW', *Proceedings E-CSCW 1995*, Stockholm: ACM Press, pp. 325–40.

Randall, D., Twidale, M. and Bentley, R. (1996) 'Dealing with uncertainty—perspectives in the evaluation process', in P. J. Thomas (ed.) *CSCW Requirements and Evaluation*, London: Springer, pp. 141–55.

Randall, D., O'Brien, J., Rouncefield, M. and Hughes, J. A. (1996) 'Organisational memory and CSCW: Supporting the 'Mavis' phenomenon', *Proceedings of OzCHI 96*, Hamilton, New Zealand.

Randall, D., O'Brien, J., Rouncefield, M. and Tolmie, P. (1998) 'Getting to know the customer in the machine', paper given at *Financial Services Workshop*, Lancaster University, February.

Rands, T. (1992) 'Information technology as a service operation', *Journal of Information Technology*, 7, 189–201.

Reed, M. (1992) *The Sociology of Organisations; Themes, Perspectives and Prospects*, Hemel Hempstead: Harvester Wheatsheaf.

Rheingold, H. (1992) *Virtual Reality*, London: Mandarin.

Rice, A. K. (1958) *Productivity and the Social Organization*, London: Tavistock.

Rittel. H. and Webber, M. (1973) 'Dilemmas in a general theory of planning', *Policy Sciences*, 4(2), 155–69.

Reiss, M. (1996) 'Grenzen grenzenloser Unternehmen', *Die Unternehmung*, 50(3), 195–205.

Robins, K. (ed.) (1992) *Understanding Information: Business, Technology and Geography*, London: Belhaven Press.

Rodden, T., King, V, Hughes, J. and Sommerville, I. (1994) 'Supporting the software process as a social process', *Proceedings of EWSPT 94, 3rd European Conference on Software Process Technology*, 7–8 February 1994, Amsterdam: Springer Verlag.

Rose, N. (1990) *Governing the Soul: The Shaping of the Private Self*, London: Routledge.

Rouncefield, M., Hughes, J. A., O'Brien, J. and Rodden, T. (1995) 'Ethnography, communication and support for design', COMIC Working Paper, Lancaster: Department of Sociology.

Rouncefield, M., Hughes, J. and Rodden, T. (1994) 'Working with "constant interruption": CSCW and the Small Office', in *Proceedings of CSCW '94*, Chapel Hill, North Carolina: ACM Press, pp. 275–86.

Roy, D. (1960) 'Banana time: Job satisfaction and informal interaction', *Human Organization*, 18, 156–68.

Sayles, L. R. (1958) *Behaviour of Industrial Work Groups*, New York: Wiley.

Schein, E. H. (1965) *Organizational Psychology*, Englewood Cliffs, NJ: Prentice Hall.

Schmidt, K. (1993) 'The sociological bonanza?', COMIC Working Paper, COMIC-RISØ-2-3, Lancaster: Department of Sociology.

Schmidt, K. and Carstensen, P. (1993) 'Bridging the gap: Requirements analysis for system design', COMIC Working Paper, COMIC-RISØ-2-2, Lancaster: Department of Sociology.

Schwartzman, H. B. (1993) *Ethnography in Organizations*, Newbury Park, California: Sage Publications.

Scott Morton, M. (ed.) (1991) *The Corporation of the 1990s: Information Technology and Organizational Transformation*, New York: Oxford University Press:

Sellen, A. J. and Harper, R. (1996) 'Can workflow tools support knowledge made?: A case study of the IMF', RXRC Technical Report No. EPC-1997, Cambridge, UK.

Sellen, A. J. and Harper, R. (forthcoming) *The Myth of the Paperless Office*, Boston: MIT Press.

Shaoul, M. (1997) 'The acrobat of desire: Consumer credit and its linkages to modern consumerism', in G. Knights and T. Tinker (eds) *Financial Institutions and Social Transformations*, Basingstoke: Macmillan, pp. 68–91.

Shapiro, D. (1993) 'Ferrets in a sack? Ethnographic studies and task analysis in CSCW', paper given at *12th Schaerding International Workshop on Design of Computer Supported Cooperative Work and Groupware Systems*, June 1–3, Amsterdam: Elsevier Press.

Shulman, A. D. (1995) 'Putting group information technology in its place: Communication and good workgroup performance', in S. R. Clegg, C. Hardy and W. R. Nord (eds) *Handbook of Organization Studies*, London: Routledge.

Silverman, D. (1968) 'Formal organizations or industrial sociology: towards a social action analysis of organizations', *Sociology*, 2, 221–38.

Silverman, D. (1970) *The Theory of Organizations,* New York: Basic Books.

Silverman, D. (1985) *Qualitative Methodology and Sociology*, Aldershot: Gower.

Silverman, D. and Jones, J. (1976) *Organizational Work: The Language of Grading/ The Grading of Language*, London: Collier Macmillan.

Simon, H. A. (1964) 'On the concept of organizational goals', *Administrative Science Quarterly*, IX, 1–22.

Sless, D. (1981) *Learning and Visual Communication*, London: Croom Helm.

Smith, C. (1989) 'Flexible specialisation, automation and mass production', *Work, Employment and Society*, 3(2), 203–20.

Smith, R. C. and Walter, I. (1997) *Global Banking*, Oxford and New York: Oxford University Press.

Smith, S. and Wield, D. (1988) 'New technology and bank work: Banking on IT as an organizational technology', in L. Harris, J. Coakley, M. Croasdale and T. Evans (eds) *New Perspectives on the Financial System*, London: Croom Helm.

Spinardi, G., Graham, I. and Williams, R. (1996) 'EDI and business network redesign: Why the two don't go together', *New Technology, Work and Employment*, 11(1), 16–54.

Storey, J., Cressey, P., Morris, T. and Wilkinson, A. (1997) 'Changing employment practices in UK banking: Case studies', *Personnel Review*, 26(1–2), 24–2.

Stovel, K., Savage, M. and Bearman, P. (1996) 'Ascription into achievement: Models of career systems at Lloyds Bank, 1890–1970', *American Journal of Sociology*, 102(2), 358–99.

Stowell, D. M. (1991) 'Appendix' to H. J. Harrington, *Business Process Improvement: The Breakthrough Strategy for Total Quality, Productivity and Competitiveness*, New York: McGraw-Hill.

Strauss, A., Fagerhaugh, S., Suczek, B. and Wiener, C. (1985) *The Social Organization of Medical Work*, Chicago: University of Chicago Press.

Sturdy, A., Morgan, G. and Daniel, J. P. (1997) 'National management styles: A comparative study of the strategy of bancassurance in Britain and France', in G. Morgan and D. Knights (eds) *Regulation and Deregulation in European Financial Services*, pp. 154–77.

Suchman, L. (1983) 'Office procedures as practical action: models of work and system design', *ACM Transactions on Office Information Systems*, 1(4), 320–8.

Suchman, L. (1987), *Plans and Situated Action: The Problem of Human-Machine Communication*, Cambridge: Cambridge University Press.

Suchman, L. (1994) 'Working relations of technology production and use', *CSCW*, 2: 21–39.

Suchman, L. (1995) 'Making work visible', *Communications of the ACM*, 38(9), 46–61.

Suchman, L. and Wynn, E. (1984) 'Procedures and problems in the office', *Office Technology and People*, 2, 133–54.

Taylor, F. W. (1947) *Scientific Management*, New York: Harper and Row.

Thompson, P. (1983) *The Nature of Work*, London: Macmillan

Thompson, P. and McHugh, D. (1990) *Work Organizations*, Basingstoke: Macmillan.

Thorsrud, E., Sorenson, B. A. and Gustavsen, B. (1976) 'Sociotechnical approaches to industrial democracy in Norway', in R. Dubin (ed.) *Handbook of Work, Organization and Society*, Chicago: Rand Macnally.

Trist, E. L. and Bamforth, K. W. (1951) 'Some social and psychological consequences of the longwall method of coalmining', *Human Relations*, 4(1), 3–38.

Twidale, M., Randall, D. and Bentley, R. (1994) 'Situated evaluation for cooperative systems', in *Proceedings of CSCW '94*, Chapel Hill, NC: ACM Press.

Urry, J. (1990) 'Work, production and social relations', *Work, Employment and Society*, 4(2), 271–80.

Vincent, D. (1990) *The Information Corporation*, Dow Jones Irwin.

Vroom, V. H. (1964) *Work and Motivation*, New York: John Wiley.

Walker, C. J. and Guest, R. H. (1952) *The Man on the Assembly Line*, Cambridge, Mass.: Harvard University Press.

Warr, P. (1994) 'A conceptual framework for the study of work and mental health', *Work and Stress*, 8, 84–97.

Weber, M. (1947) *The Theory of Social and Economic Organisation*, New York: The Free Press.

Webster, F. (1995) *Theories of the Information Society*, London: Routledge.

Weick, K. (1995) *Sense Making in Organizations*, Thousand Oaks, California: Sage.

Weigert, A. J., Smith Teitge, J. and Teitge, D. W. (1986) *Society and Identity: Towards a Sociological Psychology*, New York: Cambridge University Press.

White, W. F. (1959) 'An interaction approach to the theory of organizations', in M. Haire (ed.) *Modern Organization Theory*, New York: Wiley.

Williamson, B. (1989) 'Review article: Sentiment and social change', *The Sociological Review*, 37(4).

Wilpert, B. (1995) 'Organizational behaviour', *Annual Review of Psychology*, 46, 59–90.

Winder, C. C. A. (1988) *Modelling Intertemporal Consumer Behaviour: Theoretical Results and Empirical Evidence*, Amsterdam: Free University Press.

Wittgenstein, L. (1958) *Philosophical Investigations*, 2nd edn, transl. by G. E. M. Anscombe, Oxford: Blackwell.

Woodward, J. (1965) *Industrial Organisation: Theory and Practice*, London: Oxford University Press.

Workflow Management Coalition (1994b) *Information Pack*, Grenoble, Switzerland, July.

Yates, J. (1989) *Control Through Communication: The Rise of System in American Management*, Baltimore: Johns Hopkins University Press.

Yourdon, E. and Constantine, L. C. (1979) *Structured Design: Fundamentals of a Discipline of Computer Program*, New York: Prentice-Hall.

Zey, M. (1992) *Decisionmaking: Alternatives to Rational Choice Models*, London: Sage.

Zuboff, S. (1988) *In the Age of the Smart Machine*, Oxford: Heinemann.

Index

'accountable' character of work 70–71
accounts 'out of order' 129–34
'action frame of reference' 28, 151
  see also agency and structure
activity theory 50
advice of borrowing terms (AOBT) 143
'aesthetic reflexivity' 8, 11
affordance, notion of 60, 159, 162
agency and structure 4, 22, 28, 37, 39–40, 151
air traffic control 59–60
Anderson, R.J. 162
anecdotal knowledge 137
anthropology, social 63
Argyris, C. 26, 32
Aston studies 26
Austrin, T. 159–60
automation 54, 138
'awareness' of participants in work processes 71, 160

back office work 102–3
balanced business scorecard (BBS) 143
Bamforth, K. W. 26
Berger, P. 141
Bertrand, O. 11, 159
Bilderbeeck, R. 12
Bittner, E. 94
Blau, P. 34
Blomberg, J. L. 126
Bloomfield, B. P. 154
Blythin, S. 14
Braverman, H. 10, 51, 159
Brooks, Frederick 56
Buitelaar, W. 12
Burns, T. 30
Burrell, G. 24–5, 28–9, 31, 34, 44
Burton, D. 8, 11–12
business process, definition of 48

Business Process Reengineering (BPR) 3, 5, 22, 43–9, 55–61, 64, 157–8
Button, G. 13, 66
bypassing of specifications 47

call centres 142
Callon's theory of translation 7
Casey, C. 9–10
cash point machines 126
CATWOE (mnemonic) 53
centralisation in banking 109–10, 156–7
  and decentralisation 115–16
centres for specialist work 128, 138–40, 142
change management programmes 1–5, 16–17, 21–3, 42, 62, 64, 71, 74–7, 81, 158
CHAPS 113
checking before decision-making 133.
Checkland, P. 52–5, 60
Chicago school 63
chronic problems 47, 57
Clegg, S. 35
cognitive science 50
cognitivism 38
collaborative analysis 53
collaborative tasks 13, 160
collective resources approach (CRA) 51
competence 5
  interpersonal 160
  organizational 102–3, 121
  see also skill
computer-supported co-operative learning (CSCL) 50
computer-supported co-operative work (CSCW) 2, 4, 13–16, 63, 71, 105, 151, 160
consensus 61, 158
consumer orientation 12

contingency theory 36–7
'critical' theory 34–5, 40–41, 150–3
culture 50–51, 128, 160
    see also selling culture
customer care 110, 112
customer confidence 84–5, 89, 98, 124
'customer in the machine' see virtual banking
customer notes 148, 163
Czarniawska-Joerges, B. 38

data-gathering 42–3, 61, 64, 123
Davenport, T. H. 46–7
deconstructionism 151
'demeanour work' 84–9 passim, 108, 110, 121, 123–4
'design' discourse 49–50, 152–53
deskilling 11, 157, 159–60
determinism, 'technical' or 'social' 27–8
'difficult' customers 113
Dingwall, R. 67
disasters 64
discretion in applying rules 88
distributed cognition 50
distributed co-ordination 14–15, 163
Ducatel, K. 10
Dunkerley, D. 35

'economistic' perspective 45, 48–9
Emery, F. E. 26
empirical investigation 5, 10, 13, 16
ethnography, organizational 5–6, 43, 46–7, 51, 57, 62–6, 74, 158–59
    ethnomethodologically-informed 63, 66–9, 152–3, 155
    post-disciplinary approach to 158–59
    problems with 76–7
    value of 107
Etzioni, A. 34
'everyday' phenomena 67, 74, 82
expert systems 9, 134

face-to-face contacts with customers 81–91, 94, 118, 123–4, 155–6
Feldman, M. S. 137–8
'feminisation' of the workforce 11
feminist research 35
Fielding, N. 65
Fitzgerald, G. 50
'flexible firm', the 9, 11
Foucault, Michel 34–5
Frankfurt school 34
fraud, indicators of 113–14, 121
front stage activity 86

functionalism 4, 22–31, 35, 151
    alternative forms of 25, 28

'gambits of compliance' 94
Garfinkel, Harold 40, 57, 67, 148
Gates, Bill 145
Gibson, J. J. 162
Giddens, A. 151
Goffman, Erving 83, 86, 150
Goldthorpe, John 150
Gouldner, Alvin 150
grading and pricing policy (GAPP) 134–7, 163
Greenbaum, J. 50–51
'grounded theory' 50
group performance 26–7
Guest, R. H. 26

Hackman, J. R. 32
Hammer, M. 45
Handy, C. 33
Harper, R. 145
Harrington, H. James 45–9
Hawthorne experiments 28–9
Hertzberg, F. 32
Hochschild, A. 11, 84–5
'human-centred design' 53
human-computer interaction (HCI) 2
'human relations' school 26, 28
Hutchins, E. 50
'hygiene' 32

identity, personal 34
information, accumulation of see data-gathering information pick-up 162
information systems 60, 162–3; see also management information systems
information technology (IT) 12–13, 45–6, 54–6, 64–6, 159
    failures of 44
    sense-making about 37
    'supply led' and 'demand led' strategies 55
information theory 53–4
innovation 47, 54
interdependence of work activities 66
intersubjectivity 37, 39
interviews 95–8

Jacobson, I. and A. 43, 46
job characteristics model 32
job design 32–3

Karpik, L. 33

Kensing, F. 51–2
King, V. 66
Knights, D. 35
knowledge, social nature of 162
Kyng, M. 50–51

'labour process' studies 159–60
Lancastrian school 14
large-scale systems and organizational change 76
Lash, S. 7–9, 11
Lawler, E. 32
legacy systems 128, 145–49
lending 6, 129, 161
life cycle analysis 8
local knowledge 57–9, 66, 88–98 *passim*, 103–6, 110–11, 123, 136–7, 140, 144, 148–9, 156–60 *passim* distributed use of 103–4
local logics 136, 140
local rationalities 5–6, 66, 81, 89, 157
Lockwood, D. 10
Luckmann, T. 141

McGregor, D. 32
McHugh, D. 33–4
management information systems 128, 142–5
'Managing Local Markets' strategy 116–17
Manning, Peter 23–4
March, J. G. 137–8
Marxism 34
Maslow, A. 32
'maturation' model of the personality 32
Mayntz, R. 150–1, 153
measurement, significance of 45–6, 49, 60
Miles, L. D. 45
Miller, P. 35
Mills, A. J. 35–6, 150
Mills, C. Wright 1
money laundering 113
Morgan, G. 24–5, 28–9, 31, 34–5, 40, 44
motivational factors 26–8, 32–4, 151
Mount, M. K. 32
'multiple buffers' 49
Mumford, Enid 26, 50
Murgatroyd, S. J. 35–6, 150
'mystery shoppers' 84–5

needs of individuals 31–2
Noyelle, T. 11, 159

objectivism 152–3
O Brien, Bart 56
Oldman, G. R. 32
'open-desk' group working 140
O Reilly, J. 154
organisational change 74, 108, 149
organisational knowledge 159, 162
organisational memory 140–1
organisational studies 4
 'new' 34
 'sociologically-informed' or 'economistic' 45
organizational theory 21–9, 34–6, 40, 49, 54, 150–2
 failure of 42
 value of 151
ownership of processes 48

paper, use of 6, 105
'parachuting-in' of new systems 129
paradigm matrix 25
Participative Design 5, 26, 43–5, 49–56, 59–61, 64, 158
part-time workers 11
Patching, D. 54
Penn, R. 159–60
Peppard, J. 55
Perrow, Charles 29–31, 39, 153
personal identity 34
philosophy of science 153
'plans and procedures' 15
political analysis 53
Polley, D. 27
Porter, L. W. 32
post-Fordist organizational structure 7, 9
post-modernism 7, 9, 34, 151
power relations 152–3
Prandy, K. 126
prescriptive discourses 150–2
Pressman, R.S. 145–6
'prestructuring' 37
'problem specifications' 47
process, definition of 48
process innovation 47
'process' model of transactions 82
process walk-throughs 46, 159
productivity paradox 54–5; *see also* technology paradox
psychology 22
 organisational 28, 33–4
 social 31–5

Index

queues, management of 86–8, 91–4, 98

radical subjectivism 155
Rajan, A. 11, 159–60
rationalism 154–5
'real world' character of work 62, 64–6, 72, 74, 76, 107, 163
'reflexive accumulation' 7–8
regulation, sociology of 24
relationship management 108, 117
'remembering', organizational 140–1
requirements analysis 59
Rice, A. K. 26
'rich pictures' 53
risk-grading 134
Rose, N. 35
rule-driven work 132
rules, applicability of 88

satisficing 77
Sayles, L. R. 26
Schein, E. H. 33
Schoenherr, A. 34
Scholes, J. 52–5
scientific management 30–32, 138
segmentation of markets 8, 117
'selling' culture 82–3, 161
'sense-making' activity 37–40, 70, 160
service desks 86, 88
Sharrock, W. W. 162
Shulman, A. D. 26–7
Silverman, David 22, 35–6
skill, concept of 160;
    see also competence
  skill requirements 159–62
  social construction of 161
Sless, D. 27
Smith, C. 11
Smith, S. 11, 81
social anthropology 63
social change, sociology of 24
social organization and relationships 6, 53, 64–71, 163
socio-technical systems 26–7, 45, 47, 49, 51
sociology 1–16 *passim*, 21–2, 151, 154, 164
    interactionist 52
    of work 40
    'subjective' or 'objective' 24–5
Soft Systems Methodology (SSM) 5, 43–4, 52–5, 60–61, 64, 158
stakeholder problem 59–60

Stalker, G. M. 30
Stovel, K. 10
Stowell, D. M. 46–7
structuration thesis 152
structures, organizational
    'formal' and 'informal' 37
    see also agency and structure
subjectivity 35
Suchman, L. 6, 74
symbolic interactionism 63
system functionality 106
systematicity, socio-technical 45, 47
systems analysis and design 46, 54–5, 138
systems theory 52–3

tacit knowledge 158–60
'taken for granted' information 38, 63, 68
Tavistock Institute 26
Taylorism 25–6, 28, 31–2, 48
teamwork 103–5, 136, 140
    new forms of 9–10
technology 6, 43, 45, 124, 126–7, 157, 159
    relationship with skill 159–62
technology paradox 44, 56, 60; *see also* productivity paradox
TecSec system 138–9, 163
telephone banking 128, 142
    training for 110–11
Theory X and Theory Y 32
'thick' descriptions 61, 158
Thompson, P. 33–4
Thorsrud, E. 26
total quality management (TQM) 33
Trist, E. L. 26
trust 125

Urry, J. 7–9, 11–12
'usability' 58
user involvement 43, 50, 158

value analysis 45
value chain concept 81
van Dyne, L. 27
virtual banking 5–6, 9–10, 13, 73, 98, 108–24 *passim*, 156
Vroom, V. H. 32

Walker, C. J. 26
'walk-throughs' 46, 159
Warr, P. 32

Weick, K. 22, 37–40, 70
WEO58 process 132–3
Whyte, W. F. 26
Wield, D. 11, 81
Wiener, Norbert 53
Williamson, B. 69
Wittgenstein, L. 88, 152
Woodward, Joan 26

work-arounds 57
workflow systems 49–50, 127, 138, 149, 157, 160

Yates, J. 163

Zuboff, S. 9